Trading Options
FOR
DUMMIES®

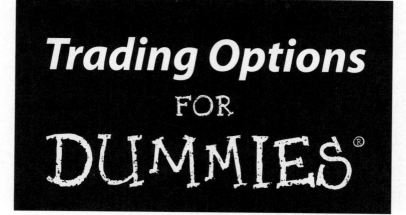

Trading Options
FOR
DUMMIES®

by George Fontanills

WILEY

Wiley Publishing, Inc.

Trading Options For Dummies®

Published by
Wiley Publishing, Inc.
111 River St.
Hoboken, NJ 07030-5774
www.wiley.com

WILEY

About the Author

Since 1993, Optionetics has provided investment education services and trading tools to more than 250,000 people from over 50 countries. Every day, Optionetics helps traders navigate the markets and chart paths to financial security. In fact, it not only stands by its pledge to provide the highest quality investment education possible, but it also guarantees it.

Optionetics high-profit, low-risk, low-stress strategies are based on over dozens of trading techniques perfected by master trader George Fontanills, founder of Optionetics. Avoiding overly theoretical or technically complicated material, Optionetics represents a practical, balanced approach to trading profitably in today's markets. Optionetics diverse range of educational offerings includes seminars, publications, workshops, CDs and DVDs, home-study materials, books, and software.

Choose Optionetics for the premier educational resources and tools to help you become the successful trader you've always wanted to be.

Visit www.optionetics.com for more information.

Dedication

This book is dedicated to the students of Optionetics and the readers of this book who may follow in their footsteps.

Author's Acknowledgments

Special thanks to Clare White, C.M.T., for all her hard work in creating an excellent options education tool.

Publisher's Acknowledgments

We're proud of this book; please send us your comments through our Dummies online registration form located at www.dummies.com/register/.

Some of the people who helped bring this book to market include the following:

Acquisitions, Editorial, and Media Development

Project Editor: Jennifer Connolly

Acquisitions Editor: Stacy Kennedy

Copy Editor: Jennifer Connolly

Technical Editor: Noel Jameson

Senior Editorial Manager: Jennifer Ehrlich

Editorial Supervisor: Carmen Krikorian

Editorial Assistants: Erin Calligan Mooney, Joe Niesen, Leeann Harney, and David Lutton

Cartoons: Rich Tennant
(www.the5thwave.com)

Composition Services

Project Coordinator: Kristie Rees

Layout and Graphics: Reuben W. Davis, Melissa K. Jester, Christine Williams

Proofreaders: Jessica Kramer, Tricia Liebig

Indexer: Potomac Indexing, LLC

Publishing and Editorial for Consumer Dummies

Diane Graves Steele, Vice President and Publisher, Consumer Dummies

Joyce Pepple, Acquisitions Director, Consumer Dummies

Kristin A. Cocks, Product Development Director, Consumer Dummies

Michael Spring, Vice President and Publisher, Travel

Kelly Regan, Editorial Director, Travel

Publishing for Technology Dummies

Andy Cummings, Vice President and Publisher, Dummies Technology/General User

Composition Services

Gerry Fahey, Vice President of Production Services

Debbie Stailey, Director of Composition Services

Contents at a Glance

Table of Contents

Introduction

Welcome to *Trading Options For Dummies*. This book brings you option strategies for managing risk and navigating a variety of market conditions. I truly believe that by taking care of risk first, profits will follow. With that in mind, the approaches you find here focus on reducing potential losses from traditional stock positions and building an option strategy repertoire that allows you to gain whether the markets are moving up, down, or sideways. To incorporate the comprehensive steps required when trading, it also provides discussions on market and sector analysis, as well as things to look for when trying out a new strategy.

An option contract is a unique security that comes with contract rights and obligations. When used correctly, an option contract provides you with leverage while still allowing you to reduce overall trade risk. Of course there's another side to that leverage, which is why you want to take the time to read through this book to understand the risks and characteristics associated with these contracts.

 When applying for options trading with your broker, your broker will send you the reference guide *Characteristics and Risks of Standardized Options.* This publication written by the Options Clearing Corporation (OCC) must be distributed by brokers to their clients prior to allowing them to trade options. It describes option contract specifications, mechanics, and the risks associated with the security. That publication, when coupled with *Trading Options For Dummies,* will give you the tools you need so you can understand your risks and use options effectively.

About This Book

There are a ton of trading titles out there, including those focusing on option strategies. This book focuses primarily on approaches aimed at managing risk, the consistent theme throughout. By setting it up this way, you can cover different topics while keeping that key objective in mind. So go ahead, jump around to areas that interest you most.

This book can be read from cover to cover or used as a reference guide. Each strategy provided identifies risks and rewards associated with the position. It also identifies alternative strategies to consider for risk management, when applicable. There are a million ways to successfully trade the markets, but certain challenges are universal to all of them. Tools and techniques focused on addressing these challenges are also provided throughout.

This book allows you to move from topic to topic in any order or serves as a start to finish guide for option trading. Use it whatever way best suits your needs.

Conventions Used in This Book

To make reading and understanding the world of options trading a bit easier, I've used some conventions to help you along the way:

- *Italics:* I provide newly defined terms in italics in all parts and chapters.
- **Acronyms:** I repeat the full name for acronyms quite a bit so you don't have to flip around a bunch to find out what VIS (very important strategy) stands for — I hate when I have to do that, too.
- **Glossary:** I include a glossary at the end of the book so you can find the definitions that you need fast.
- `Monofont`: Any time I reference a Web site that may provide additional information or make a task easier, those addresses appear in `monofont`. And if you ever see a Web site split from one line to the next, rest assured that I've added no extra hyphens, so type the site in your browser just as it appears.

What You're Not to Read

Because trading is not a skill that's typically mastered with a basic checklist, I've included comments along the way to provide additional insight for the strategy or approach. I've enclosed these comments in sidebars (gray-shaded boxes) as well as with an eye-catching Technical Stuff icon. However, you can successfully implement the strategies I describe without looking at these not-to-read pieces. They are there to reinforce ideas or provide technical detail and interesting information aimed at adding to the core discussion. These sidebars and Technical Stuff icons allow me to provide a little more detail, but they are at your disposal or for your disposal. However, I have to say, you must be a little curious?

Foolish Assumptions

In writing this particular book, I made some assumptions about you that may explain the level at which this book is written as well as show you how *Trading Options For Dummies* can be the resource you've been searching for. Here's what I've assumed about you:

✔ **You have experience.** If you've chosen this book, you have some familiarity with the stock market and the risks and rewards it presents to you. As a self-directed investor, you seek ways to manage those risks and rewards. However, if you're not familiar at all with options or you've just had a little exposure to them, option fundamentals and mechanics are covered here. Even if you've traded these instruments before, you can consider it a review if you're looking for one.

✔ **You hold longer term investments.** Regardless of whether or not you choose to actively trade options, I've assumed you hold longer term investments. For that reason, core strategies aimed at managing risk associated with longer term holdings are included. The small amount of time needed to implement them may be well worth it.

✔ **You already decided how to allocate your investment and trading dollars.** Although I distinguish investment assets from trading assets, I don't address how to allocate those dollars because everyone's financial situation is different. I do assume this is something you've already completed, because plans should strike a balance between the two (long-term and short-term) to grow assets.

✔ **You have computer and Internet access.** I can't imagine trading or investing without a computer and reliable access to the Internet . . . so I assume you have both.

✔ **You use a broker.** I assume you contact a broker to further manage your risk when needed. I assume you also have a comfort level with your broker's web platform. It may serve as a resource for some of the ideas covered in this book.

How This Book Is Organized

I've broken this book into five main parts, any of which provide you with option-focused trading insights. Whether you want an options primer or review, basic strategies or those that are more advanced, or insights from the options market, each one has its place in this book and can be found in the following parts:

Part 1: Getting Started

This part provides you with an introduction to option contracts, including rights and obligations for option buyers and sellers. It identifies how you trade these securities on exchanges, along with how your rights and obligations are satisfied. As with any security, you must understand the risks and rewards associated with these contracts. Part I provides foundational risk and reward information for you.

Part II: Evaluating Markets, Sectors, and Strategies

Trading options don't begin by running out to buy a call or put. It's the culmination of your analysis on the markets, sectors, and the underlying security for your trade. This part provides market assessment methods using breadth and sentiment analysis then moves on to technical analysis of sectors. It also incorporates the options market in this analysis. Because you may be exploring new strategies, you also want to evaluate those strategies in a systematic way to reinforce your understanding of them while also addressing the unique characteristics of options, such as trading costs and order placement methods, which I provide in this part.

Part III: What Every Trader Needs to Know About Options

Options provide you with some distinct trading advantages, but as with other types of securities, they are not without risk. In fact, used the wrong way, they can be very risky. By understanding option styles and the risks associated with each you can manage that risk. Even if you choose to use options on a limited basis, you can consider a few core strategies to limit your overall market risk. These can be implemented with existing stock positions, single option positions, or through combination option positions.

All the strategies provided in this part focus on alternative, reduced risk approaches to stock positions. Exchange-traded funds (ETFs) and option strategies using ETFs are also discussed here to provide some insights on ways to reduce portfolio volatility as well as single stock risk.

Part IV: Advanced Strategies for Option Traders

Option strategies go beyond stock trading alternatives. When trading options you can benefit from large moves in a stock, regardless of the direction of the move when using the right strategy. There are also ways you can create a perfectly hedged position that has minimal risk from moves in the underlying. Through position adjustments you can maintain a completely neutral market view, but still profit. The key to these strategies is changing volatility — a topic addressed throughout this part.

Part V: The Part of Tens

The chapters in this part include summaries for great option strategies aimed at reducing your risk. After you reduce your risk, you can look toward increasing reward . . . . also covered here. I also address key elements all traders must address to be successful with a bent toward option traders.

Glossary

All types of trading have terms unique to it, along with those that are more universal to investing. To remain true to the resource goal of this text, a nice glossary is provided that focuses on options to help you find the information you need quickly.

Icons Used in This Book

To supplement the topics discussed in *Trading Options For Dummies*, I've also added different comments aimed at reiterating core ideas and giving you some trading insight. I use the following icons to point out these insights:

 When encountering this icon, you'll find slightly more detail-oriented tools and considerations for the topic at hand, but the information included with icons aren't necessary to your understanding of the topic at hand.

 The Tip icon is used to give you experienced insight to the current discussion. I consider these asides any trader would mention to you along the way.

 Items previously discussed or assumed as part of your base knowledge are identified by the Remember icon. If you hesitate for a moment when reading the core content, check for one of these to keep you progressing smoothly.

 Concepts that reiterate ways to manage potential risks appear with this icon. It highlights important reminders in case you missed them in the text.

Where to Go from Here

Whether you're seeking to improve longer term investing or shorter term trading results, strategies geared toward both are included in this book. By using the techniques in the book and viewing yourself as a risk manager, your losses should decrease allowing you to move forward to increased profits.

You may decide to pick up this reference while evaluating your investments on a quarterly basis or keep it handy at your desk for weekly trading assessments. During your regular review routine you may also find that current market conditions that once kept you on the sidelines, are now ideal for strategies you reviewed here. Consider it a reference.

Ready to go? You have lots of options ahead. (No pun intended.)

If you've recently been perplexed with action in the markets, you may want to start with the sentiment discussions covered in Chapter 5. It identifies different things happening in the options markets that may clarify stock market activity.

Those new to trading options or who feel you can benefit from a refresher, should consider perusing Part I. Because the markets are ever-evolving, Chapter 3 gets you up to speed on current conditions.

If you have a basic handle on option contracts and want to quickly access unique ways to capitalize on different stock movement, consider jumping to Part IV. This part includes a variety of approaches you just can't match with stocks.

Chapter 18 provides my thoughts on what it takes to be a successful option trader. Because trading options comes with many of the same challenges encountered when trading any security, you may want to make it the first thing you read to help you succeed with your current trading.

Part I:
Getting Started

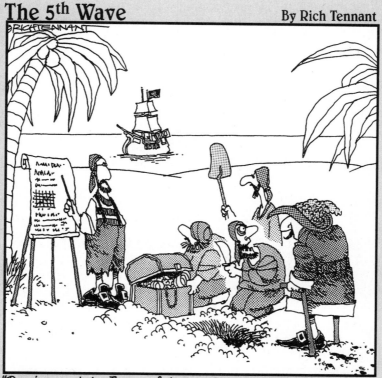

The 5th Wave   By Rich Tennant

"Precious metals? Energy futures? Currency speculation? I say
we stick the money in the ground like always, and then feed
this guy to the sharks."

In this part . . .

This part provides you with an introduction to option contracts, including rights and obligations for option buyers and sellers. It identifies how you trade these securities on exchanges, along with how your rights and obligations are satisfied. As with any security, you must understand the risks and rewards associated with these contracts. Part I provides foundational risk and reward information for you.

Chapter 1

Options Trading and Investing

*W*hether you're new to trading or an experienced investor, listed stock and index options are great vehicles for managing risk and growing your assets. The wide variety of strategies available using these securities make them suitable for just about everyone — providing you understand how they work and apply them properly. I started trading options decades ago and found that by using different strategies I could implement trades with reasonable risk-reward profiles throughout all those years.

Trading and investing are typically distinguished by timeframes. I consider investing to be something you carry out to meet longer term financial goals. Regardless of the plan you personally create to satisfy those goals, options offer a means of protecting longer term assets during periods when the markets work against them. Parts I and III provide you with insights towards these goals. It is also a main focus for Chapters 10 and 13.

Although I primarily use the term *trading* for investing or trading, I consider the latter an approach to the markets aimed at obtaining superior returns to help build those longer term investments. Superior returns mean taking additional risk, but I definitely mean measured risk. If nothing else, the approaches offered in this book should reinforce the focus you must maintain on risk, reward, and effective position management regardless of the financial asset you decide to use. An option specific risk primer can be found in Chapter 4.

The timeframes for trading may be shorter, but don't get the wrong idea . . . I'm not talking about hyperactive day-trading where you're glued to your screen. Stock and index options offer strategies requiring daily management, as well as those that can be reviewed weekly or longer. It's up to you to implement those approaches that are suitable to your risk tolerances and preferences, along with your schedule.

Understanding Options

Options are financial instruments that derive their value from another underlying asset or financial measure — here I focus on stocks and stock market indexes. Because options come in two forms, calls and puts, adding them to your current investing and trading tools allows you to benefit from both bullish and bearish moves in either underlying you select. You can do this to limit your total assets at risk or to protect an existing position.

To truly understand stock and index options, you must also have a solid understanding of the asset in which they're based. This may mean looking at stock or index movement differently — for example, volatility is a key component in option value. By comparing options to its underlying security or other securities, your learning curve is geared toward applying them. Chapter 9 distinguishes this for stocks and index options.

The primary focus for trading any security is to understand its risks including all the following:

- Knowing what conditions to consider when analyzing a trade
- Using proper trade mechanics when creating a position
- Recognizing trading rules and requirements for the security
- Understanding what makes the position gain and lose value

The sections that follow address these key components of options to give you a good platform to create rewarding positions.

Knowing option essentials

A listed stock option is a contractual agreement between two parties with standard terms. When creating a new position, buying an option gives you rights and selling an option leaves you with obligations. These rights and obligations are guaranteed by the Option Clearing Corporation (OCC) so you never have to worry about who's on the other end of the agreement.

A primary risk you encounter with options is time risk because contracts have a limited life. A call option gains value when its underlying stock goes up, but if the move in the stock is too late the call can expire worthless. On the plus side options have expiration periods as late as 9 months to 2½ years.

Your rights as a call owner include all the following:

✔ Buying a specific quantity of the underlying stock

✔ Buying by a certain date (expiration)

✔ Buying at a specified price (known as the strike price)

That's why the call price goes up when the stock price goes up — the price you have rights to is fixed while the stock itself is increasing in value.

A put option gains value when its stock moves down, but the timing issue is the same. The move has to occur before the option contract expires. Your put contract rights include selling a specific quantity of stock by a certain date at a specified price. If you have rights to sell a stock at $60, but bad news about the company pushes its price below $60, those rights become more valuable.

Gaining skill as an options trader means selecting options with expiration dates that allow time for the anticipated moves to occur. This may sound too challenging at the moment, but there are some basic trading rules of thumb that help. Among those rules is proper trade management which means exiting a position if it moves against you and reaches your pre-determined exit point.

Each stock with options available has a variety of expiration dates and strike prices. When researching options you'll find the following:

✔ An option with more time until expiration is more expensive.

✔ An option with a more advantageous strike price is more expensive.

Information about all available options can be found on the Internet from a variety of sources, including your broker. Selecting the best ones given current conditions and your outlook for the stock takes a little bit of time, but it's not rocket science. Your biggest challenges are those associated with any type of trading: managing your own emotions and using discipline.

Gaining comfort with option mechanics

Options differ from stocks in terms of what they represent and how they are created. This results in additional rules for trading and decision-making beyond the basic buy or sell considerations. You may decide to exercise your rights under the contract or simply exit the position in the market. Fortunately market prices will help you with those decisions as will some thoughts from Chapters 9 and 18.

Are these extra complications worth it? For many people, yes. The differences in stock and option mechanics are pretty straightforward and manageable. A big advantage to these securities is the way they provide you with leverage. By controlling rights to the stock rather than the stock itself, you significantly reduce your risk.

From the very start of this book, I identify factors impacting the value of an option as well as conditions that are best suited for buying and selling different contracts. By understanding the way options provide leverage and reduce your trading risk, you begin appreciating why I use the term measured risk at the start.

Recognizing option risks and rewards

The primary risk associated with options is time risk. You have the potential to lose your entire investment if the move you're expecting is too small or occurs too late. It's not an all or nothing proposition for you though. You can exit an option position if an adverse move occurs in the underlying stock before expiration. It comes down to disciplined trading.

Assessing stock risk versus option risk for a call or a put builds a solid foundation for understanding the risk and rewards created by more complex option positions. Viewing these risks on a chart develops your skill for evaluating an option trade. Risk graphs, which plot the position value against the price of the underlying stock, is a tool of the trade that will be invaluable to you throughout your trading career. I use throughout the book, especially in Chapters 4 and 10 through 17 which are strategy oriented.

Incorporating Options into Your Routine

Understanding options and what drives their prices gives you an alternate view of the stock market. In addition to sentiment information provided by option trading, the conditions you more thoroughly understand as an options trader can aide your stock market analysis. These market characteristics also help you analyze and select sectors aimed at achieving your goals. Chapter 5 includes specific discussions on this topic.

As with any new strategy or market approach, adding options to your trading means the following:

- ✔ Understanding the risks and rewards associated with them
- ✔ Testing them out in a no risk or low risk manner

Options can be "test driven" by monitoring price changes, using paper trading strategies, and focusing on a limited number of strategies that are well suited to current conditions. In addition to these steps, it helps to consider the costs of trading associated with this security. See Chapter 7 for more on this.

Adding options to your analysis

Option analysis for trading can readily fit into your current market analysis, even supplementing it with sentiment tools. Market breadth tools and sentiment analysis generally focus on extreme conditions to identify periods when there is a greater potential for market reversals. Basically, when the last person trading turns bearish it's a bullish sign for the future. Option measures that help you recognize such extreme conditions include contract volume and implied volatility readings for major stock indexes. So by adding sentiment analysis to breadth analysis, you get nice confirmation of pending changes. See Chapter 5 for more on this.

Options analysis focuses on two aspects of the market:

- ✔ Trending conditions
- ✔ Volatility conditions

Although stock traders are also aware of trending conditions, they may be less in tune with volatility conditions. Or perhaps there is a strong emotional sense of increased volatility, but not a quantitative one.

Technical analysis aimed at providing both trend and volatility information helps you whether you're concentrating on option or stock trading. Adding the information to sector analysis enables you to use underlying groups that behave differently so you can better diversify your holdings and spread your risk. The combination of sector and option analysis also provides nice low-risk alternatives for capitalizing on bearish moves through the use of puts. I cover core technical analysis concepts in Chapter 6.

Trying out investing and trading strategies

Option values are not solely based on the price of the underlying stock it tracks. There are other factors impacting an option's market price. Reading about these other factors is a great start, but to a get a better handle on pricing dynamics before you have money on the line, there are additional steps you can take. Chapter 7 highlights this information.

There are different techniques available to you designed to provide the following:

  ✔ A better intuitive understanding of the changes in the underlying stock (and market in general) that affect the price of an option

  ✔ Improved working knowledge of strategy mechanics through simulation

So becoming proficient with option strategies requires practice through paper trading — similar to trading stocks. But before that, you really have to understand how real market changes impact option values over time. After you accomplish this, you can get a lot more out of paper trading. You can focus on other trading costs including slippage and margin requirements, as well as ways to best execute transactions.

Paper trading is not the only technique you can borrow from stock trading to check out a new strategy. Backtesting an option approach may take a little more time than a stock approach, but it certainly could save you a lot of money. By having a plan that slows down your pace so you address different option trading nuances in advance, you will be setting disciplined trading skills in stone.

Putting Options to Work

Option contracts can be used for financial hedges or tools for speculating. When purchasing an option contract you have the ability to exercise your rights or simply trade those rights away. Different needs and conditions will dictate different actions. You want to be prepared to properly assess the situation so you do what's best. Exercising an option to minimize stock risk is just one way you put options to work for you.

Reasonably reducing risk is the name of the game in investing, so it's very useful to know ways you can protect existing positions and strategies by adding options to them. Protection can be put in place on a position by position basis or by hedging the whole portfolio. If instead of a bearish short-term outlook that requires hedging, your view becomes so negative that you're seeking bearish trading opportunities, options offer a much safer approach than short selling a stock or sector. Chapter 10 identifies some hedging techniques.

Another way options can do some heavy lifting for your investments is through the use of leverage. By spending less on an initial investment you satisfy a reduced risk approach, but that doesn't mean you must realize reduced returns. Basic strategies can help you accomplish both. And if speculating is part of your modus operandi, you can risk even less when willing to cap your profits.

Understanding option styles

There is a primary focus on stock options in this book, but it's hard to ignore another big segment of the stock market . . . that is the index market. The glaring difference between a stock and an index is that stock is a security that can be traded. An index cannot. This means index option exercise takes on a whole new dimension. Because this is not the only difference between the two option types, it's important to grasp how your rights and trading are affected by the style of the option you decide to use. See Chapter 9 if you want to know more.

Using options to limit your risk

Comparing stock and option risk profiles is a nice start to appreciating the value options bring to your investments, but using strategies to capitalize on these securities is that much better. Evaluating the many options available for protection is one of the first steps you take in implementing all strategies. Spending time upfront understanding why some will suit your purposes better than others switches theory discussions to real applications:

- ✔ **Risk for an existing position:** Risk for existing positions can be reduced by varying degrees ranging from moderate protection to full hedges that are adjusted as market conditions change. (See Chapter 10.)

- ✔ **Risk for a new position:** Risk for new positions can similarly be reduced to a very small amount using a combination of options or less significantly with single long-term options. (See Chapters 1 and 12.)

Account approvals for strategies that use long options combined with stock or individually are generally available to most traders. As you gain experience and have more strategies available to you, you can really customize a position risk profile using option combinations. These include:

✔ Vertical debit spreads

✔ Vertical credit spreads

✔ Calendar spreads

✔ Diagonal spreads

Access to multiple strategies means implementing approaches that are best suited to existing market conditions.

Applying options to sector approaches

Exchange-traded funds (ETFs) may be one of the best investment products created in decades. They offer great diversification such as mutual funds (MF), but far outshine them in two areas:

✔ Ability to exit an ETF as needed with a quoted market price during the day (not end of day value calculation)

✔ Existence of options using ETFs as the underlying security

Needless to say, I really love that second one. Portfolios can be constructed using ETFs and ETF options for protection or using ETF options for the entire portfolio. In keeping with one of the book's objectives to provide both investors and traders with option tools, this topic definitely had to be included and is found in Chapter 13.

Using Options in Challenging Markets

Stocks and ETFs offer a great way to participate in bullish or bearish markets, but there remains a third potential trend for prices — that's sideways. By adding strategies that allow you to capitalize on this third trending alternative, you're taking one more step toward letting the market dictate your approach.

In addition to addressing a third potential market trend, option strategies allow you to reduce directional risk by profiting from moves upward or downward rather than in just one direction. You can create a combination position and adjust it over time as prices change. Such an approach responds to market movement rather than trying to predict it. See Chapter 14 for more on this.

Reducing your directional bias

Stock positions, whether long or short, have directional bias because they rely on movement in one direction for profits. Options allow you to reduce directional bias by creating combination positions that can profit if the underlying moves up or down.

So not only can you better control maximum losses with options, but you can also reduce directional risk by using strategies that can gain from two of three possible directional moves. Such approaches are based on delta neutral trading styles which introduce a whole new way of thinking about the market. Chapter 15 adds to similar strategies introduced in Chapter 14.

Benefiting when the markets go nowhere

A stock can stay in a sideways trending channel for an extended period of time, providing option traders a way to profit when most stock traders can't. Although the sideways pattern may be longer term, the option strategies that capitalize on them are shorter term in nature. These extended patterns also tend to result in strong moves away from the channel that retrace and often test the pattern before continuing on. This sets you up for a strategy change early on in a new trend. Chapter 15 provides more insight to this.

Considering your obstacles

Whether you're trading stocks, ETFs, currencies, or options, there are similar obstacles to success that must be overcome. The main one is your make-up. Trading evokes certain emotions that can wreak havoc on your results unless you actively manage them. There are a variety of ways to do this, many of which are discussed (and reiterated) throughout the book. It seems to me the topic also warrants its own space so consider periodically reviewing Chapter 18 to keep your plan on track.

Chapter 2

Introducing Options

....

....

*O*ptions come in many forms and sizes, but in this book I focus on two specific types of options: listed stock options and listed index options. Both of these types of options are traded in the options market. They provide you with flexibility to capitalize on opportunities while limiting losses. To best appreciate the benefits of options trading, having a good handle on what exactly an option is and its associated risks and rewards is a must. So in this chapter, I provide detailed information on the components that identify an option and how you recognize them in the market as well as compare options to securities you may already be trading.

Understanding Option Contracts

To best understand option contracts, you need to understand the basics as well as how options differ from other derivatives in the market. The sections that follow give you the basics you need know to best balance the risks and rewards of option contracts so you can begin trading with confidence.

Getting a grasp on option basics

A *financial option* is a contractual agreement between two parties. This book focuses on stock and index options that use standard agreements and trade on exchanges. Stock and index options are referred to as *listed options* and provide the owner with the rights and the option seller with obligations. Using a stock option, these follow:

- ✔ **Stock option owner rights:** The right to buy a specific amount of stock at a predetermined price (call option) *or* the right to sell a specific amount of stock at a predetermined price (put option).

- ✔ **Stock option seller obligations:** The obligation to sell a specific amount of stock at a pre-determined price (call option) *or* the obligation to buy a specific amount of stock at a predetermined price (put option).

In this chapter, however, I focus on monthly stock options. To ensure you stay on the same page with me, the following bullets give you the formal definitions as well as the benefits for the two types of stock options you can trade — a *call option* and a *put option:*

- ✔ **Call option:** Call options give the owner (seller) the right (obligation) to buy (sell) a specified number of shares for the underlying stock at a specified price by a predetermined date. A call option allows you to invest a smaller amount and still benefit from an upward move in stock value.

- ✔ **Put option:** Put options give the owner (seller) the right (obligation) to sell (buy) a specified number of shares for the underlying stock at a specified price by a predetermined date. A put option on a stock you hold for the long-term gains value during those downturns you find so painful to watch.

To minimize risk and maximize reward with any financial asset, you must understand how the asset works. After you begin trading a new security, always consider the risk involved with the worst-case scenario

Stock options allow you to do the following:

- ✔ Benefit from upside moves for less money
- ✔ Benefit from downward moves without the risk of short-selling
- ✔ Protect a stock position or portfolio during market downturns

However, you have to consider the downside as well:

- ✔ **Limited life:** Each contract comes with an expiration date, so if the move you anticipate is late, you will lose your entire initial investment. Proper option selection and position management helps minimize this negative effect.

- ✔ **Improper aggressive trading strategies:** Such strategies cap rewards while exposing you to unlimited losses — the same risks you have when you short a stock. I don't advocate using options in that manner.

Comparing options to other securities

The primary factor determining the market value of an option is the stock price in which it's based. So an option derives its value from the underlying stock. These types of securities are known as *derivatives*. To best understand option valuations, you should know more about other derivatives in the market, including commodities and futures contracts and a quasi-derivative: the exchange-traded fund (ETF):

✔ **Commodities and futures:** As with stock options, commodities and futures contracts are also agreements between two parties. The main distinction is that a stock option gives you rights as an owner while a commodities or futures contract obligates you regardless. That's an important distinction if you are already trading these securities.

Commodities are contracts that fix the price for a set amount of a physical item such as gold or livestock. Each contract is scheduled to be executed on a pre-determined date unless you exit the agreement by trading out of the contract. So as with a stock option, a commodity contract locks in the price and quantity of an asset. Unlike an option it identifies a specific delivery date.

✔ **Indexes:** An *index* is a tool used to measure prices for a group of stocks, bonds, or commodities. As a result, you derive an index value using the price of the different components that make it up. I cover indexes and options on indexes in much greater detail in Chapter 9.

An index isn't a security though. You can't buy one. What you can do is buy a security that tracks the ups and downs of an index, such as a mutual fund. A mutual fund often imitates changes in the index it tracks by owning the same mix of stocks, bonds, or commodities. You won't get a perfect one-for-one match with the index, but it works pretty well.

✔ **Exchange-traded funds (ETFs):** In the same way an index derives its values from its components, so does the index mutual fund. Another security that behaves similarly is the exchange-traded fund (ETF). It's similar to a mutual fund because it represents a partial investment in a basket of stocks, bonds, or commodities. I refer to it as a *quasi-derivative* because not all ETFs actually hold the component assets of the index it tracks. Some of them do it using more exotic securities. ETFs differ from mutual funds because they can be traded throughout the day just as with a stock. You're probably familiar with two of the original ETFs:

  • SPYDR S&P 500 Trust (SPY) which tracks the S&P 500 Index

  • Nasdaq-100 Index Tracking Stock (QQQQ)

Both of these ETFs regularly top the most active volume lists on different stock exchanges. That means these particular ETFs are easy to sell after you own them. The best thing though, is that there are options available on them. I'll be using these ETFs along with the associated stock options throughout the book.

✔ **Stocks and bonds:** When you buy a stock you partially own the company's assets. Purchasing a bond makes you a part holder of the company's debt. Each come with different rights, risks, and rewards. Table 2-1 gives you a breakdown of how stocks and bonds compare with options.

Table 2-1	Stock, Bond, and Option Comparison	
Stock	*Bond*	*Option*
Asset ownership	Hold company debt	No ownership
Exist indefinitely	Has maturity date	Has a limited life
Total loss possible	Total loss possible	Total loss possible

Uncovering an Option's Value

Knowing your potential risks and rewards means you understand how an investment is valued, what makes it go up and what makes it go down. You determine appropriate market values for listed options based on the following:

✔ The option type (call or put)

✔ The market value of its underlying security

✔ How the underlying security traded in the past — volatile or calm

✔ The time remaining until it expires

Puts increase in value as the underlying stock declines.

In this section I provide the option contract details you need to know to successfully navigate through market information to uncover how each of these factors impact an option's value.

Understanding options rights and obligations

Options come in two types: calls and puts. When you own a call, you have the right to buy a certain stock at a specific price by a certain date. As a put owner, you have the right to sell certain stock at a specific price by a specific date.

The rights you have as an option owner are at your discretion — you don't have to exercise them when the option expiration date approaches. Between the time you purchase an option and the date it expires you can do as follows:

✔ Sell it for a profit

✔ Sell it for a loss

✔ Exercise it

✔ Let it expire with no value (for a loss)

As an option seller, you're obligated to complete certain transactions. You have less choices and the market generally dictates your fate in terms of meeting those contract obligations. As expiration approaches you can do as follows:

✔ Buy it back for a profit

✔ Buy it back for a loss

✔ See it expire with no value (for a profit)

 To remember your call and put rights, think about *calling* the stock away from someone (buying) and *putting* the stock to someone (selling).

Taking in some terminology

Here is some important option terminology to understand before you move forward:

✔ **Underlying security:** The stock which you buy or sell.

✔ **Strike price:** The price you pay if you exercise your rights.

✔ **Expiration date:** The date the option goes away, along with your rights.

✔ **Option package:** The number of shares and name of the security you call away or put to someone.

- ✓ **Market quote:** The most current price offered by buyers to purchase the option and the being asked by sellers to give up the option.

- ✓ **Multiplier:** The number used to determine how much money you pay when you call away stock and how much you receive when you put stock to someone. It also is used to determine the total value of the option.

- ✓ **Premium:** The total value of the option you buy or sell. It's based on the market quote for the option and its multiplier.

- ✓ **Exercise value:** Your cost when you exercise your call option rights, also known as the exercise cost. Obtain the exercise value by: multiplying the strike price by the multiplier.

Options have expiration dates so the rights you buy don't last forever. To determine the time until expiration, just identify the expiration date and figure out how many days or approximate months you are from that date.

Accessing All Your Options

Many people trade in and out of options without ever considering buying or selling the underlying stock. Regardless of whether you want to just trade options or actually exercise them to buy or sell a stock, understanding option rights is an important part of valuing them. Knowing exactly how a security works is also critical to managing your risk.

There are many places to access option market information online. Free sites usually provide listings of all options available for a particular stock, with a 15 to 20 minute time delay for quote and trading data if the option markets are open. In addition to the option exchanges, you can access this data from your broker's Web site and financial information sites such as Yahoo and Optionetics.

Identifying options

Not all stocks have options, but those that do offer multiple strike prices and expiration months for you to check out based on your expectations for the stock and time horizon. The list of options for each stock is referred to as the *option chain*. Reviewing option chains allows you to see all the calls and puts available for a stock as well as option specific data including the following:

> ✔ How many contracts exist; known as open interest
>
> ✔ A market quote that is current or delayed about 15 minutes
>
> ✔ Recent trading levels for the option, either current or delayed

Options currently have a unique identifier known as its *option root* which is one to three letters long, matching stock symbols with one to three letters (i.e. General Electric's stock symbol and option root is GE). Four letter stock symbols currently require a different three letter option root (i.e. Microsoft's stock symbol is MSFT and its option root is MSQ).

Option identification is more complex than stocks because the option type, strike price, and expiration all need to be specified. Currently, options have a root symbol plus two additional letters to identify them. A new option identification system will be finalized in 2008 and implemented in 2009 that will improve shortfalls in the current system and make option symbols more intuitive.

Under the current system, an option symbol includes an option root and two additional letters to designate the option type and expiration month (first letter) and the option strike price (second letter). See Table 2-2 for an example of this system. As of the writing of this book, the Options Symbology Initiative is working on updating this system. A new option identification system is expected to be approved in mid-2008 for implementation in 2009.

Table 2-2	Letters Identifying Option Type and Month	
Month	*Call Option*	*Put Option*
January	A	M
February	B	N
March	C	O
April	D	P
May	E	Q
June	F	R
July	G	S
August	H	T
September	I	U
October	J	V
November	K	W
December	L	X

Given the option root of MSQ for Microsoft, all October call options will include the letters MSQJ in the symbol. There are always options available for the current month (*near month*) and the following month (*next month*), as well as two additional months following one of three cycles as detailed in Table 2-3. Microsoft follows cycle 1, so even if you're searching for options in May, you can review October call and put options for MSFT.

Table 2-3	Option Expirations by Cycle
Cycle	**Months**
I	January, April, July, October
II	February, May, August, November
III	March, June, September, December

Option strike price designations are more tricky because the range is so large. Searching an option chain on-line, you find that the strike prices available for a specific stock cluster around the stock trading price. A stock trading at 20 will have options with strike prices near this level, while those for a stock trading at 120 will be in that range. Option strike prices can still be stated as fractions, but the new initiative will update strike prices to decimal formats.

Double-check option details when you see a quote that doesn't seem quite right. You can accidentally bring up a call chain when you meant to view a put chain. Also, there are times when corporate actions for the underlying stock require the option to be adjusted resulting in a non-standard option package. The Options Symbology Initiative will improve, but not completely fix this issue.

Option strike prices are available in as little as $1 increments. For the most part though, the increments start at $2.50 and move up to $10 depending on the stock price. Table 2-4 provides common strike price identifiers.

- Stock at $30: Strike prices generally available at $2.50 increments
- Stock at $80: Strike prices generally available at $5 increments
- Stock at $140: Strike prices generally available at $10 increments

Table 2-4	Common Letters to Identify Strike Price
Letters	*Strike Price*
A	05
B	10
C	15
D	20
E	25
F	30
G	35
H	40
I	45
J	50
K	55
L	60
M	65
N	70
O	75
P	80
Q	85
R	90
S	95
T	00
U	7.5
V	12.5
W	17.5
X	22.5
Y	27.5
Z	32.5

Expiring options gracefully

An approaching expiration means decision time is also approaching for you, if you're still holding an option position. By this point you should have a good handle on whether you expect to do the following:

- ✔ **Take advantage of your contract rights:** When you take advantage of the rights under the option contract, you are *exercising* the option. This can be accomplished by contacting your broker and submitting *exercise instructions* to them. I cover this topic in detail in Chapter 9.

- ✔ **Trade out of the position**

Monthly stock option expiration dates are always the Saturday that follows the third Friday of the month. Because trading doesn't take place on Saturdays, you need to submit exercise instructions or exit the position on the last trading day before expiration — typically a Friday.

Each month the expiration for stock options occurs on the Saturday following the third Friday of the month:

- ✔ **Last trading day:** Because the stock market isn't open on Saturdays, that means the last trading day for the stock is that third Friday. An option derives its value from the underlying stock, so they also stop trading on the same Friday. Occasionally holidays push this last trading day even further up the week to Thursday.

- ✔ **Last day to exercise:** The last day to trade is usually the last day for a retail trader (you and me) to exercise stock option rights. Typically the cutoff time to submit instructions is one hour after the markets close, but that time varies by broker. You must contact your broker to obtain their specific cutoff times and instruction requirements.

Dissecting your rights

Purchasing a stock call option gives you the right, but not the obligation, to buy a certain amount of stock at a set price (strike price) at any point up to the option's expiration date. From the time you buy it until (just about) the day of expiration, you can either exercise your option rights or trade out of the position.

Purchasing a stock put option gives you the right, but not the obligation, to sell a certain amount of stock at a set price (strike price) at any point up to the option's expiration date. From the time you buy it until (just about) the day of expiration, you can either exercise your option rights or trade out of the position.

You may never actually exercise an option. Establishing an option position may simply be part of an overall trading strategy for you. Because you have rights but not obligations under the contract, how you proceed is entirely up to you.

Advantages to exercising options include the following:

- ✔ **Call:** Benefiting from shareholder rights including receipt of cash and stock dividends and fully participating in other corporate actions such as mergers, acquisitions, and spinoffs.

- ✔ **Put:** Exiting a stock position when bad news comes out about a company after the close of regular trading in the stock market.

- ✔ **Call or put:** Minimizing commissions if you hold an option and want to buy or sell the underlying stock. Selling the option then buying or selling the stock in the market typically generates an added commission.

The last item may seem confusing – why sell away your rights to buy a stock if you want to own it? There are times when it's just more profitable to sell the option and complete the stock transaction in the market. I lay out the decision-making process for you in Chapter 9.

Creating Contracts

Stocks have a set number of shares available for trading referred to as its *float*. To increase this number, shareholders vote to authorize the issuance of additional stock. Options are more flexible because new contracts are created to meet the demand for that particular contract. This flexibility impacts how you place an option order and makes it easier to sell an option you don't own.

The total stock issued for a company is referred to as the *authorized shares*. Shares available for trading are referred to as the stock's float. The possible number of option contracts available to trade is limitless because they are created by demand. The actual contracts in existence for a specific option is referred to as its *open interest*.

Opening and closing positions

When you enter an order to buy an option, there may or may not be an existing supply available. If there isn't a new contract is created to meet the new demand — it's pretty seamless; you won't really know whether you're buying an existing contract or a newly created one.

What it does impact is how you create and exit option positions. In order for the option exchanges to keep everything straight, you need to identify whether you're opening a new position or closing an existing one. You purchase a call option by entering the following order:

Buy to Open, 1 ABC Apr 08 30.00 strike call option

Exiting the position at any point down the road you:

Sell to Close, 1 ABC Apr 08 30.00 strike call option

Because you can sell an option you don't own, you just need to designate what type of transaction you're completing by using the same terminology to enter and exit the position:

✔ Sell to Open, 1 FGH Jun 08 17.50 strike call option

✔ Buy to Close, 1 FGH Jun 08 17.50 strike call option

Completing an order to sell an option you don't own is pretty straightforward. Understanding the risk associated with it is the really important part.

By entering and exiting orders this way, the exchanges and clearing company for all stock options are able to track the actual numbers of contracts that exist for each option. This contract value is known as *open interest*. As with stock, option volume data is also reported to identify the number of total contracts traded on any given day.

Because open interest is a record-keeping amount generated from that day's trading activity, any open interest value you see with quotes reflects a value up to and including the previous day's contract level. There is a one day lag in this number.

Identifying whether an order opens or closes a position is important for contract recordkeeping. If you make a mistake during order entry and the trade is executed, the error should be readily fixable. Contact your broker as soon as possible to get the transaction corrected in your account and at the exchanges.

Selling an option you don't own

Selling a stock call option as an opening transaction obligates you to sell a certain amount of stock at a set price (strike price) at any point through the option's expiration date. From the time you sell it until expiration weekend, you are required to satisfy that obligation if a call option holder chooses to exercise their rights. If and when this happens it is referred to as being *assigned* the option. Typically your broker contacts you informing you of the assignment.

Assuming you're assigned on a call option contract, one of two possibilities exist:

✔ You owned shares of the underlying stock in the account which are then sold at the strike price; this results in closing the stock position in your account

✔ You did not own shares of the underlying, but the shares are sold at the strike price creating a short stock position in your account.

Selling a call option when you own the underlying shares is referred to as a *covered* transaction because the stock is said to *cover* the short call position. If you don't own the stock, the option position is referred to as a *naked call*. Your risk associated with a naked call option is the same as your risk when you short stock — unlimited.

When selling a call option as an opening transaction without owning the stock, your risk is the same as holding a short stock position. Because a stock can technically keep rising, your risk is unlimited.

Selling a stock put option as an opening transaction obligates you to buy a certain amount of stock at a set price (strike price) at any point up through the option's expiration date. From the time you sell the put until expiration weekend, you are required to satisfy the obligation if a put option holder chooses to exercise their rights.

Typically you're assigned on a short put when the stock has suffered a decline. So you're purchasing stock at a higher level than its current market value. Short put transactions can also be covered or naked.

When selling a short put, you're obligating yourself to buy shares so you cover the option with a short stock position in the underlying. Buying the shares closes this short stock position. If the short put is naked, assignment of the put creates a new long stock position in your account.

Creating a short option position takes a little time to fully grasp for two reasons:

✔ The obligation associated with the position takes you out of an active decision-making role for transactions in the underlying stock

✔ The risks associated with the short option transaction change significantly when it represents a covered versus naked position

I include much greater risk-reward considerations for long and short option positions in Chapter 4.

Keeping Some Tips in Mind

You not only want to get off on the right foot when you begin trading options, but you also want to keep both feet firmly grounded throughout the process. The following tips should help:

- ✓ **Get approval.** When you want to start trading options, you need to get approval from your broker . . . the Securities & Exchange Commission (SEC) requires it. They need to make sure that trading these securities is appropriate for your financial situation and goals. It's part of the process and means you typically get approved for basic option strategies if you haven't traded them in the past.

- ✓ **Be disciplined.** When you enter a trade for a specific reason, i.e. an earnings announcement, pending economic report or a particular value for an indicator you use, you must exit the trade when conditions change or your original reason for purchasing the security no longer exists. Don't let a stock or option position you intended to hold for three weeks become part of your long-term portfolio. Being disciplined and following your rules is a must for all traders.

- ✓ **Keep track of the expiration date.** Many option chains include the actual expiration date for each month along with the option quote data. The expiration date may also be included with your account position information. Knowing when the option expires is critical to managing the position.

- ✓ **Practice.** Always remember that you can paper trade a security that is new to you. Although the emotions you experience trading this way don't exactly mimic having real money on the line, it will help you get familiar with new types of securities.

Chapter 3

Trading Places: Options for Stocks

● ●

In This Chapter

▶ Finding your way around the option markets

▶ Leveraging your investment while managing risk

▶ Valuing options with the Greeks

▶ Looking at the past to gauge the future

● ●

*Y*our trading career probably started with the stock market. Because there are plenty of similarities between stocks and options, comparing the two takes advantage of your base knowledge to expand firmly into a new trading environment, so I do that when possible here.

Covering options from a trader's standpoint, this chapter provides information about the option exchanges you encounter, the different market participants impacting your transactions and the market conditions that affect your trades. All these things have some influence on your trading success. The biggest key to success though, is really getting a handle on the factors that come into play when valuing options. With that in mind I introduce formal option pricing components, known as the "Greeks."

The U.S. Options Exchanges

There are six option exchanges in the U.S., which is pretty amazing for a security that just started trading in the 1970s. Two of these were launched since 2000 and all six offer some form of electronic execution:

- ✔ **American Stock Exchange (AMEX):** www.amex.com
- ✔ **Boston Options Exchange (BOX):** www.bostonoptions.com
- ✔ **Chicago Board Options Exchange (CBOE):** www.cboe.com
- ✔ **International Stock Exchange (ISE):** www.ise.com
- ✔ **New York Stock Exchange (NYSE/ARCA):** www.nyse.com
- ✔ **Philadelphia Stock Exchange (PHLX):** www.phlx.com

There is common information on the different option exchange Internet sites, along with information specific to the exchange's listings. Each also seems to have a unique strength. Periodically check the sites for new tools and insights.

Navigating the Markets

In this section, I give you information on how to get around the options market including executing trades, understanding key players in the options game, and recognizing some of the more unique characteristics of options trading.

Trade execution

Entering an order through the Internet on your broker's system triggers an extremely fast series of events:

- ✔ The order is routed to one of six exchanges where it gets executed if it satisfies the current market quote or is reflected in the market if it improves the current quote.

- ✔ If your order is routed to an exchange with a less favorable market quote, that exchange can either improve their price or send it to the exchange with the best quote because the exchanges are linked electronically.

- ✔ If and when your order is executed, a report is sent back to your broker with the trade details. This information appears almost immediately in your account when received by your broker.

- ✔ Orders that improve the best market quote are posted quickly on the exchange where it was routed. It is reflected across all exchanges as the best bid when buying or the best offer (ask) when selling. It remains there until it is executed or a better bid or offer replaces it.

So much of the order process is completed electronically that you can have an execution report in seconds. If your experiencing regular delays, you need to consider what role your Internet connection plays in that problem.

Option market participants

The option market includes market participants similar to the stock market:

- ✔ **Brokers:** A broker with a specialized license needs to approve your account for option trading. Not only does the firm need to protect you, they also need to protect themselves because unlimited risk option positions, such as short naked calls, could expose you both to high losses. Be patient with the approval process and only trade strategies in which you fully understand the risks associated with a worst-case scenario. If you want to trade options, you need to complete an additional application for each brokerage account you want to include. There are different approval levels for option trading that reflect an increasing amount of risk for the strategies approved. Typically you can receive approval for basic strategies when starting out.

  Brokers must follow minimum rules and regulations, but can also operate under ones that are stricter. Communicate with your broker to understand key trading items such as margin and maintenance rules, minimum balances for option trading, cut-off times for submitting exercise instructions, and similar issues.

- ✔ **Market makers and specialists:** Market makers and specialists are responsible for providing a market for your orders — meaning they're required to take the other side of your trade at the quoted level. You may not always agree with their quotes, but they are key to the exchanges by providing liquidity and assuming risk. They also keep the markets orderly so your orders are handled by price and time priority, even when chaos erupts during buying frenzies and selling panics.

  When trading options you want to lean toward those contracts that are more actively traded. This allows you to get into and (much more importantly) out of the position more easily. You can find the most active options for each exchange on its Web site.

- ✔ **Options Clearing Corporation:** I don't know about you, but when I enter into a financial contract I want to know a little something about the person on the other side agreement. So if you were a little concerned about who's protecting your option rights, this part is for you. The Options Clearing Corporation (OCC) is the clearing firm that guarantees option sellers will meet their obligations. So when you buy an option contract on an exchange, you don't have to seek out the seller when it's time to exit the position. When you buy an option that trades on multiple exchanges it has the same terms regardless of whether you bought it on the CBOE, ISE, or any of the six exchanges listed. All of these exchanges clear through the OCC (www.optionsclearing.com).

✔ **Options Industry Council:** The OCC and six option exchanges all participate in an investor education partnership known as the Options Industry Council (OIC). The mission for this organization is to educate the investing public about listed stock options. The OIC Web site is www.optionscentral.com and should definitely be on your list of ones to check out.

Transactions unique to options

Because option contracts are created as needed, there is a unique way to enter option orders. You identify whether you are creating a new position or closing an existing position by including the following with your order:

✔ Buy to Open

✔ Sell to Open

✔ Sell to Close

✔ Buy to Close

In addition, exercising contract rights create a buy or sell transaction in the underlying stock that goes through the OCC.

The exercise process

Exercising your option contract is accomplished by submitting exercise instructions to your brokerage by its cutoff time. Check with your brokerage for this information. It usually takes one day for the option exercise and associated stock transaction to appear in your account.

When you exercise a put and do not own the underlying stock in your account, you are creating a short stock position. Be sure you understand all the risks and rewards associated with submitting exercise instructions.

The assignment process

When you are short a stock option contract, you are at risk of assignment from the time you create the position through expiration of the contract. The only way you can alleviate yourself of the obligation is to exit the position by entering a Buy to Close order for the option. Basically, when *assigned* you are on the receiving end of the transactional flow:

✔ When holding a short put, the assigned option is removed from your account and a Buy transaction occurs for the underlying stock.

✔ When holding a short call, the assigned option is removed from your account and a Sell transaction occurs for the underlying stock.

Contact your broker to find out the method they use to assign short options. Almost all use a random selection process.

Trading rules you should know

Whenever you begin trading a new market you likely get some butterflies until the first few trades go off without a hitch. It's always nice to find everything unfolds as you expected. That actually requires some advance work on your end and this short list of trading rules hopefully helps your comfort level with initial executions, as well as considerations down the road:

✔ **Contract pricing:** Options in general trade in $0.05 and $0.10 increments rather than $0.01 increments as with stocks. The exchanges began trading a pilot group of stocks and ETFs at $0.01 increments in 2007. Additional securities have been added to the program in a trend that will likely continue.

✔ **Transaction premium:** The premium value you pay for an option is obtained by multiplying the option price quoted in the market by the option's multiplier. This value is usually 100 for stock options. So when you purchase an option quoted at $2.80, you are actually paying $280 for the option, plus commissions.

✔ **Market conditions:** There are different market conditions that impact both the stock and options markets. These include:

- **Trading halts for a security or entire market:** If you hold options for a halted stock, the options are also halted. You still have the ability to exercise your contract rights when this occurs before expiration. Generally, a trading halt will not restrict your right to exercise at all.

- **Fast trading conditions for a security or securities:** When this happens, you can expect to see quotes that are changing quickly and you'll likely experience significant delays in order execution and reporting. Unless you must exit a position for risk reasons, I strongly advise against using market orders for options in fast markets.

- **Booked order:** A *booked order* is one that improves the current market quote and updates it. The market maker isn't necessarily willing to take the trade at the quoted level, but another trader is. You can encounter problems with such orders because the size can be as small as one contract. If you enter a ten-contract order that matches the booked order price, you may only be filled on one contract. The rest of your order may or may not be filled.

SEC Execution Quality Rules

In 2001, the Securities and Exchange Commission (SEC) adopted rules requiring market centers, including brokerage firms, to report on the execution quality and handling of its retail order flow (order flow from you and me). SEC Rule 11ac1-5 and Rule 11ac1-6 are the two primary rules that set the standards for reporting to the public. Option trades were originally excluded from this reporting, but exchanges do need to report any trades not executed at the National Best bid or Offer (NBBO).

SEC 11ac1-5 provides a monthly report on a variety of speed and execution measurements for all orders (collectively) covered by the rule which includes covers retail orders for market and marketable limit orders that are received during regular trading hours, and specifically excludes orders with special handling requirements. SEC 11ac1-6 is a quarterly reporting identifying where the brokerage firm sent its covered order flow, along with any material relationships the firm has with that market venue (i.e. any payment it receives from an exchange for its orders.)

Execution quality reporting focuses on two key elements: how close to the NBBO was your order executed and how long did it take. The NBBO measurement is calculated using the *effective to quoted spread* (E/Q%), which is equal to 1.00 or 100% when your order is executed at the midpoint of the NBBO spread. An E/Q% of 98% indicates a trade that was executed at a price better than the NBBO (price improvement) while an E/Q% of 105% indicates a trade that was executed at a price that was worse than the NBBO (price disimprovement).

The time for order completion begins when the market center receives your order (the trading department acting as market maker or specialist if your brokerage firm completes that portion of the transaction). The time measurement ends when the order is executed in the market place, not when you receive the trade report back via the web or your broker.

The SEC requirements are specific, but there are enough vagaries for firms to highlight their strengths and down play their weaknesses. You may find firms using best-ex reporting as part of their marketing campaign. Since order flow routing information provides summary information rather than specific order details, the results you experience on your order execution may seem vastly different from what you see reported from 1-5, 1-6 or marketing literature.

✔ **Best-execution:** *Execution quality* is a general term used to describe a broker's ability to provide trade completions at, or better than, the current market for the security. This means when you place an order to buy an option with an asking quote of $2.00, your order is filled in a timely manner at $2.00 or better. Execution quality reports use the National Best Bid and Offer (NBBO) for all exchanges trading the security. Option exchanges are required to send a daily report to your broker whenever a trade is executed at a price other than the NBBO, referred to as *traded-through*. They must also provide an exception reason for the trade through. Even with the reporting, you may feel you're not getting the best possible executions on your option trades.

If you are not satisfied with the execution you receive on a specific order, or you have an order that was marketable and is still open, contact your broker immediately. The broker can check the status of the order (it may be executed but the trade report is delayed) and market condition details that are more difficult to track as time passes. More often than not, your broker really wants to get you the best execution possible.

Because an option eventually expires you really need to understand option valuations so you don't pay too much for the time remaining. You can manage this time risk by exiting a long option at least 30 days before it expires. Within 30 days, the option's time value erodes at an accelerated pace.

Weighing Option Costs and Benefits

There are benefits to using options, but you don't get those for free. The biggest risk associated with an option is its limited life because an option can expire worthless. You could lose your entire investment. Clearly this is a risk that needs to be addressed, which I do throughout the book. Other option cost factors to be considered include:

- ✔ Costs associated with the trading process
- ✔ Cost of future movement for the stock

By understanding the basic cost structure for an option that I discuss in the following sections, you can see how options provide leverage at a reduced risk. The extent to which options do this is very powerful.

Option prices are partially based on probabilities. For stock options, you want to consider the likelihood a particular option will be in-the-money at expiration given the type of price movements the underlying stock has experienced in the past.

Identifying costs unique to options

Because options are a little different than other securities, it's important to recognize that these securities have certain characteristics that make them more expensive than trading more commonly held securities such as stocks. The main costs to consider include:

- ✔ **Liquidity:** The ease you can enter and exit a trade without impacting its price, varies by option. Low liquidity securities are more expensive.

- ✔ **Time:** The more time you are purchasing, the greater the cost of the option.

- ✔ **Volatility:** Stocks with greater price movement in the past are expected to continue such movement in the future. The more volatile the stock, the more expensive the option.

The ways each of these items impact your trading costs follow in this section.

Paying for less liquidity

Although many option contracts are actively traded with high open interest, the sheer number of contracts available to trade means there will also be those that have limited daily volume and open interest levels. This results in a wider spread which translates to higher costs for you.

The *spread* is the difference between the market bid and the ask. When liquidity is low, the spread widens. *Slippage* is the trading term associated with money lost due to the spread. The best way to think about this cost is if you were to buy on the ask then immediately turn around and sell the option on the bid you would have a loss. This loss is referred to as slippage.

Lean toward higher open interest contracts with higher volumes when trading options to reduce the impact of slippage costs. These liquid contracts can be more easily entered and exited without widening the spread and increasing your costs.

Compensating for time

All option contracts have a time value associated with them. The more time until the contract expires, the more the option costs. The only problem is, everyday you own the contract, time to expiration is decreasing as is the option's value associated with it. *Theta* is the measure that provides you with the estimated value lost on a daily basis and is covered in the section, "Grasping Key Option Pricing Factors," later in this chapter.

When first reviewing option chains, be sure to compare options that have the same strike price but different expiration months to note the cost of time.

Paying for time means you need to consider options that reasonably reflect potential movement for the underlying. Given the wide range of strike prices and expiration months available to you, this is certainly possible.

Shelling out money for high flyers

Some stocks are more volatile and regularly swing a few percentage points each month, while other more quiet stocks take a few months for those kinds of moves. Generally, the cost of time for an option increases if the stock has proven to be more volatile in the past.

Valuing options benefits

By keeping the rights associated with a particular option type straight, you can often figure out a quick estimate of an option's value from the option's strike price and the market price of the stock. The three primary factors for valuing any stock option include the following:

- The type of option, call or put
- The option strike price
- The price of the underlying stock

Understanding these basic structural valuation features allow you to then appreciate the limited risk and unlimited reward potential options possess. Although I reiterate the fact that you can lose your entire option investment, you have to compare that to the losses accumulated when owning the underlying stock. By substantially limiting the investment amount through the options market you also substantially limit risk.

Stock values and option premiums

You need to consider two things when valuing an option:

- The value of the option rights given the current price of the stock
- The potential for stock movement between now and expiration

Option prices are broken into two pieces:

- **Intrinsic value:** The value of the contract rights if the contract is exercised and the resulting position is then exited in the market. With a call option, this value is the profits realized if you were to exercise the call then immediately sell the stock. When these two transactions result in a gain, that gain is the option's intrinsic value. When there's a loss, intrinsic value equals zero. Intrinsic value is calculated differently for calls and puts:

  Intrinsic Value (Call) = Market price of stock – Option strike price

  Intrinsic Value (Put) = Option strike price – Market price of stock

> ✔ **Extrinsic value:** The remaining value, which is attributable to time — this is also known as *time value* because it adds potential value for the option based on future moves for the stock. The extrinsic value is what remains after you account for intrinsic value. To determine the time value for an option contract, subtract the intrinsic value from the option price:
>
> Extrinsic Value = Option Price – Intrinsic Value

An option's intrinsic value cannot be less than zero. Whenever the calculation used to determine intrinsic value falls below zero, intrinsic value equals zero.

Option moneyness

Options are said to have a certain *moneyness,* which describes relative information about the intrinsic value of a contract. The calculation for intrinsic value can lead to three different results in terms of moneyness:

✔ In-the-money (ITM) when Intrinsic Value > 0

✔ At-the-money (ATM) when Intrinsic Value = 0

✔ Out-of-the-money (OTM) when Intrinsic Value < 0

These three terms are used regardless of whether an option is a call or a put. Whenever an option is OTM, its market price reflects only time value.

Options that are out-of-the-money (OTM) have only extrinsic value. This is also referred to as time value.

Leverage with reduced risk

The greatest benefit of trading individual options is the type of leverage you access. First, consider leverage with the stock market — when buying on margin you borrow from your broker to buy stock which gives you the opportunity to own more shares. As you probably know, using leverage this way is a double-edged sword:

✔ When using leverage to buy stock you reap additional rewards when the stock moves in your favor, but

✔ You also reap additional losses when the stock goes down.

Just because your broker is helping finance a stock transaction doesn't mean he shares in the losses — those are all yours. On top of that, you still have to pay the broker's financing fees in the form of margin interest whether you have a profit or loss.

When you access leverage with an option, you gain control of a certain number of shares of stock through your rights at a cost that is much, much lower than purchasing (or selling) those shares outright. This significantly amplifies gains and losses resulting from the position.

When using margin to leverage a stock position, both your gains and losses accelerate. Gains must outpace financing costs in the form of margin interest.

An example of leverage with reduced risk

The best way to get a feel for how to leverage with reduced risk is through an example. Using stock ABC trading at $43, assume you purchased 100 shares at this price with a 50% margin position and the stock moves up to $47 in one month. The value of a $40 strike call option was $4. After the move to $47 the call will be at least $7 because this represents its intrinsic value.

- ✔ Option rights (purchase rights) = $40
- ✔ Market value (sale price) = $47
- ✔ Call intrinsic value: $47 − 40 = $7

Calculating the returns for the stock using a 50% margin purchase:

- ✔ Initial investment: $43 × 100 × 0.50 = $2,150
- ✔ Gains: ($47 − 43) × 100 = $400
- ✔ Gain as percent of initial investment: $400 ÷ 2,150 = 18.6%

Calculating the returns for the option:

- ✔ Initial investment: $4 × 100 = $400
- ✔ Gains: ($7 − 4) × 100 = $300
- ✔ Gain as percent of initial investment: $300 ÷ 400 = 75%

Both the stock and option position provide you with leverage. Assuming the stock dropped $4 instead of moving upward and the option lost all its value. Instead of gains there would be losses of 18.6% and 100%, respectively.

The real power for the leveraged option position is its limited loss nature. Assuming a third scenario, really bad news is released for the stock and it dropped $13 instead:

Calculating the losses for the stock using a 50% margin purchase:

- ✔ Initial investment: $43 × 100 × 0.50 = $2,150
- ✔ Losses: ($43 − 30) × 100 = ($1,300)
- ✔ Loss as percent of initial investment: ($1,300) ÷ 2,150 = (60%)

Calculating the losses for the option:

- ✔ Initial investment: $4 × 100 = $400
- ✔ Losses: ($4 − 0) × 100 = ($400)
- ✔ Loss as percent of initial investment: ($400) ÷ 400 = (100%)

Although the loss percent is higher for the option, it is capped. The losses can continue with the stock position and can even generate margin calls requiring you to deposit additional funds to hold the position.

Grasping Key Option Pricing Factors

Option prices are determined by the type of option (call or put), its strike price, the price of the underlying stock, and the time remaining to expiration. Prices are also determined by the volatility of that underlying stock. It turns out this last pricing component plays a pretty big role in options analysis and strategy selection.

There are option valuation measures available to you that help you determine whether an option price quoted in the market represents a reasonable value or not. The measures provide you with a feel for how decreasing time or changes in the stock's price or volatility impact the option's price. These measures are available for each individual option and are referred to as the option because most of their names are derived from Greek letters.

Introducing option Greeks

An option's Greeks provide you with the value of expected changes in the option, given changes in the underlying stock. They are derived from one of several option valuation models and are available to you from various sources, such as an option calculator. Most option exchange Web sites provide this tool.

Using an option calculator, you enter the price of the underlying stock, the option strike price, time to expiration, and the option quote. The calculator then provides each of the Greek values listed. The insight you gain from the Greeks include the following:

- ✔ **Delta:** Represents the expected change in the option value for each $1 change in the price of the underlying stock.
- ✔ **Gamma:** Represents the expected change in Delta for each $1 change in the price of the underlying stock.

- **Theta:** Represents the option's expected daily decline due to time.

- **Vega:** Represents the expected change in the option value due to changes in volatility expectations for the underlying stock.

- **Rho:** Estimates changes in the option value due to changes in the risk-free interest rate (usually T-bills). Option price changes attributable to interest rates are much smaller, so this last measure receives less coverage.

Option valuation models can be used to determine whether a particular option is relatively expensive or cheap. A model is best applied when you understand its assumptions and recognize the Greeks provide expected values that by no means guarantee the future.

Delta

Delta is probably the most important Greek value for you to initially understand because it connects changes in the underlying stock's value directly to changes in the option value. Delta values range from:

- Calls: 0 and 1.00 or 0 and 100
- Puts: 0 and –1.00 or 0 and –100

Gamma

Gamma provides you with the expected change in delta for each $1 change in the price of the underlying stock. By understanding and checking gamma, there's less of a chance that delta values will get away from you.

The delta for an ATM option is approximately +/–0.50 regardless of the stock's past volatility. Option valuations assume that there's a 50% chance the stock will move up and a 50% chance it will move down.

Assuming ABC is trading at $20 and moves to $21, Table 3-1 provides option data before and after the move for a 20 strike call and put:

Table 3-1	Option Values for ABC Call and Put			
Type	**Moneyness**	**Value**	**Delta**	**Gamma**
Stock at $20: Call	ATM	$1.10	+0.50	0.1962
Stock at $20: Put	ATM	$1.00	–0.50	0.1931
Stock at $21: Call	ITM	$1.60	+0.70	0.1438
Stock at $21: Put	OTM	$0.50	–0.30	0.1467

Connecting past movement to the future

Past movement in the underlying stock is used to determine the probability that a certain minimum or maximum price will be reached. As you know, past movement doesn't provide you with a map of what's going to happen during the next month, next week, or even next day, but that doesn't mean you can't look at past movement to evaluate the potential for certain price targets to be reached. This section takes a look at two key measures that relate past movement in a stock to movement that is expected in the future.

Historical volatility

Historical volatility (HV) is a measure of past movement in a stock and is also referred to as statistical volatility (SV). To calculate HV you must do the following:

1. **Calculate the daily price change over a set number of days.**

2. **Calculate the average value for price change over that period.**

3. **Determine how each daily price change compares to that average value by taking the standard deviation for the price changes in the set.**

4. **Divide the value in step 3 by 0.0630 to approximate an annualized standard deviation.**

It's next to impossible to avoid statistical lingo when discussing option valuations. Don't get hung up on the math — HV is calculated in this manner so you can make an apples-to-apples comparison of a stock's most recent movement versus its past movement. It also allows you to compare two different stocks.

Standard deviation measures how dispersed data is from its average value. When applying this measure to stocks, those with a higher HV are expected to make bigger daily moves that are less predictable than those with a smaller HV. Lower HV stocks have daily changes that stay close to the average daily change.

Past stock movement is used as a basis for future expectations. Expected values don't use just this information though. Each day news is released that impacts expectations going forward. This is where implied volatility (IV) enters the picture.

Implied volatility

Implied volatility (IV) is one component of an option's price and is related to the time remaining until expiration. On a given day, you can identify as follows:

- ✔ Current price for a given stock
- ✔ Nature of past movement for the stock
- ✔ The type and strike price for a particular option
- ✔ The number of days until that option expires

What you don't know of course is what the stock is going to do between now and expiration. Don't let anyone kid you, no one does. However, what everyone in the market knows, including you, are the previous four things listed.

IV is based on historical volatility, but there is more to it than just that. It also incorporates supply and demand pricing pressures for the individual option. IV is part of the extrinsic value and provides you information about what market participants expect to see happen in the underlying stock.

The biggest distinction between HV and IV is that there is a specific formula for HV — it uses past data for the stock. IV is based on this calculation, but is more abstract and reflects new information about the market. There's also a psychological component to IV. A large one-day move in a stock has some impact on its 100-day HV calculation, but the impact on the option's IV will likely be much more pronounced because of the uncertainty this one-day event brings.

IV is the volatility implied by the current market price for the option.

Modeling option values

An option pricing model uses stock and option data to provide you with a theoretical value for the option. A few similar models exist, such as the one available on the OIC's Web site (www.optionscentral.com), and you can access them via an options calculator. By comparing an option's theoretical value to its market price, you get a feel for whether the option is relatively expensive or cheap.

The difference between the option's model value and actual value reflects the difference between historical and implied volatility.. An option model incorporates historical volatility, while the market value reflects IV. You may be able to identify a good reason for an option to be expensive or cheap — expensive isn't always bad and cheap isn't always good.

Different historical volatility (HV) values are available using a variety of time frames and typically include 10-day, 20-day, and 100-day. IV is an option specific value based on its current price. Both HV and IV values are available to you from a variety of sources, including option analysis software.

There are two ways an option calculator can be used (Figure 3-1 displays an option pricing calculator with sample inputs):

> ✔ Using HV to get the option's theoretical value
>
> ✔ Using the current market price of the option to get IV

The first option pricing model was developed by Fisher Black and Myron Scholes, earning them a Nobel Prize in Economics.

Figure 3-1:
Sample
inputs for
OIC option
pricing
calculator.

An option calculator that uses HV in the volatility field will provide you with the following when you click Calculate:

> ✔ The theoretical value for both the call and put at that strike price
>
> ✔ The theoretical Greeks for both the call and put

Nice, eh? This is good information and you can compare the theoretical price to the actual price in the market. When first starting out, change-up the inputs to see how they impact option prices.

Figure 3-2 displays the option pricing calculator results when you click the Calculate button.

Now you have a sense of appropriate option prices assuming the stock moves the way it did in the past. At those prices, you can use the Greeks to estimate option prices changes based on changes in the underlying or changes in interest rates.

Figure 3-2:
Sample
results for
OIC option
pricing
calculator.

Something that will actually provide you with better information in terms of
the Greeks though, is to calculate the implied volatility using this feature on
the OIC calculate. Now when you click Calculate you obtain the implied
volatility for the call or put which can be used to get the Greeks expected
when you buy or sell the call and put.

Theoretical option values are based on historical volatility versus actual
option market prices which are based on implied volatility. These values are
compared to artfully determine if future expectations reasonably reflect
what's happened in the past for the stock. Even when actual prices exceed
model prices, the option may still represent a trading opportunity.

Chapter 4

Option Risks and Rewards

Most traders identify an exit price prior to entering an order for a new position as part of their risk management. The exit is executed through an advanced order type or manually by the trader as they monitor the position. A major problem with this approach is that the stock may gap down below the exit level at the open creating greater losses. Manual execution is generally worse because then the trader can rationalize not executing the exit at all.

The fact of the matter is that the maximum risk for stocks is the entire investment and more when trading on margin. Stocks get halted or can decline rapidly and traders can create long-term investments from short-term positions. It's the nature of the beast. So when trading stocks or options, you need to acknowledge the true risk for these securities. This chapter looks at both risk and reward for stocks and options by identifying them, then quantifying them.

Understanding Your Trading Risks

Risk is related to reward, but it is possible to be subject to more risk given the same reward potential. It depends on the risk characteristics of the security you trade. Understanding your risk means you know the following:

- ✔ The maximum loss possible
- ✔ The conditions that create this maximum loss

Knowing your risk comes before knowing your reward potential and managing your risk comes way, way before thinking about what you can do with those gains.

Risk includes both the potential for losses as well as the lack of gains. In the latter case, investments that don't keep up with rising costs of living may be depleted.

Risking money with stocks

I recently heard a trader mention that as soon as they put money into a stock trade, they assume their maximum allowed risk for that trade is the entire investment, acknowledging the fact that the entire position can go to zero before he can respond. Although you may use stops to reduce your perceived maximum risk, the truth of the matter is the entire position has the potential for loss.

Long stock

There are two ways for you to establish a long stock position:

✔ Purchasing the stock with 100% cash

✔ Purchasing the stock on margin with 50% cash

Although you can limit the amount of margin used to some number below 50%, this is the maximum amount allowed for an initial position and a good place to start.

When buying stock ABC at a 32, it can move up, down, or sideways the next day. Losses accrue with continued downward moves. Usually stocks vacillate up and down, but it is possible for you to get in on a really bad day when the ABC experiences only declines going forward. Or worse yet, it is possible for ABC to stop trading, preventing you from exiting at any level.

Although you will likely exit at some point, the fact remains that when purchasing a stock with 100% cash, the stock can move downward to zero resulting in a complete loss of your investment. So the maximum risk you have when buying a stock is:

$$\text{\# of Shares} \times \text{Price of Stock} = \text{Risk}$$

Purchasing a stock on margin provides you with leverage, allowing you to own more stock for a set initial investment. This magnifies both gains and losses and is often referred to as a double-edged sword.

Assuming you purchased ABC on margin rather than using 100% cash, your risk increases by 1 divided by the initial margin percentage or 1 / 0.50 = 2. Welcome to leverage.

To calculate your maximum risk when buying stock on margin, you can start by multiplying the initial investment by 1 divided by the initial margin percentage. You need to also add the cost of using margin which is the margin interest rate for the stock holding period.

The maximum risk you have when buying a stock using 50% margin is:

$$\text{Risk} = (\text{\# of Shares} \times \text{Price of Stock}) \times (1 \div \text{Initial Margin \%})$$

Use of margin to purchase stocks must consider the downside for the strategy.

Short stock

When you short a stock you reverse the order of the typical stock transaction. Rather than buying first and selling later, you sell first and buy the stock at a later point. You still want to buy low and sell high, but a bearish outlook for a particular stock means you have to sell first to capitalize on this view.

To sell a stock you don't own, you need to borrow the shares from your broker. If the stock is a popular one to short, shares may or may not be available to you. You need to check your broker's short sale list or contact them directly to determine this. Traders using brokers that specialize in active trading accounts will likely find it to be less of a problem for them.

When completing brokerage account paperwork you may be providing them with authorization to lend out shares in your account which are then made available to short sellers.

You can only hold a short stock position in a margin account — short selling stock is not allowed in retirement accounts such as Individual Retirement Arrangements (IRAs). Although a credit is received for the sale of stock, a 150% margin is required to establish the position. This basically translates to a 50% margin after deducting the initial credit you receive for the sale.

Where does that put you in terms of risk? In a position that is very high risk. There is no limit to how high a stock can move upward; shorting a stock is an unlimited risk strategy. Granted you can buy back a stock before it goes to infinity and beyond, but in the same way a stock can gap down, it can gap up. Consider how many short positions feel pain after an intra-meeting Fed rate cut occurs.

Long stock represents a limited, but high risk position. It is limited because a stock can only move down to zero, it can't trade below that. The risk remains high because a stock can do just that — move to zero. This risk increases when margin is used and creates a situation where you can lose more than your initial investment.

Calculating option risks

Both call and put options have risk that is limited to the initial investment. This initial investment can vary in size, but is less than the investment required to control the same number of shares of the underlying stock. Although the risk is relatively smaller in terms of dollars, it's important to recognize the likelihood that an option will go to zero is much higher than the underlying stock going to zero.

The chance that an option will go to zero is 100%. Remember an option is a limited life security that eventually expires. At expiration, the option value goes to zero.

Call option

A call option provides the buyer with rights to purchase the underlying stock at the contract's strike price by its expiration date. When the strike price for the call option is below the price for the underlying stock, it will lose time value as expiration nears. Assuming the stock remains at the same price level, this time decay can result in losses for the trader. The losses will be limited because the option retains its intrinsic value.

However, when the stock is trading below the strike price the option's value is all time value. Assuming the stock remains at the same price level, time value diminishes as you get closer to expiration. Continuing in this manner will result in a total loss of the initial investment.

Most of the time a stock doesn't stand still, it does that vacillation thing. That means that although there's a chance the underlying stock will increase in value rising above a call strike price, the stock may also decline in value and fall below the strike price. Once again that puts you in a situation where you can lose your entire investment as expiration nears.

Put option

A put option provides the buyer with rights to sell the underlying stock at the contract's strike price by its expiration date. The option will lose time value as expiration nears, which can result in losses for the trader when the stock is trading above the option strike price. When trading below the strike price, the losses will be limited because the option retains intrinsic value.

However, when the stock is trading above the strike price the option's value is all time value. Assuming the stock remains at the same price level, time value diminishes as you get closer to expiration. Continuing in this manner will result in a total loss of the initial investment.

Because the stock has the same chance of rising as falling, there's a chance the underlying stock will increase in value rising above a put strike price. As a result, you can lose your entire investment as expiration nears.

Reaping Your Rewards

So with all this stock and option risk, just why do you do it? Because the interest you receive on a regular money market account can often be below the rate of inflation, the only way for your savings to keep up or outpace your expenses in the future is by assuming this risk. You should expect rewards that are better than a money market rate. Both stocks and options provide this potential.

Benefiting from stocks

As a stock holder you can benefit by receiving dividends and/or gains in the price of the stock. This often results when a company's sales or profits increase, when new products or technologies are introduced, and other countless reasons. There are also approaches that allow you to benefit from downward moves in the stock.

Long stock

A long stock position by purchasing shares of stock in the market. Because stock can continue to exist indefinitely, it can continue to rise without limit. What ultimately happens is a function of the company prospects and general market conditions. So your potential reward with stock is unlimited.

Not all companies distribute profits in the form of dividends to stock holders. Many growth stocks retain profits to fuel continued growth.

Short stock

You create a short stock position by reversing the standard stock transaction; you sell first with the expectations that the price of the stock will go down. In this situation you profit when you buy the shares back. You complete such transactions in a brokerage account that allows margin trading.

The rewards you reap for a short stock position is similar to the risks assumed for a long stock position — it is high, but limited. A stock can continue to decline, but only until it reaches zero. This is the downside limit that caps your rewards.

Call options increase in value when the underlying stock rises while put options increase in value when the underlying stock falls.

Breaking even with options

A call option provides you with similar profits as long stock while a put option provides you with similar profits as short stock. This makes sense given your rights as an option holder it allows you to buy or sell stock at a set level. There is one slight difference between stock rewards and option rewards; options require an initial premium payment that you must consider when identifying potential gains.

Calculating potential option rewards requires you to add option premiums to call strike prices and subtract option premiums from put strike prices to come up with a price known as the position's *breakeven* level. A stock must:

- Rise above the breakeven for call option profits to kick in
- Fall below the breakeven for put option profits to kick in

In each case, this results in profits that are slightly less than your stock profits.

A stock's breakeven point is your purchase price when buying stock or your sell price when shorting a stock. As soon as the stock moves away from this price, you have gains or losses.

Call option

Purchasing a call option gives you rights to buy stock at a certain level. As a result, the option increases in value when the stock moves upward. After a stock moves above your call option's strike price, the option has intrinsic value which increases as the stock continues to rise. Calls with strike prices below the price of the stock are referred to as in-the-money (ITM).

For a call position you own to be profitable at expiration, it must remain above the strike price plus your initial investment. At this level option premiums will minimally equal your cost when you bought the call.

The breakeven for a call option is:

Call Breakeven = Call Strike Price + Call Purchase Premium

After a stock is at the option's breakeven level, it can continue to rise indefinitely. Your call option can similarly rise indefinitely until expiration. As a result, call option profits are considered to be unlimited, just like stock.

An option's moneyness is determined by the option type and the price of the underlying stock relative to the option strike price. Call option's with a strike price that is below the stock price is out-of-the-money (OTM) and its premium is all time value. After the stock moves above the strike price, it is referred to as in-the-money (ITM) and has intrinsic value along with the time value.

Put option

Purchasing a put option gives you rights to sell stock at a certain level. As a result, the option increases in value when the stock moves downward. When a stock moves below your put option's strike price, the option has intrinsic value which increases as the stock continues to fall. Puts with strike prices above the price of the stock are referred to as in-the-money (ITM).

For a put position you own to be profitable at expiration, it must remain below the strike price minus your initial investment. At this level option premiums will minimally equal your cost when you bought the put.

The breakeven for a put option is:

Put Breakeven = Put Strike Price – Put Purchase Premium

When a stock is at the option's breakeven level, it can continue to fall until it reaches zero. Your put option can continue to increase in value until this level is reached, all the way to its expiration. As a result, put option profits are considered to be high, but limited, just like a short stock.

Call options have risks and rewards similar to long stock while put options have rewards that are similar to short stock. Put option risk is limited to the initial investment. The reason your rewards are similar rather than the same is because you need to account for the premium amount when you purchased the option.

Profiling Risk and Reward

Profiling risk and reward means you're using a visual to get a feel for potential gains and losses for the trade. By doing this you can quickly assess strategies you already trade as well as new ones. *Risk graphs* or *risk profiles* are graphical views of potential risks and rewards in option trading. You can create a generic graph that excludes prices to identify the risks and rewards for any asset type. In addition, you can also create a more specific risk graph that includes stock price levels, with breakeven levels, profits, and losses for a particular position.

Profiling stock trades with risk graphs

Although risk graphs are more commonly used in option trading, it's important for you to get a good picture of stock risk graphs. Such basic profiles simply look at maximum potential risks and maximum potential rewards.

Long stock

The maximum potential risk for long stock is high, but limited to the downside. This is because a stock can only decline to zero. The maximum potential rewards for a stock position is unlimited because a stock can technically rise without limit.

The long stock risk graph displayed in Figure 4-1 reflects this risk-reward profile.

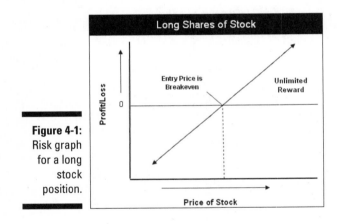

Figure 4-1: Risk graph for a long stock position.

By profiling the risks and rewards this way for long stock, you quickly see that losses (which are limited to the initial investment amount) accumulate as the stock price declines while profits continue to rise as the stock price rises.

Short stock

The maximum potential risk for short stock is unlimited because a stock can technically rise without limit. The maximum potential reward for a short stock position is high, but limited to the downside. This is because a stock can only decline to zero.

The short stock risk graph displayed in Figure 4-2 reflects this risk-reward profile.

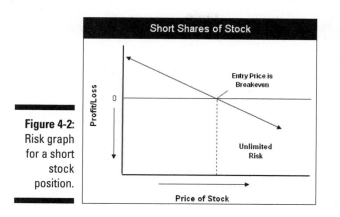

Figure 4-2:
Risk graph
for a short
stock
position.

The short stock risk graph quickly displays losses that rise without limit as the stock rises and profits that are high, but limited as the stock declines.

Profiling option trades with risk graphs

Basic call and put option risk graphs incorporate the risk and reward for the security, along with the breakeven level. Position specific profiles will include stock prices on the x-axis and profits/losses on the y-axis. The profile also identifies the following:

- The option strike price
- The position breakeven

Although it's less obvious when you're viewing generic risk profiles, the main benefit of using options to limit losses can be viewed in these risk graphs.

Call option

A basic call option risk graph is similar to a long stock risk graph with two distinctions:

- You need to account for the call option premium in the breakeven level.
- Your losses are capped to the downside before a stock declines to zero.

The potential risk for a call option is limited while the potential rewards are unlimited. This is displayed by a generic call option risk graph displayed in Figure 4-3.

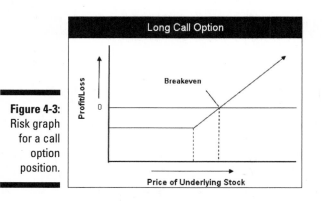

Figure 4-3:
Risk graph
for a call
option
position.

The call option risk graph provides you a visual of losses that are limited to the initial investment as the stock declines. This amount is much smaller than those for a long stock position. It allows unlimited profits that are similar to a long stock position, but must also account for the call option breakeven level.

Put option

A basic put option risk graph is similar to a short stock risk graph with a couple of distinctions. The second one is extremely valuable if you're bearish on a stock:

✔ You need to account for the put option premium in the breakeven level.

✔ Your losses are capped with an upside move and are therefore limited.

The potential risk for a put option is limited while the potential rewards are limited, but high. This is displayed by a generic put option risk graph displayed in Figure 4-4.

Figure 4-4:
Risk graph
for a put
option
position.

The put option risk graph provides you a visual of losses that are limited to the initial investment as the stock rises. As a trader, you have to prefer this graph to the short stock profile. It also provides profits that are similar to a short stock position which are high, but limited. The put risk graph also accounts for the put option breakeven level.

When you buy a put option, the most you can lose is this initial investment. Although that's pretty undesirable, you need to remember that this initial investment is much smaller than a short stock position which is also used when you have a bearish outlook for the stock.

Combining option positions

Many investors use put options as a form of insurance for existing stock positions. You can buy puts for stocks you own, as well as for those you don't own because holding the underlying asset is not a requirement in the listed option markets.

A *combined position* is one that is made up of one of two things:

- ✔ Stock and options for a single underlying stock
- ✔ Multiple options for a single underlying stock

In addition to creating a risk graph for a single stock or option position, you can also create ones for combined positions. This definitely helps you easily access the reward profile for the position and more importantly, its risk profile.

Trading options with stock

Three basic combination positions for long stock and options include the following:

- ✔ A married put position
- ✔ A covered call position
- ✔ A collar position

In each case long stock is paired with a long put, a short call, or both to improve the risk and/or reward potential. Similar combination positions can be applied to a short stock position.

You can hold a stock position and purchase options on that same stock to change the risk or reward profile for the stock or you can hold option positions without holding a position in the underlying.

Trading options with options

There are many combination positions that use multiple options to capitalize on market conditions or improve the risk and/or reward potential. Different market conditions include:

- High relative volatility
- Low relative volatility
- Sideways stock movement
- Directional stock movement (up or down)

After a market outlook is identified, different strike prices and options can be combined to vary risk and reward.

Profiling a combined position

You can draw risk graphs for combination positions by drawing the risk graph for each individual position and overlaying them. You then check to see if the risks or rewards for any one position provide a cap for the unlimited or limited, but high risks or rewards for the other position.

This is better understood through example. Figure 4-5 displays the risk graph for a married put position, one that combines long stock and a long put for the same stock.

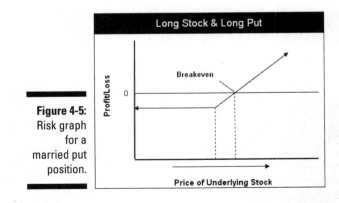

Figure 4-5:
Risk graph for a married put position.

In this figure, you create a risk-reward profile that is similar to a long call. By adding the put, you minimize losses for the stock. At the same time, your potential rewards remain unlimited after accounting for the new breakeven point.

Considering the worst-case scenario

Before looking at your potential gains, you must look at the downside if you want to continue trading for any extended period of time. By managing your risk, you stay in the game long enough to master different strategies that are appropriate for changing market conditions. That's why considering the worst-case scenario is so important — these worst-case scenarios can and will happen during your trading career.

All new traders assume they'll do the right thing when the time comes — exit a position when their predetermined exit level is reached. But after you've been trading awhile you know how hard this seemingly simple action can be. Never assume you will completely control the emotions you experience when trading. The best traders know that all they can do is manage them.

Start with single position risk graphs

Looking at the worst-case scenario means looking at the lower portion of the risk graph; the one that profiles your losses. After you have a certain stock or market outlook, you can select the position or strategy (i.e. long stock or long call option) that has the most desirable risk graph.

Look to trade strategies that do the following:

- ✔ Limit losses
- ✔ Allow unlimited profits

In Chapter 10 I discuss more specific position risk graphs that will make this more intuitive for you.

Improve existing risk graphs

There's a lot more to cover before exploring advanced strategies using combination positions with just options. Throughout the strategy review process, consider those option additions that improve the risk profile first. This can be done by:

- ✔ Capping losses that are limited but high and even better,
- ✔ Capping losses that are unlimited.

By managing your risk first, you get the opportunity to realize gains.

Part II:
Evaluating Markets, Sectors, and Strategies

The 5th Wave   By Rich Tennant

"Right now I'm working with a combination of charting techniques. Japanese Candlesticks, some Elliot Waves, and a dash of Magic 8-Ball."

In this part . . .

Trading options doesn't begin by running out to buy a call or put. It's the culmination of your analysis on the markets, sectors, and the underlying security for your trade. This part provides market assessment methods using breadth and sentiment analysis then moves on to technical analysis of sectors. It also incorporates the options market in this analysis. Because you may be exploring new strategies, you also want to evaluate those strategies in a systematic way to reinforce your understanding of them while also addressing the unique characteristics of options, such as trading costs and order placement methods, which I provide in this part.

Chapter 5

Tapping Into the Market's Mood

In This Chapter

▶ Digging deeper into market results

▶ Using option activity to determine market mood

▶ Assessing indicator levels

*U*sing breadth tools and sentiment analysis, you gain insight on the strength of a market move and the level of fear or complacency driving it. By looking at statistics such as volume and the number of advancing versus declining stocks, you know whether gains were due to just a handful of stocks or if a large number of them fueled the advance. The latter suggests continued strength while the former may be a warning sign of weakness ahead.

The options market can also be used to gauge the health of a stock market move. Monitoring option activity gives you a sense of the degree of fear or greed associated with an advance or decline. It helps you decide whether the trend has more room to go or may be stalled in the near future.

The name of the game with many sentiment analysis tools is extremes. Using past data to identify atypical readings, you can identify levels associated with unsustainable advances or declines. In this chapter, I sort through the different ways you can monitor the market to help make better trading decisions.

Assessing the Market's Bias

The stock market has a mind of its own and it pays to remember that . . . especially when you think you have the next move figured out. You might expect a decline when weak economic numbers are released only to be surprised by the rally that follows. Or you expect to see a boring day after a profitable earnings report is released, and then your jaw drops with the ensuing decline that's attributed to this news. When following market breadth and sentiment data, you get a sense of the market's mood before these seemingly crazy swings — they alert you to pending changes.

Judging the strength of a move

All market advances and declines are not the same. Advances can occur at a moderate pace with lots of sectors rising together, in a frenzied manner with some stocks and sectors strongly outperforming others, or any variation in between. What you want to do is assess the odds of that advance continuing.

It's similar for declines — you want to keep the odds in your favor by trading in the direction of the trend, but it's hard to create new positions when you feel you may have already missed the move. Looking at market breadth helps you decide whether conditions are improving or there's more room on the downside.

Keep the odds in your favor by using a variety of tools to confirm your market assessments, and then use strategies consistent with such assessments.

Defining market breadth

Market breadth focuses on the nature of market rises and declines. By monitoring the number of advancing versus declining stocks for a specific index you can gauge the health of the move for that index. During rising markets, you want to see a variety of companies participating in the advance. On declines you look for signs that there's so much participation the bear exhausts itself.

Breadth indicators use statistics based on the following:

- Number and volume for advancing and declining issues
- Number of issues reaching new highs or lows
- Up and down volume
- Issues trading above or below moving average lines

An advancing market with declining stocks outpacing advancing stocks in both number and volume is bearish — it suggests that a select group of stocks may be doing well, but overall the market is not healthy. On the other hand, market advances accompanied by stocks in a variety of sectors trading above their 200-day moving average is more bullish suggesting a healthy rise that will likely continue.

The advance-decline line breadth indicator

A commonly used breadth indicator is the advance-decline (Adv-Dec) line using the New York Stock Exchange (NYSE) Composite Index. You won't be looking for a specific bullish or bearish level for this indicator — you use it more as a confirming or diverging tool. You construct the line by keeping a daily cumulative total of:

Adv-Dec Line = # of Advancing Issues – # of Declining Issues

You may note an index is rising even when the Adv-Dec Line is falling. This happens when:

✔ Component stocks with more influence on the index increase even if a majority of the component stocks decrease

✔ A smaller number of stocks advance, but the value of gains from advancing stocks is greater than the value of losses from decliners.

The number of unchanged issues are excluded from this indicator. When using the tool, focus on trends rather than absolute values for this tool. Figure 5-1 displays the daily Adv-Dec Line with the NYSE Composite Index (NYA).

From June to mid-July in 2007 NYA was rising, but this move was not confirmed by a large number of advancing issues. The Adv-Dec Line was diverging from NYA, which eventually suffered some serious declines.

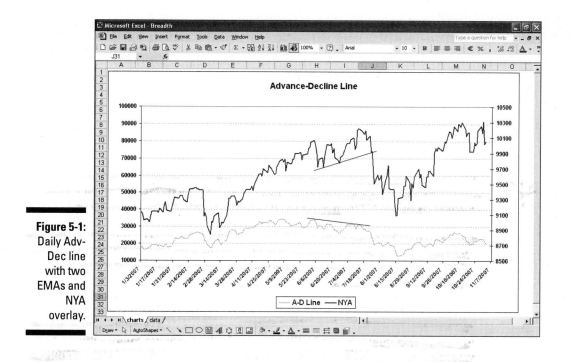

Figure 5-1:
Daily Adv-Dec line with two EMAs and NYA overlay.

Calculating the advance-decline line as a ratio

The Adv-Dec line may also be calculated as a ratio rather than a cumulative value (Adv/Dec). This results in an oscillating indicator with the following characteristics:

✔ Oscillates around the value one.

✔ When there are more advancers, the ratio is greater than one (more common).

✔ When there are more decliners, the ratio moves between zero and one.

Oscillator crosses of the center line, divergent movement, or movement into extreme ranges are monitored for potential turns.

When an indicator suggests weakness as a stock or index is moving upward or strength when either is moving downward, the indicator is diverging from the price or index level.

Adv-Dec indicators can be calculated on any index that provides daily advancing and declining statistics. When monitoring the Adv-Dec line, look for advancers to outpace decliners in rising markets and decliners to outpace advancers in falling markets to confirm index changes. When the indicator diverges from index action, the current trend may be in trouble.

Recognize that *contrarian strategies* are those that are counter to existing market trends. These represent higher risk trades because they anticipate a change in momentum and direction.

Adding volume as a key tool

Volume is a key tool used in market analysis — it provides fuel for upside moves and animates fear as declines pick up steam. Increasing volume confirms the current trend. Without it, the move becomes very suspect.

Splitting volume by movement type allows you to incorporate it into breadth analysis. During a bullish move you see whether a handful of advancers are leading the way with strong participation or if interest in even these popular shares is tapering off. It lets you know if the trend is in good shape or if you should start looking for other signs of weakness.

When markets are moving downward, the volume for declining issues is like a panic meter. You can practically see traders scrambling to hit the Enter button for sell orders. But then a funny thing happens . . . the decline continues, but there is a shift in these two volume components. Advancing volume starts to pick up, particularly for the favored stocks of the day.

Viewing advancing and declining volume separately provides one picture of market strength, but they can also be combined as ratios with the number of advancing and declining issues to display overall market breadth. The result is in interesting battle between the bulls and the bears. A breadth indicator using all this information is the Trader's Short-Term Index described next.

If you have easy access to index component quote lists, you can create advance-decline indicators for the index.

Measuring breadth with the Arms Index

The Arms Index, also known as the Trader's Short-Term Index (TRIN), is a widely used breadth indicator developed by Richard Arms, Jr. Incorporating volume provides additional insight about the strength of a market move. Calculating the Arms Index is pretty straightforward:

> [# of Advancing Issues ÷ # of Declining Issues] ÷ (Advancing Volume ÷ Declining Volume]

Once again the NYSE Composite Index is used; however readings for the Nasdaq Composite Index and AMEX Composite Index are also available. A daily close of 1.0 is neutral, although daily readings between 0.70 and 1.30 could be classified as neutral.

The Arms Index is primarily used for short-term alerts and trend indications, but it can also be used to assess the market. This is definitely one of those indicators that you should look at past data to help in understanding its movement. Be sure to include an overlay chart of the index to get the most out of the review.

Checking out an Arms chart

Arms noted that adding moving averages (MAs) to the indicator helped with market assessments. By also highlighting key levels with horizontal lines showing neutral areas and extremes, your analysis is more complete. It makes for a pretty ugly chart at first, but speeds up things in the long run. For more information on chart scaling and MA techniques used here, see Chapter 6.

Figure 5-2 provides a daily chart for the Arms Index (light, thin line) with NYA (dark, thick line) as an overlay. The Arms Index (TRIN) is shown as an inverted, log chart. Inverting it allows extremely high readings (bearish) to spike downward as the NYA sells off. A log scale displays relative readings more clearly. The chart also includes a 21-day EMA (lighter) and 55-day EMA (darker), as well as the following horizontal lines displaying key levels:

Figure 5-2:
Daily TRIN
with NYA
overlay and
EMA trend
lines.

✔ 1.0 (dark, solid line) designates a neutral area for the index.

✔ 0.70 designates an extreme daily reading that generally indicates a lower opening the next day (values less than 0.70 which are above the line).

✔ 1.30 designates an extreme daily reading that generally indicates a higher opening the next day (values more than 1.30 which are below the line).

✔ 2.85 designates an extremely bearish day.

✔ 1.10 designates oversold conditions for the EMAs.

The TRIN chart displayed in Figure 5-2 coincided with a strong decline in the fall of 2007. Note the movement of the MAs.

Taking a long-term look back

When viewing past conditions to gain insight on the here and now, it also pays to look further back at periods resembling the current one. As of late 2007 a long-term bull market is in place, so you want to compare the current situation to two types of mature bull trends:

✔ One associated with continued bullish conditions (late 1998)

✔ One signaling a major trend change (early 2000)

Regardless of the different scenarios you consider, focus on managing risk for existing conditions rather than betting on an anticipated move. Breadth indicators are extremely useful in identifying bottoms because market declines occur much faster. But there are no guarantees for a reversal.

(Psycho)-analyzing the market

Embracing the idea that the market has a mind of its own is easier when you consider that human behavior drives it. Some argue the market is efficient because people respond rationally to all available news about stocks, the economy, and prospects for both. That sounds great, but all you have to do is watch the way an index moves after big reports are released and you get the feeling that something very irrational is going on.

There are many rules-based approaches allowing you to make money in the markets, but that doesn't mean the market moves in a predictable way. Because buying and selling securities translates to making or losing money, you have to figure that market participants bring a good amount of irrationality to the game. Multiply one irrational person by many irrational people and you have a crowd moving prices up or down, quickly or slowly, depending on the day.

Crowds can behave in very strange ways when feeding on each other's greed or fear. There are ways to monitor market conditions and crowd behavior to better understand why the market reacts the way it does. One helpful step in this process is identifying which human emotion is in command at the time: greed or fear.

Defining sentiment

Sentiment broadly describes the overriding bias for the market, be it bullish or bearish. Greed (with a touch of fear) generally drives the former while it's all about fear when markets decline. Month after month, year after year, and decade after decade, these greed-fear patterns repeat regardless of economic changes that occur along the way.

Sentiment tools use stock and options statistics to provide you with information about crowd activity during advances and declines. Most of this data is available from exchange Web sites or charting packages. It's a matter of identifying which tools to monitor along the way.

When employing sentiment analysis, you try to identify periods when greed has gotten unsustainable or fear is just about exhausted. It's sort of like musical chairs . . . at some point the music stops and everyone is scrambling for a spot so they can participate in the next round or move. You just want to be prepared so that you can respond quickly when a change in direction does take place. Focusing on market sentiment may allow you to do just that.

Always remind yourself of what *is* happening in the market versus what you anticipate happening next.

Measuring investor actions

Sentiment analysis attempts to measure bullish and bearish actions versus what's being said about the market or even it's current direction. Watch for things, such as the following:

- Bullish commentary contradicted by unusually high put volume
- A mild economic report that produces a wild swing in the market

The options market gives you quick indications about trader sentiment:

- Are traders bullish (buying calls/selling puts)?
- Are they bearish (buying puts/selling calls)?

Option data primarily provides insight to fear. Historical volatility and volume measures give you a feel for how much emotion was involved with moves in the past. Implied volatility levels let you know what's anticipated for the road ahead.

Watching Call and Put Activity

Investors are generally bullish. Because the markets spend more time going up rather than down, this is a pretty rational result. Wait a minute . . . does that mean I think investors are rational? I guess they are at times, but I digress. The reason it pays to note market bullishness is because typically call volume exceeds put volume, reflecting the tendency for the market to advance. It provides you with an option activity baseline.

When people start getting nervous, as they will do, put volume increases. Monitoring the put-to-call relationship, you can identify extreme levels corresponding with market reversals. Indicators may use call and put volume, or put volume alone, to measure fear or complacency in the market.

Consider using extreme sentiment readings to reduce positions in the direction of the trend and slowly establish counter-trend positions.

Understanding put-to-call ratios

Martin Zweig is credited with creating put-to-call (P:C) ratios, deriving them by simply dividing put contract volume by call contract volume. A wide variety of such ratios are available to you. Alert levels have changed over the years, but the emotion they signal remains the same: fear.

A P:C ratio focuses on bullish and bearish action taken by various market participants. Many are also contrarian measures, meaning the implications for the indicator are opposite of market sentiment. When everyone is excessively bearish, conditions are right for a reversal. And when everyone is exuberant about market prospects, signs of a pending decline are overlooked. You interpret P:C ratio readings the following way:

✔ Extremely low readings are bearish.

✔ Extremely high readings are bullish.

Now for the good stuff. A select list of ratios using call and put volume follow, with information about the indicator construction and readings:

✔ **CBOE equity put/call ratio:** Total volume for all stock options trading on the CBOE. Readings from the former option volume leader are now less comprehensive given significant gains from the International Securities Exchange (ISE). In the past readings above 0.90 suggested increased fear in the market and oversold conditions. More recently readings above 0.80 reflect growing fear.

✔ **CBOE index only put/call ratio:** Total volume for all index options trading on the CBOE. This measure includes SPX and OEX index volume which remain important market barometers. A distinct aspect of this indicator is the type of trader it reflects — the index options trader is considered more sophisticated and on target with market moves. As a result, high readings reflect pending bearishness for the market. Readings above 2.4 reflect approximately three standard deviations (SD) above the mean and have occurred immediately before short-term and intermediate term tops.

Drops in the market typically happen faster than increases.

✔ **ISE Sentiment Index (ISEE):** This tool is actually a call:put ratio with two other important distinctions noted by the ISE:

- It focuses on new buys only, versus total volume which reflects short sellers too.

- It excludes market maker and other professional trader activities, leaving customer activity only (money managers and retail).

Because this index is an inverse of the typical ratios, low readings coincide with extreme bearishness. Since 2002, readings less than 85 are 2SD below the average and have coincided with short-term and intermediate term bottoms.

✓ **ISE index and ETF put/call ratio:** Total volume for all index and ETF options trading on the ISE. Consider augmenting the CBOE index-only ratio with this tool to round out your assessment of broad hedging activity.

Three keys to getting the most from all these sentiment tools are

✓ Knowing basic indicator construction information

✓ Understanding the historical extremes and implications for the tool

✓ Recognizing significant market changes and impact on indicator data

If you're zeroing in on the sentiment for individual security, be sure to capture the data from all exchanges that trade options for that underlying. Rather than a specific reading, identify atypical readings for the data by calculating the average value and standard deviations, then add lines to identify extreme levels.

Certain ETF and index options trade past 4:00 p.m. eastern time — be sure to track the correct closing time and price.

Figure 5-3 provides a daily chart for the S&P 500 exchange-traded fund (SPY) and its put/call ratio with a five-day moving average and a +1SD line.

Figure 5-3:
Daily SPY chart with P:C ratio.

When the 5-day simple MA for the SPY put:call ratio reached more than +1SD, a near term bottom was signaled six of eight times.

Indicators may behave differently during bull and bear markets and even during different stages of bull or bear markets (early, mid, late). When using a new indicator, check its performance during similar periods in the past.

You can also use these SD lines when identifying extremes for exchange data, particularly when market changes impact volume.

Using the put volume indicator

The put volume indicator (PVI) is a sentiment tool created by John Bollinger that measures relative put activity levels. It's similar to a P:C ratio with extreme readings used to identify periods of excessive fear or complacency. PVI can also be applied to individual stocks, indexes, or an entire exchange.

The PVI is calculated using daily put option volume data which is available from a number of sources, including the OCC and options analysis software. It's calculated by dividing daily put volume by the 10-day simple moving average (SMA) of that volume. A rising ratio indicates the following:

- Put volume is increasing
- Bearish sentiment is increasing

Figure 5-4 displays a daily chart of PVI values for the S&P 500 Index (SPX) with an overlay of SPY, the exchange-traded fund (ETF) based on the index. Very high readings identify extreme pessimism which sets the tone for a reversal.

Figure 5-4:
Put volume
indicator.

The chart includes the following:

- ✔ Daily price data for SPY
- ✔ PVI line across the bottom
- ✔ Central mean line at approximately 1.0
- ✔ +2SD line above the mean at 1.80 & -1SD line below it at 0.60

The vertical lines help view bearish extremes. Four of six of these extremes coincided with, or occurred shortly before, a bottom reversal in the market.

If you have data to create a put to call ratio, you can also create the PVI.

Using Volatility to Measure Fear

Market participants generally head for the exit much faster than committing new money to stock positions. The result . . . markets generally fall much faster than they rise. This can be seen with increased volatility as daily and weekly swings move in a larger range. Using volatility sentiment measures helps you recognize declines that are nearing exhaustion.

Measuring volatility

Volatility really just gives you information about the price range for a particular security. You can use a variety of trading periods to calculate an annualized value allowing you to compare movement for different securities. Historical volatility (HV) can be plotted on a chart enabling you to view trends and gain a sense of how current HV stacks up to previous periods.

Implied volatility (IV) is an option pricing component that is referred to as a plug figure. It's the volatility level that accounts for the current option price after all other, more tangible pricing factors (i.e. price, time and interest rates) are valued. IV incorporates HV because it's reasonable to expect the stock to move in a similar manner than it has in the past, but not necessarily the same.

IV can also be plotted on a chart allowing you to view trends and relative levels. Such charts highlight strong seasonal tendencies for certain stocks.

Recognizing impact from changing volatility

You want to understand IV so you can make the best decisions when buying and selling options. It can be advantageous to buy options when IV is relatively low and sell them when it's relatively high, but there are no guarantees that seemingly low or high conditions won't persist.

Clearly there's always a chance of being wrong about the direction of an index or stock (two out of three really), but generally:

✔ When IV is relatively low and increases quickly, it adds value to both calls and puts.

✔ When IV is relatively high and decreases quickly, it decreases value for both calls and puts.

Pending news and reports, along with unexpected events can spike IV. After the news or event is in the past and an initial reaction occurs in the stock, IV declines as quickly as it spiked. Changes in IV that are more gradual may also occur, in either direction.

Spelling fear the Wall Street way: V-1-X

VIX stands for volatility index. It is a blended implied volatility value calculated using specific S&P 500 Index option contracts and is used as a sentiment indicator. You may have heard references to the VIX by market analysts commenting on conditions.

Because statistical volatility usually climbs when securities decline, you should expect IV to increase too. By viewing the VIX and SPX on the same chart, you can see just how often it does. The following holds for VIX readings:

✔ A climbing VIX reflects bearish conditions in SPX and typically the market as a whole.

✔ A declining VIX reflects neutral to bullish conditions in SPX and typically the market as a whole.

Overly bearish sentiment is reflected by high VIX levels. Eventually the bearish fear is exhausted, a reversal in stocks occur, and the VIX declines.

The Volatility Index (VIX) was previously calculated using the S&P 100 (OEX) Index. This former VIX measure can be accessed using its new symbol: VXO.

Figure 5-5 displays a weekly chart for VIX with an SPX overlay.

Figure 5-5:
Weekly VIX
chart with
SPX overlay.

The relationship between the two indexes appears pretty strong when viewed together. The two are negatively correlated so when SPX goes down, VIX goes up and vice versa. Look for VIX reversals to confirm market bottoms.

Two other stock indexes with implied volatility data to watch include the Nasdaq Composite Index (COMPQ) and the S&P 100 Index (OEX). The corresponding volatility indexes are VXN and VXO, respectively.

When viewing a chart for the Volatility Index (VIX), readings prior to the revised S&P 500 (SPX) methodology are constructed using historic data.

Applying Breadth and Sentiment Tools

Most breadth and sentiment indicators make use of the same logic:

- ✔ Weakness in the reading is a bearish sign.
- ✔ When the reading is extremely bearish, it becomes bullish.

And thus goes the behavior of the crowd. The only notable exception is the CBOE index only P:C ratio. Because exchanges, trading platforms, and market products can potentially change over time, the nature of extremes for different indicators can also potentially change over time. Rather than using set-in-stone values for any one of them, you may want to combine a qualitative and quantitative assessment of them periodically.

When evaluating different breadth and sentiment tools, be sure to consider which indicators provide you with new information. It makes sense to include two or three option sentiment tools, but probably not five or six if that's the only type of sentiment indicator you're using. I guess it's okay if you're crazy about sentiment analysis and want to monitor everything under the sun, but try to use tools that provide different or complementary information.

To calculate the standard deviation for a column of data in Excel, use the cell formula: '=stdev(data)'.

Locating neutral areas for indicators

The Arms Index (TRIN) chart includes a neutral range between 0.70 and 1.30 — in this region there is no bias for the next day's open. When TRIN readings stay in that area you simply have to look to other indicators to confirm moves or gain insight on potential changes.

Although it might seem that 1.0 would be a neutral reading for a put/call ratio, it doesn't work that way. Under normal conditions the ratio will be less than 1.0 because markets typically move upward, reflecting a bullish bias.

One method used throughout this chapter to identify both neutral areas and extremes for different indicators is an average +/– standard deviation approach. Here are some things to keep in mind when applying this:

- ✔ The calculations require a data set from some series — the data selected must be representative of the series.

- ✔ When you move forward in time by a significant amount, you run the risk of applying outdated conditions to current conditions.

- ✔ Consider calculating values for clearly defined bullish and bearish periods to see if the indicator behaves differently in each.

This is where qualitative judgment comes in — you don't necessarily want to include all possible data points in your assessment because conditions change over time. But they don't change often, so you need to include enough data so you're capturing information that is truly representative.

Stock and index price data is not normally distributed so commonly used statistical rules for this data won't apply. You need to use returns.

By calculating an average value (mean) and standard deviation value, you're able to create bands around the central value to identify a region where most of the data is found. Points outside of that area are atypical — when focusing on these areas you're pinpointing times when emotions are running high and decisions are far from cool and calm.

Identifying indicator extremes

When analyzing data sets you can complete different statistical tests directly on the data including:

✔ Mean and median calculations for information about central tendencies

✔ Standard deviation calculations to identify extreme levels

Most often you'll use mean levels, but if one or two very extreme data points skew the results, you may opt to use a median value. When outliers are present, the mean value and median value will not be very close together.

In addition to applying these calculations directly to the data, you can apply them to smoothed segments of the data — namely moving averages. When doing this you want to keep the moving average period pretty short so that you don't overly smooth the values. Remember, you want to view extreme behavior, not smooth it over.

An outlier is a data point that is a good distance away from the other data points in the set and can't be dismissed.

A last look at advancing and declining breadth data is completed here using the advance-decline ratio, which oscillates around 1.0. This value is reached when the number of advancers on the NYA equals the number of decliners.

Figure 5-6 displays daily Adv-Dec ratio values along with the NYA. Two horizontal lines appear with the data: a darker average line, a +1SD line and a −1SD line near the very bottom of the chart.

Compared to the P:C ratios, the extreme high values for the A/D Ratio lag a bit. That's to be expected because put buying reflects pending doom and gloom while improvement in breadth occurs with a broad market rally. After that, things settle back to normal. The upward spikes don't exactly identify bottoms. Two light vertical lines are drawn to help you view this lag.

Figure 5-6:
Daily advance-decline ratios along with the NYA.

REMEMBER

When an indicator diverges from the index or stock you're evaluating, it may be an early warning of trend trouble.

The darker vertical line toward the beginning of the chart captures strong fear and coincides with the short-term market low. Although the number of extreme values is limited in both directions, the low extremes provide more timely information. The upward spikes confirm the reversal after the fact.

When applying SD lines, consider using multiples of 1, 2, and 3 to see what extremes are highlighted. It may be necessary to use one multiple for spikes on the high end and a different multiple for those on the low end, depending on how fast the values used in the indicator respond to market changes.

Chapter 6

Targeting Sectors with Technical Analysis

In This Chapter

▶ Understanding chart advantages

▶ Selecting sectors with strength

▶ Projecting price movement

*W*hen the broad averages move strongly up, so do most stocks and sectors, and when they move strongly down, most stocks and sectors follow. Sectors don't move in exact tandem with indexes though. Often economic conditions favor one group for a period of time, then as conditions change, so do the sectors displaying strength or weakness. Focusing on strong or weak sectors allows you to apply strategies that are best suited for conditions. First, of course, you have to know how to find them. Technical analysis provides you with tools for analyzing sectors, including those geared toward identifying relative strength and weakness. In this chapter, I give you the technical analysis basics you need to accomplish this to build your sector trading strategies.

Getting Technical with Charts

Chart analysis is one aspect of technical analysis that uses price and volume data to provide a view of trends for market evaluation purposes. There are a variety of chart types and data displays, providing you with an extremely large list of tools for analysis. By focusing here on a handful of technical tools and techniques geared toward sector and option trading, traders new to chart analysis should get up to speed quickly while those more familiar with it will get a bit of review.

Chart basics

Charts use price data to provide you with a view of trading activity during a given period. A short list of common chart types include the following:

- **Line chart:** Uses price versus time. Single price data point for each period is connected using a line. It typically uses a closing value, which is generally considered the most important value for the period (day, week, etc.) Line charts provide great "big picture" information for price movement and trends by filtering out noise from more minor moves during the period.

  Disadvantages to line charts is that they provide no information about the strength of trading during the day or whether gaps occurred from one period to the next. A gap is created when trading for one period is completely above or below trading for the previous period. This happens when significant news impacting the company comes out when the markets are closed. Doesn't that seem like good information for you to have when you're trading?

- **Open-high-low-close (OHLC) bar chart:** Uses price versus time. The period's trading range (low to high) is displayed as a vertical line with opening prices displayed as a horizontal tab on the left side of the range bar and closing prices as a horizontal tab on the right side of the range bar. A total of four price points are used to construct each bar.

  OHLC charts provide information about both trading period strength and price gaps. Using a daily chart as a point of reference, a relatively long vertical bar tells you the price range was pretty big for the day. Another way to look at it is to say the stock was volatile that day — good information for option traders. It also hints at strength in the stock when the stock closes near the high of the day and weakness when it closes near the low for the day.

- **Candlestick chart:** Uses price versus time. Similar to an OHLC chart with the price range between the open and the close for the period highlighted by a thickened bar. Patterns unique to this chart can enhance daily analysis.

  Candlestick charts have distinct pattern interpretations describing the battle between bulls and bears. These are best applied to a daily chart. Candlesticks also display price ranges and gaps.

View charts using both:

- Longer term line charts noting price trends
- OHLC or candlestick charts for better understanding price action during the period, including security strength and volatility

A wide variety of technical charting packages are available as independent software programs or web-based applications. The cost ranges from free to thousands of dollars depending on the package features. When first using technical analysis, consider starting with a free web-based package then identify your specific needs and expand from there.

Adjusting your time horizon for the best view

Before focusing on one specific chart interval, consider your investment or trading horizon. What you want to view when evaluating your 401(k) investment is different than your focus for active trading.

Technical analysis places different emphasis on timeframes. Longer term trends are considered stronger than shorter term ones. To get the best view of trends, it's extremely helpful to change the time interval used for your charts. The typical chart default is a daily chart, but others exist as well.

When completing a market analysis to locate strong sectors, an ideal progression includes evaluating the following:

- ✔ Long-term, major trends using monthly charts on indexes and sectors
- ✔ Intermediate-term, major and minor trends using weekly charts on broad market indexes and sectors
- ✔ Short-term, minor trends using daily charts on sectors

By first recognizing major and intermediate trends, you're less likely to get caught up in the emotion associated with shorter term moves.

A horizontal support line can be drawn after price moves down to touch a price level twice. The line is confirmed when a third touch of that price level successfully holds and buying demand returns to the security sending the price up.

Visualizing supply and demand

Charts can be thought of as a display of supply and demand:

- ✔ Buying demand pushes prices upward
- ✔ Supply creates selling pressure that drives prices downward
- ✔ Volume displays the magnitude of supply or demand

Markets don't just move straight up and down — the battle between the bulls (demand) and the bears (supply) results in different types of price movement.

A horizontal resistance line can be drawn once price moves up to touch a price level twice. The line is confirmed when a third touch of that price level successfully holds and selling supply returns to the security sending the price down.

Areas of support and resistance

Price support and resistance halt the trend that is in place:

- ✔ Support represents a transition from declining prices driven by supply to climbing prices when renewed demand kicks in at that price level.

- ✔ Resistance represents a transition from climbing prices driven by strong demand to declining prices when selling pressure comes in at that price.

When trading, notice that these transitions line up over time, sometimes creating sideways trading channels as price moves between the two. The longer the price serves as support or resistance, the stronger it's considered.

Using support and resistance to identify entry and exit points is one basic trading system. Consider also using them in price projections to identify stop-loss and profit-taking exits, as well as calculating risk-reward ratios.

Price areas that previously served as support often serve as resistance areas in the future and vice versa.

Trend analysis

I use the concept of trend quite a bit before reaching this formal definition. That's because I'm pretty sure you have a sense of what an upward trend and a downward trend is for any asset. Painfully so if you were holding on to that asset in the latter trend. More formally, trend identifies price direction:

- ✔ **Upward trend:** Prices climb and pullback in such a way that a rising line can be drawn under the pullbacks which display higher lows. Higher highs are also characteristic of uptrends.

- ✔ **Downward trend:** Prices fall and retrace in such a way that a declining line can be drawn above the top of retracement peaks which display lower highs. Lower lows are also characteristic of downtrends.

Create a trend line by connecting two higher lows (uptrend) or two lower highs (downtrend). When price successfully tests the line a third time, the trend is confirmed. Using these lines as entry and exit points is a valid application of the tool, similar to support and resistance levels.

Consider drawing two trendlines using a longer term chart such as a monthly chart, to highlight an area of resistance versus a subjective single trend line. One may use closing data while the other uses market lows. Follow market action near each.

Moving averages

Moving averages are lines constructed on a chart using an average value of closing prices during a certain number of days. These lines are considered *lagging* indicators because the historical data follows price action. The two main types of moving averages include as follows:

- ✔ Simple moving averages (SMA) which use a basic average calculation
- ✔ Exponential moving averages (EMA) which incorporates all available price data providing greater weight to more recent data

Simple moving averages equally weigh all closes for the time period selected while exponential moving averages are calculated in such a way that more recent data carries greater weight in the line.

Both SMAs and EMAs can be constructed using a variety of settings and chart intervals. So you can view a five-day SMA on a daily chart or a ten-week EMA on a weekly chart. Moving average lines are considered unbiased trend indicators because the lines are derived from objective calculations.

The three most common settings for either moving average include the following:

- ✔ 20-day moving average displaying short-term trends
- ✔ 50-day moving average displaying intermediate-term trends
- ✔ 200-day moving average displaying long-term trends

You may have heard financial media reporting that price is approaching the 200-day moving average. That's because a break of this line is considered significant and may confirm a trend reversal.

Exponential moving averages (EMA) incorporate all available price data for the underlying security, with more recent data having a greater weight on the EMA value for the period. As a result, they are more responsive to price changes.

Identifying Relatively Strong Sectors

Strong market moves up or down generally result in gains for most sectors and securities too. However, during more moderate trending certain sectors and securities perform better than the market while others perform worse. A sector or security can also move in the opposite direction during these periods. Your objective as a trader is finding those relatively strong and weak groups so you can apply profitable sector strategies.

Relative ratios

You construct a relative ratio line by dividing one security into another. This allows you to objectively view the performance of one security relative to the other because the line rises when the primary security is outperforming the second one and falls when it is underperforming. Adding an overlay chart to a relative ratio allows you to view both securities on one chart. Log scales typically provide a better view for the movement of each.

Trend lines drawn on a log chart will appear differently when you switch to an arithmetic scale.

Figure 6-1 displays a weekly log chart for XLF (dark solid line), an exchange-traded fund (ETF) comprised of S&P 500 financial companies. It also displays an overlay of SPY (light, thinner line), which is the S&P 500 Index ETF. The 10-week and 40-week EMAs (two dashed lines) are also included for XLF, displaying intermediate and long-term trends respectively. Finally, the bottom portion shows the relative ratio line for XLF/SPY.

Figure 6-1: Weekly chart for XLF with EMAs and performance relative to SPY.

Shorter moving averages (i.e. low setting) are considered faster and move more closely with price. You can distinguish these lines on a chart because they are somewhat jagged.

When including relative ratios on a chart you have a clearer view of the performance for two securities. In Figure 6-1 it appears that the two indexes moved pretty similarly until very recently. But a look at the relative ratio line tells another story. Throughout a good portion of the three-year period SPY outperformed XLF, very significantly from June 2007 through October 2007.

Relative ratio lines are also referred to as relative strength comparisons.

Within a month after the deterioration in the relative ratio line, XLF dropped below its 200-day EMA and shortly after the 50-day EMA followed. Although not labeled, the shorter EMA is identified by noting which one moves more closely with the price. When downward trending conditions are ideal, prices and MAs line up with price data appearing lowest on the chart followed by the shorter EMA, then the higher EMA — just like this chart is showing.

Some traders use moving average crosses as trading system signals. This approach has its place in trading, but note where price was when the cross occurred — almost at its lowest point. Remember, moving averages lag price data. I like to use crossovers to identify a change in conditions for the stock and as a strategy filter. Once that cross occurs, I favor bearish strategies.

Before moving away from this particular chart, note that trend lines can be applied to relative ratios. The same rules apply:

- ✔ Draw uptrends using the low points in the trend
- ✔ Draw downtrends using the high points in the trend

Also, previous areas of support can become resistant and vice versa.

When using overlay capabilities on a chart, indicators added to the chart are based on the primary security.

When using relative ratios, it's good to identify a group of related indexes or sectors to monitor. Cash flows from one outperforming market or sector to another as economic conditions change. Portfolio allocations should favor outperforming markets and underweight underperforming ones. This results in reversals for one market leading another market by varying amounts of time.

The wide range of ETFs that track different assets (i.e. the U.S. dollar or oil) allows you to employ an asset allocation plan across markets using a single security type. Add the existence of options for many ETFs and you have reduced risk access to the commodity and foreign exchange markets.

Trend lines can be used on relative strength comparison lines to better identify changing conditions and areas of support and resistance. Similarly, support that has been broken will often serve as resistance in the future.

Focusing on sectors, selecting one optionable ETF fund family sector group
allows you to quickly evaluate sector trends and relative performance. As an
example, the Select Sector S&P Depository Receipts (SPDR) include ten ETFs
based on the S&P 500 Index:

- ✔ SPY tracks the entire S&P 500 Index
- ✔ Nine ETFs track each of the nine major sectors that make up the index

Collectively the nine sector ETFs make up the SPY ETF. By analyzing ten
charts, you can complete a broad market and sector assessment which can
serve as a basis for comprehensive sector investing or trading. Seeking an
ETF fund family that is liquid and optionable is your first objective, then you
follow-up by confirming liquidity in the ETF options.

A relative ratio line only compares performance of two securities — it does
not indicate the trend for either security. A rising line can indicate the primary security is trending upward at a faster rate than the second security or
that it is trending downward at a slower rate.

Rate of change indicator

Relative ratios provide you with a good visual approach for assessing sectors. A rate of change approach allows you to also quantify and rank performance for those sectors. The rate of change (ROC) for a security is the speed
in which it moves — when calculating security returns you are using one type
of ROC. There is also an ROC indicator that can be drawn on charts for analyzing, trading, or ranking securities.

To calculate a ten-day ROC, you use the following formula:

(Today's Price ÷ Price 10 Days Ago) × 100

Using the nine sector ETFs, you can rank the sectors by strength using a 14-
day ROC value for each as follows in Table 6-1.

Table 6-1	14-Day ROC Sector Rankings on 8-16-07		
ETF	*Sector*	*14-Day ROC*	*Rank*
XLU	Utilities	1.020	1
XLP	Consumer Staples	1.003	2
XLV	Healthcare	1.002	3
XLF	Financials	0.994	4
XLI	Industrials	0.962	5
XLK	Technology	0.959	6
XLY	Consumer Cyclicals	0.953	7
XLE	Energy	0.950	8
XLB	Materials	0.935	9
SPY	Entire Index	0.979	--

XLU, XLP, and XLV are considered relatively strong while XLY, XLE, and XLB relatively weak compared to price 14-days ago. Does this mean XLV is trending upward or XLB trending downward? Not at all — it's simply a way you can compare the performance of a group of securities using a specific criteria. It turns out each of these ETFs hit a short-term bottom on the day the ROC was calculated. Round out your analysis by evaluating each sector chart, starting with the extremes.

As an alternate approach to sector trading you can expand the list to include industry groups, investment styles (small or large cap, value or growth), or countries, among others. The main goal is to develop a group of ETFs that experience related capital inflows and outflows.

When using ROC trends, you really want to capture money flows from one market or sector to another. Consider checking out different periods such as weekly or monthly ROCs and see how the rankings change each week. Relative strength trading approaches seek to establish bullish positions in relatively strong performers and bearish position in relatively weak performers. This works best when the periods used result in rankings that persist more than a week or two, so you remain in a strong position.

When trading, the ROC is used with a simple moving average (SMA) as a trade alert. Crosses of the ROC up above its SMA is a bullish alert and crosses of the ROC down below its SMA is a bearish alert. An example of this is shown in the next section.

The term *normalize* refers to the process of expressing data so that it is independent of the absolute value of the underlying. This allows comparison to other securities.

Using Sector Volatility Tools

Technical analysis displays volatility in a variety of ways including basic range bars and historical volatility (HV) plots. Objective technical indicators available in many charting packages and covered in this section include the following:

- ✔ Statistical volatility
- ✔ Average true range
- ✔ Bollinger bands
- ✔ Bollinger %b

These tools provide you with different volatility views and allow you to scan the markets for securities that may be gearing up for a change. Although volatility can remain high or low for extended periods of time, these measures may provide you with the following:

- ✔ A buy alert when declining
- ✔ A sell alert with jumps higher
- ✔ A tool to help identify appropriate strategies
- ✔ Detection of seasonal movement

The value used for technical indicators is referred to as the *setting*. Commonly used settings are referred to as *default values*.

Displaying volatility with indicators

Statistical volatility and the average true range are two different displays of price movement. Here's how they differ:

- ✔ **Statistical volatility (SV):** SV, another term for historical volatility, uses closing values to plot an annualized standard deviation line that represents the degree of price movement in the security. Because various time periods can be used on a chart, SV reflects the chart period, not necessarily a daily calculation as you see on option HV or SV charts.

✔ **Average true range (ATR):** The ATR uses a true range (TR) value to define price movement and was developed by Welles Wilder. TR incorporates extreme movement such as gaps, so it better reflects volatility. TR uses the previous close and current high and low values to calculate three different ranges. The biggest range for the three is the TR for the period.

A rate of return calculation is one measure of rate of change. It allows comparisons for securities with different prices by creating a value that is independent of price.

Figure 6-2 provides the three TR range calculations and a bar chart example of each.

Figure 6-2:
Daily true range calculations and display.

Daily True Range

Greatest of the following absolute values:

1. High (today) – Low (today)
2. Close (yesterday) – High (today)
3. Close (yesterday) – Low (today)

ATR is an exponential moving average that smoothes TR. A strong move in the ATR incorporates price gaps and provides traders with important information about price volatility that can be missed by other smoothed indicators. Because ATR uses historical prices and a smoothing process, it's a lagging indicator and does not predict volatility. However, a sharp move upward in a security's ATR is often accompanied by an increase in IV for its options.

When using rankers to identify stocks with narrowing bandwidth, be sure to check the chart to see what's happening with the stock. Price may have flattened due to a pending corporate action such as a stock buyout and is less likely to move from that point.

Figure 6-3 displays a daily OHLC bar chart for SPY, the S&P 500 Index ETF with the 14-day ATR and 14-day SV.

Figure 6-3:
SPY daily
OHLC bar
chart with
ATR and SV.

In the late July — early August period, the volatility for SPY increased as seen by range bars increasing in length. In this particular decline, SV peaked approximately five days before SPY bottomed which was followed by a peak in the ATR one day later.

All nine sector ETFs bottomed on the same day with each ATR peaking within one day of this bottom. The SV profile for the ETFs varied more, but most also peaked a few days prior to the bottom. When reviewing the charts, you note the following about XLI:

✔ Price moved in a very wide range, closing the day at its high with a slight net gain

✔ SV was pulling back from a peak two days prior

✔ ATR was still moving upward

✔ The SMA for the 14-day ROC was flattening suggesting a possible end to the decline

Although XLI ranked fifth on a 14-day ROC basis, closing at its high for the day was extremely bullish given the range of trading for that day. The situation merited monitoring to confirm a reversal. By following conditions for a couple of days, you would have seen the following for XLI displayed as Figure 6-4.

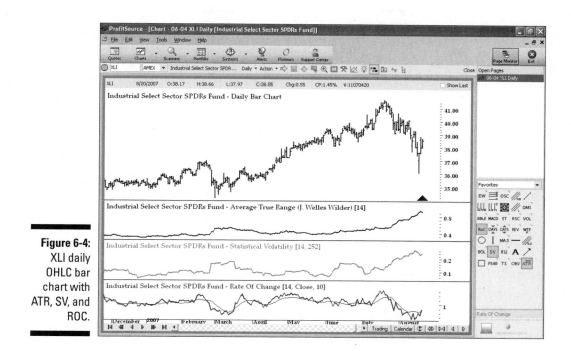

Figure 6-4:
XLI daily
OHLC bar
chart with
ATR, SV, and
ROC.

Price continued upward while ATR appeared to be pulling back and SV conditions remained elevated. ROC crossed up above its ten-day SMA, which was a bullish signal. The only strategy briefly discussed so far that suits these conditions (bullish, high volatility) is a long stock, short call position.

Buying the ETF near the close at $38.55 and selling the Sep 39 strike price call for $0.80, you've created a moderately reduced risk position. Rather than $3,855 on the line, you've reduced your exposure to $3,775 or by 2%. There are actually better strategies to capitalize on this situation — ones that allow you to limit your risk much more — but this one is suitable for now.

You can establish a short-term covered call strategy with the goal of being called out of the position. That's the case here so you want XLI to be trading above 39 at September expiration. This is, exactly what happened. On expiration Friday XLI closed at 40.63 and you would have been assigned. This means you bought the position for $3,775 and sold it for $3,900.

Analyzing volatility with Bollinger bands

Bollinger bands provide you with another nice visual of relative volatility levels. This technical tool uses a simple moving average (SMA) surrounded by upper and lower bands, both derived from a standard deviation calculation. John Bollinger, the tool's developer, uses the following as default settings:

- 20-period SMA
- Upper band (SMA + two standard deviations)
- Lower band (SMA – two standard deviations)

The bands contract and expand as price volatility contracts and expands. Two additional Bollinger band tools include the following:

- **Bandwidth (BW)** to measure the distance between the two bands using the calculation: BW = (Upper BB – Lower BB) ÷ Moving Average

  According to Bollinger, when BW is at its lowest level in six months, a squeeze candidate is identified. That's a security that is consolidating before a potentially strong breakout higher or lower. It is not uncommon for a false move to occur so straddle strategies (see Chapter 14) can provide a way to play this situation.

- **%b** to identify where the price is relative to the BW, calculated using a variation of George Lane's Stochastic indicator, with values ranging from:

    - 0 to 100 when price is at or between the bands
    - Less than 0 when below the lower band (bearish)
    - Greater than 100 when above the upper band (bullish)

Review the news when you see a chart with a big price jump or decline along with narrow bandwidth on the Bollinger bands.

A value of 75 reflects price that is within the bands and one quarter below the lower band from a total bandwidth standpoint. %b normalizes price relative to band-width size and allows you to make an apples-to-apples comparison of different stocks for ranking purposes.

Different sectors experience bullish and bearish trends at different times. Although strong rallies and declines in the broad markets often move all securities in the same direction, the strength and duration of the moves for these different securities can vary greatly. In general, the following apply:

- Securities and sectors with very high values for %b are bullish when confirmed by other technical tools.
- Securities and sectors with very low values for %b are bearish when confirmed by other technical tools.

Bollinger noted that rather than prices being extended when near a Bollinger band, the condition actually reflects strength and a breakout that can continue. Look for pullbacks toward the moving average line to establish new positions in the direction of the trend after such a breakout.

Projecting Prices for Trading

There are no guarantees in the markets. Options with low implied volatility levels can remain low, stocks in a downtrend can continue dropping, and options with a 75% chance of being in the money at expiration according to the models can expire worthless. That's why risk management is your first order of business as a trader. Using support and resistance areas and trend lines is a straightforward way to manage your risk.

Price projections can include those identifying exits for a loss or a profit. Both are important. Sometimes we focus so much on managing risk that we forget to also be on the alert for profit taking. By identifying areas above and below the current price prior to establishing a position you simplify trade management. Consider using objective techniques such as price channels, retracements and extensions for identifying exit levels. The following sections give you both sides of the coin: methods for projecting price moves (magnitude and time), as well as risk-management tools. Just what's needed for option traders.

Support and resistance

Support and resistance provide you with subjective tools that identify:

✓ Concrete exit levels for a loss

✓ Potential exit levels for a profit

Although support and resistance lines are subjective, they do represent a reasonable approach to managing your risk because they identify a maximum loss. As your skills develop applying such tools and exit points will improve.

The reason I use "potential exit" on the profit side is because changing conditions may warrant an early exit for partial profits or they may allow you to extend gains depending on the change. Suppose you hold a bullish position — if your indicators become bearish you may receive an alert prompting an earlier than anticipated exit from the position. On the other hand, you may have already taken a portion of your profits when the stock reaches your original projection price. If the chart remains bullish, you can revise your price target for additional profits.

Extending the exit only applies to profit-taking, exit points for a loss have to be written in stone. You can exit the position early, but you absolutely cannot revise the exit level in a way that extends losses. It's critical for you to identify a maximum loss price for the position, and execute it if it's reached.

Because trend lines are drawn by the analyst, a degree of bias may be introduced. Consider allowing a little bit of leeway when using these price areas for entries and exits to help minimize the impact of bias.

Using a moving average crossover system, you decide to enter a long position in XLF (financials ETF) the day after the 20-day EMA crosses up over the 50-day EMA. One exit signal includes a cross of the 20-day EMA down below the 50-day EMA. Because this exit doesn't identify a specific exit for a loss, you add a support line below the current price to manage your risk.

In the previous uptrend, $36.58 served as support, but this area was broken when XLF declined a couple months ago. The market has since reversed and the same $36.58 level served as resistance when XLF started moving upward. The ETF recently broke above this level making it a reasonable stop-loss support area going forward. Because the ETF is trading around $37.10, it represents a 1.4% loss which is well within your risk parameters.

To view a 200-day moving average on a weekly chart, you must use a setting of 40 because there are five trading days in a week.

Figure 6-5 displays the daily OHLC bar chart for XLF with 20-day and 50-day EMAs, and a horizontal support line drawn at $36.58. The entire trade period is shown, including trade entry which was established at $37.12. Both exit signals that resulted are also identified.

Figure 6-5:
XLF daily
OHLC bar
chart with
support line
and 20- and
50-day
EMAs.

Price moved upward for a little more than a month then dropped, but remained above the support line. Another weaker advance failed and now price dropped below support. The trade was exited at the next open for $36.34. Assuming 100 shares were purchased, the position loss was $78, which represented 2.1% of the initial position. Unless a physical stop loss order is in place (see Chapter 8), actual losses will be greater than those calculated using the support price. Regardless, this exit did prevent an additional $44 (1.2%) loss had you waited for the EMA crossover.

When viewing the chart, you may notice that price reached an approximate double top at $38.00, then declined. An approach that took partial profits at this previous resistance level would have yielded more gains than losses.

Longer moving averages (i.e. high setting) are considered slower and less responsive to price changes. You can distinguish these lines on a chart because they are smoother. Calculating a moving average is referred to as a *smoothing process*.

Trends

Trend lines are upward and downward moving lines drawn across higher lows (uptrend) or lower highs (downtrend). These lines can similarly be used for price projection purposes. The actual price level you use with these lines is estimated because the lines are trending rather than horizontal.

Many technical analysis packages include a crosshair tool allowing you to identify the price and date for different areas on the chart. Using the same EMA crossover entry technique for XLF, a trend line exit can be identified with the crosshair tool.

Many trend-following systems have a larger number of small losses and fewer large profitable trades. These systems rely on using the system exit rather than physical stop-loss exit levels. To properly manage risk while allowing the system to perform as it should, incorporates percentage loss exits into your back-testing to determine if the system is viable when a stop loss is included.

Figure 6-6 incorporates a successfully tested trend line on a daily chart for XLF. The crosshair level one day after the trade entry date is included. Although this method uses an estimate for the stop, it represents a stop that is dynamic because it increases over time as the trend remains intact.

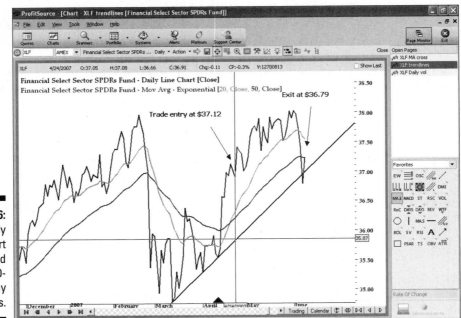

Figure 6-6:
XLF daily
line chart
with trend
line and 20-
and 50-day
EMAs.

Using the trend line approach on the example resulted in profits, but don't jump to the conclusion that it's a superior approach — it just worked out better in this case. The main point is that it's possible for you to use basic tools when identifying reasonable price levels for downside protection. Exiting a bullish trade when an upward trending line is broken makes a lot of sense.

Options come with an expiration date so the time it takes for a stock to reach a projected price is as important as the projection itself.

There are many technical tools that generate entry and exit signals, but not price projections. When identifying a maximum loss exit point, remember to consider basic techniques for managing risk.

Channels

Price channels include those drawn using two different trend lines and those constructed using a regression line — here I display the latter to focus on objective tools. A regression channel:

✔ Uses a specific number of past prices to create the channel

✔ Includes a middle regression line that represents the expected value for future prices (no guarantees)

✔ Fixes the data period, then extends the channel lines forward in time

A regression line is fixed, meaning it's constructed using data that has a start and end date rather than adding and dropping data the way a moving average does. Price is expected to revert the mean with these channels.

A regression line is also referred to as a line of best fit. It's the line that represents the shortest distance between the line and each data point.

When creating a regression channel, you use an existing trend that is expected to remain intact. Price contained by the channel confirms the trend and price moving outside of the channel suggests a change in trend may be developing.

There are a variety of ways you can construct a channel, here I focus on a basic linear regression approach. After identifying the trend period, the regression line is drawn and the boundary lines are created as follows:

✔ Upper boundary line uses the distance between the regression line and the point furthest above the line

✔ Lower boundary line uses the distance between the regression line and the point furthest below the line

Very wide channels reflect volatile trends, while narrow channels reflect more quiet trends. Often times price will remain in the upper or lower region of the channel for periods of time while it is trending. If price breaks out of the channel then returns to it without moving to the middle regression line, a change in trend may be developing.

Suppose you constructed the regression channel in Figure 6-7 using a weekly OHLC bar chart for XLB. The data range for the channel is shown above it and a long trade entry point is identified by the arrow.

As the trend progresses upward, you can identify a rising exit point using the lower channel boundaries and regression line. Your exit rules may include the following:

✔ Exit the position on the Monday after price closes outside of the lower channel line on the weekly chart (projected at 25.36).

✔ Take profits if price moves above the upper channel line, then returns to the channel.

✔ Take partial profits at the middle regression line if price fails to move to the upper channel line.

Check out the chart package help links to obtain information about indicator construction and applications.

Using the crosshairs tool allows you to identify realistic price projections that correspond to future points in time.

Consider creating regression channels on monthly and weekly charts, then moving down in time to weekly and daily charts, respectively, to apply stronger trends to the relatively shorter time period.

Although difficult to see in the image, the crosshair tool also identifies March 12 as the corresponding date for movement to the lower boundary line. That is, assuming price continues to behave as it has in the past.

You may be thinking that's a pretty big assumption, but it's the one made any time you enter a position in the direction of the trend. This approach to a time projection is subjective, but it does provide you with a nice reality check when considering potential moves.

Trends are not considered predictive. They exist in the market, but they do not predict price because they can either continue or fail. Technical tools provide guidelines for risk management and profit-taking, not guarantees.

Price retracements and extensions

Retracement tools make use of existing trends to identify potential areas of price support and resistance. As you saw in Chapter 5, market trends and conditions are largely associated with two primary human emotions: greed and fear. Technical analysis acknowledges the impact of such crowd-driven behavior and uses tools that attempt to quantify it when possible. One such application includes the use of Fibonacci ratios for retracement purposes. These ratios are derived from a numeric series of the same name, originally defined by Leonardo Fibonacci.

Examples of the series and ratios are found throughout nature and are used by many traders in various applications. Because different market participants will be taking action when certain Fibonacci price levels are reached, you should be aware of these levels. A basic understanding will likely help you assess market action.

W. D. Gann was a successful commodities trader who also developed a series of ratios and retracement and extension tools that are widely used. Gann's ratios include 0.125, 0.25, 0.50, and 1.00 among others.

Fibonacci series and ratios

The Fibonacci integer series is generated starting with 0 and 1, and adding the two previous integers in the series to obtain the next integer:

0, 1, 1 (0 + 1), **2** (1 + 1), **3** (1 + 2), **5** (2 + 3), **8** (3 + 5), **13** (5 + 8), . . .

The *Fibonacci ratios* are values reached when dividing an integer in the series by specific previous or subsequent integers in the series The primary Fibonacci ratios used in technical analysis are:

0.382, 0.500, 0.618, 1.00, 1.618 and 2.618

Because prices do not move straight up or down, retracements develop which are counter-trend moves. A retracement includes:

✔ A pullback in price during an uptrend

✔ A rise in price during a downtrend

Fibonacci ratios are often used to define retracement areas. Extensions use the same ratio process to identify projections beyond the starting point for the base trend.

Fibonacci numbers can be used for indicator settings when making adjustments to the default setting.

Figure 6-8 displays Fibonacci retracements (thinner lines occurring during the trend) and extensions (thicker lines occurring beyond the trend) for XLI.

Time extensions

A second method uses Fibonacci numbers or ratios to identify future dates for potential turning points. Projections are determined using

✔ A ratio based on the time taken to create the original trend.

✔ A count using Fibonacci integers moving forward.

Another commonly applied approach to time objectives is use of market cycles. Similar to the economic business cycle, the stock market undergoes bullish and bearish cycles that are measured from low point to low point. A cycle low can then be used to estimate the next potential low point for the market. One of the most well-known cycles for the stock market is the four-year cycle with a recent low point occurring in 2006. Projecting forward, this means another significant low should develop in 2010.

Figure 6-8:
XLI daily chart with Fibonacci retracements and extensions.

Projections and probabilities

By lining up different high probability factors, you create a situation where you put the odds in your favor for a particular strategy or trade. By managing your risk, you limit losses and realize larger gains. The process involves part science (supported by rules) and part art (supported by experience).

Weighing possibility versus probability

Even though basic tools can be subjective, a valid trend line helps you more easily identify intact trends and provides a reasonable exit point when the line is broken. Such a break is a clear signal that the original reason for entering the trade is no longer valid. However, you can still encounter problems when that time comes.

What if the trendline you drew was on a weekly chart and during the week the trend line was broken? Technically, you don't have a weekly close below the trend line, but that doesn't mean you should continue to simply watch price erode. Technical methods rely on confirming indicators to help line up probabilities.

Identifying a stop exit point before entering a position helps reduce your emotion during the trade.

During an uptrend, if volume increases as price moves down towards the trend line it's a bearish alert. A break of the line with increasing volume is more bearish evidence. Such action on a daily chart supports exiting a position established using weekly data.

Going back to Figure 6-4, a covered call position in XLI was created based on a bullish price reversal and high implied volatility. Table 6-2 presents conditions in place to assess probabilities for the strategy. The indicators narrowly favor a bullish resolution.

Table 6-2	Lining Up Probabilities	
Indicator	*Action*	*Bias*
Price	Higher close for two days	Bullish
Price	Returns to bearish channel	Bearish
ATR	Declining after peak	Bullish
ROC	Crossing above SMA	Bullish
SV	Diminishing	Neutral — Bullish

(continued)

Table 6-2 *(continued)*

Indicator	Action	Bias
IV	Recent peak	--
Volume	Bottoming pattern possible	Neutral — Bullish
Weekly Trend	Long-term uptrend intact	Bullish
20-day EMA	Downward sloped	Bearish
50-day EMA	Downward sloped	Bearish
200-day EMA	Flat	Neutral

There are no guarantees a trend will remain intact.

Waiting for every tool to turn bullish will typically result in no trades taken at all. Or those that are signaled will be created toward the end of a move. Try to assess conditions and use your experience to put the odds in your favor. Although XLI moved upward and the trade realized gains, the same conditions on a different day could result in continued bearish movement. That's why managing risk is key.

Reacting to versus anticipating a move

Anything can happen in the markets the next week or trading day . . . even by the time the market closes. Trends can continue, reverse, or simply stall. The further out in time, the more uncertain things become, so it's always good to remind yourself that you simply don't know what will happen tomorrow. The best you can do is identify rules for managing risk and keep the odds in your favor. When conditions change take the necessary action and move on.

Practice disciplined trading through these methods to gain the experience needed to hone your skills over varying market conditions:

✓ **Sector analysis:** When completing an analysis, use tools that provide objective information about current conditions for different timeframes, including moving averages and Bollinger bands. This keeps you tuned in to "what is" happening versus what may happen next. Consider broad market movement and how the sector moves in relation to the market.

After assessing current trending and volatility conditions, incorporate other tools that provide you with insight about the strength of those conditions and potential changes. Then develop your strategy accordingly.

Only take on new positions if you can effectively manage all your open trades.

✔ **Trade evaluation:** When evaluating potential trades, use tools that provide reasonable projections to assess reward:risk ratios. Only consider those positions with risk levels that are within your guidelines. Identify an absolute exit price for a loss, as well as tools used for taking profits.

✔ **Trade management:** When managing a position be sure to monitor conditions — don't walk away from a trade that requires your attention. Use order types that automatically execute a stop loss exit when possible (see Chapter 8).

Try to put the odds in your favor.

Chapter 7

Kicking the Wheels of a New Strategy

In This Chapter

▶ Understanding option price changes

▶ Practicing by paper trading

▶ Testing an approach

▶ Gaining strategy mastery

You may consider new trading strategies exciting, but be careful about jumping the gun. There's a good amount of advance preparation needed. Three steps to take before using a new strategy in the market include:

✔ Understanding the security's risks and rewards

✔ Practicing strategies

✔ Analyzing a trade

Although this book covers a lot of "learning" and "analyzing" topics, this chapter introduces tools and techniques for practicing strategies. First, by monitoring different option pricing components and paper trading you simulate live conditions. This provides a better intuitive feel for price changes and helps you avoid costly mistakes. Next, by developing your backtest skills you implement only the best approaches, allowing you to stay in the game long enough to gain valuable experience. Through practice and experience you eventually reach strategy mastery.

Monitoring Option Greek Changes

Understanding basic option strategies is a much quicker learning curve than recognizing the proper pricing for options used in the strategies. Theoretical models and conditions impacting option premiums are discussed in Chapters 3, 14, and 15. But one of the best ways to really grasp the value of these securities is by monitoring price and Greek changes under actual conditions.

Tracking premium measures

Developing your skills with any option strategy means really understanding how option premiums are impacted by changes in both of the following:

- ✔ The price of the underlying
- ✔ Time to expiration

A great way to get a better intuitive feel for the impact from both of these is by formally tracking changes in all the different components on a day to day basis. All you need to do this is access to market prices, an option calculator, and a spreadsheet program. By monitoring a few different options, you should be able to learn a lot about how changing conditions impact prices in general. By including Greeks in the process you also understand which factors play more significant roles at different times. See Chapter 3 for more on the Greeks.

Ideally you'll end up reviewing the markets and tracking prices during a period when prices are moving around a bit. This helps highlight delta, gamma, and theta impacts on price. Prior to putting your trading dollars on the line, set up a spreadsheet to track the following:

- ✔ Price of the underlying
- ✔ Prices for ITM, ATM, OTM calls and puts with varying days to expiration
- ✔ Days to expiration
- ✔ Option intrinsic value, delta, gamma, and theta

By tracking these values you can identify which measures have the biggest impact on option strategies.

Delta may be displayed based on values from -1 to +1 or -100 to +100.

Figure 7-1 displays a spreadsheet for a Microsoft (MSFT) call, and put. Although only a portion of the month is displayed, monitoring these values over an extended period helps you view varying market conditions. Note that option prices don't change by the exact amounts projected by the Greeks.

Figure 7-1:
Tracking
price and
time
changes for
option
premiums.

Tracking Price & Time

Date	MSFT	Change	Days to Expiration	Price	Intrinsic Value	Delta	Gamma	Call Theta	Strike	Put Theta	Gamma	Delta	Intrinsic Value	Price
1-Aug-07	29.30	0.31	77	1.10	0.00	45.64	0.118	-0.0097	30.00	-0.0065	0.124	-54.49	0.70	1.61
2-Aug-07	29.52	0.22	76	1.14	0.00	47.88	0.124	-0.0096	30.00	-0.0064	0.128	-52.01	0.48	1.44
3-Aug-07	28.96	-0.56	75	0.90	0.00	41.04	0.122	-0.0093	30.00	-0.0064	0.123	-58.75	1.04	1.80
6-Aug-07	29.54	0.58	74	1.09	0.00	47.77	0.129	-0.0097	30.00	-0.0065	0.133	-52.13	0.46	1.38
7-Aug-07	29.55	0.01	73	1.06	0.00	47.70	0.133	-0.0096	30.00	-0.0064	0.136	-52.16	0.45	1.35
...	...	...	...	...	...	...	...	...	...	...	...	...	...	...
28-Aug-07	27.93	-0.56	52	0.35	0.00	23.75	0.123	-0.0084	30.00	-0.0045	0.128	-79.28	2.07	2.25
29-Aug-07	28.59	0.66	51	0.45	0.00	30.57	0.149	-0.0090	30.00	-0.0056	0.159	-71.27	1.41	1.71
30-Aug-07	28.45	-0.14	50	0.43	0.00	28.95	0.143	-0.0091	30.00	-0.0056	0.153	-73.29	1.55	1.82
31-Aug-07	28.73	0.28	49	0.45	0.00	31.74	0.158	-0.0090	30.00	-0.0057	0.169	-70.01	1.27	1.57

Changing volatility and option prices

The volatility impact on option prices is a little tough to get a handle on at times because implied volatility (IV) includes pricing factors that vary during the life of the option. IV incorporates the following:

- Past volatility (historical)
- Volatility expected in the future (implied) and
- Contract demand

Past volatility

Crowd behavior can drive up option prices when demand for specific contracts increases as news on a company hits the wires. Figure 7-2 displays a similar spreadsheet for the MSFT call and put options, tracking price, and volatility changes.

Figure 7-2:
Tracking
price and
volatility
changes for
option
premiums.

Tracking Price & Volatility

Date	MSFT	Change	Days to Expiration	Price	Intrinsic Value	IV	Call Vega	Strike	Put Vega	IV	Intrinsic Value	Price
1-Aug-07	29.30	0.31	77	1.10	0.00	24.671	0.054	30.00	0.054	23.441	0.70	1.61
2-Aug-07	29.52	0.22	76	1.14	0.00	23.571	0.054	30.00	0.054	22.799	0.48	1.44
3-Aug-07	28.96	-0.56	75	0.90	0.00	23.905	0.052	30.00	0.052	23.709	1.04	1.80
6-Aug-07	29.54	0.58	74	1.09	0.00	23.129	0.053	30.00	0.053	22.395	0.46	1.38
7-Aug-07	29.55	0.01	73	1.06	0.00	22.639	0.052	30.00	0.052	22.057	0.45	1.35
...	...	...	...	...	...	...	...	...	...	...	...	...
28-Aug-07	27.93	-0.56	52	0.35	0.00	23.878	0.033	30.00	0.030	20.999	2.07	2.25
29-Aug-07	28.59	0.66	51	0.45	0.00	21.998	0.037	30.00	0.036	19.963	1.41	1.71
30-Aug-07	28.45	-0.14	50	0.43	0.00	22.690	0.036	30.00	0.034	20.338	1.55	1.82
31-Aug-07	28.73	0.28	49	0.45	0.00	21.427	0.037	30.00	0.036	19.463	1.27	1.57

Implied volatility (IV)

Implied volatility (IV) is the volatility implied by the option's price. Does that about cover it for you? Because IV is a pretty important option pricing factor, it's probably good to expand on that definition a bit.

In terms of trading and IV:

- ✔ It's better to buy options when IV is relatively low.
- ✔ It's better to sell options when IV is relatively high.

The problem with these rules of thumb is that you can't always follow them. When holding a long-term stock position you want to protect, should you just throw caution to the wind because put IV is high? Definitely not, especially when you consider that increasing IV often translates to increasing fear in the market. When faced with buying options in a high volatility environment, you may need to evaluate a broader range of expiration months and strike prices.

When implied volatility (IV) is relatively high, then drops significantly, it's referred to as an *IV crush.*

Remember that IV can vary:

- ✔ **By time to expiration,** which contributes more uncertainty to the option's value.
- ✔ **By strike price:** Usually at-the-money (ATM) IV is the lowest, but it doesn't always work out that way. Skew charts (discussed in Chapter 15) provide IV by strike price and can speed up the option selection process when you need to purchase contracts while IV is relatively high. An option price can be broken into two components: intrinsic and extrinsic value. The intrinsic value is completely determined by the option moneyness, but IV does not play a role in this value. The deeper in-the-money (ITM) the option is, the less impact IV will have on the total option premium.

When using short option strategies, time decay works in your favor. Selling options with 30 to 45 days to expiration accelerates this decay for you.

Paper Trading an Approach

Continually seeking and implementing new strategies naturally develops your trading skills. By paper trading, you make risk-free progress on the new strategy learning curve.

When paper trading, be sure to incorporate trading costs associated with the position to get the best value for strategy profitability.

Trading on paper: pluses and minuses

Paper trading is an excellent way to minimize losses when learning strategy mechanics or changing your trading routine a bit. Watching a long out-of-the-money (OTM) option deflate in value as implied volatility drops is much less painful when it's on paper. However, it doesn't really prepare you for the battle of greed and fear from within. What it does do, however, is it forces you to address the situation prior to having money on the line. Some pluses and minuses for paper trading appears in Table 7-1.

Table 7-1	Advantages and Disadvantages to Paper Trading
Advantages	**Disadvantages**
Provides feedback via profits/losses	Does not prepare you emotionally for losses
Allows you to incorporate all trade costs	There's no assignments
Identifies issues you may not have considered	Typically does not address potential margin problems
Avoids account losses	Does not help trade execution understanding

Implementing electronic paper trades

Paper trading can be done on a spreadsheet, an electronic platform, or . . . you got it, paper. Do whatever works best for you. If you plan on setting up your own log, incorporate option Greeks, too.

Many financial Web sites allow you to enter different positions in a portfolio tracker that updates at the end of the day or intra-day on a delayed basis. Unfortunately, not all of them accept option symbols. A basic tracker will provide position information that includes price changes with profits and losses. A more advanced platform can include risk chart displays and other trade management tools. Figure 7-3 displays the free Optionetics.com portfolio tracker with shares of Microsoft (MSFT), as well as the MSFT Jan 30 call and Jan 30 put.

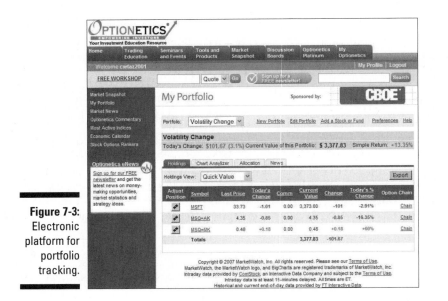

Figure 7-3:
Electronic
platform for
portfolio
tracking.

Using Trading Systems

A trading system is an approach with specific rules for entry and exit. Even if you currently use a systematic approach to a strategy — i.e. only purchasing a call when implied volatility is relatively low — a trading system is more rigidly defined. When using a system you should do the following:

✔ Establish a position for all buy signals generated by the rules

✔ Exit each position when the exit signal is generated

Knowing what you're getting

There is no decision-making when implementing the system — you never think about whether or not to accept an entry or exit signal. If accruing losses or something seems amiss, you completely stop the system. The two best things about a formal system is:

✔ It minimizes your trade emotions

✔ It allows for backtesting to get a sense of expected performance

If you start using discretion by deciding which trades to take, both of these advantages disappear. Emotions creep in and your results can vary significantly from test results. As with any trading approach, an important key to system trading is working with systems that are suitable to your trading style and account size.

Although the rules for a system are rigid, building in flexibility is common by varying indicator speeds or adding filters. A *filter* is an extra rule for trade entry or exit. Indicators and similar system components are defined as system *parameters*.

Characteristics of a good trading system include:

- ✔ Profitability across a variety of markets, securities and market conditions
- ✔ Outperforming a buy and hold approach
- ✔ Stability with manageable drawdowns
- ✔ Diversifying your trading tools
- ✔ Suiting your style and time availability

Be extremely careful about creating a system and putting it on auto-pilot. Always monitor trades.

Performing a backtest

A backtest uses past data to determine if a system generates stable profits. You can complete backtesting using data downloads or tracking trades mechanically, but the most efficient way of doing it is via a software application intended for backtesting. You just have to be sure that you're testing what you think your testing.

When performing backtesting for a system, include longer periods of time to capture bullish, bearish, and sideways moving markets. This way you generate results under worst-case conditions and experience (in a test environment) realistic drawdowns. *Drawdown* is the term used to define cumulative account losses from consecutive losing trades. Evaluating drawdown is just another way to mange your risk.

A robust trading system works for a variety of markets (commodities, stocks, etc.) under a variety of conditions (bull/bear markets).

When reviewing backtest results, you're looking for both profitability and stability. *Stability* refers to the consistency of results — you want to know if just a few trades are generating all the profits or if they are spread over a variety of trades. A stable system

✔ Has winning trades with average profits that exceed the average losses of losing trades

✔ Has an average system profit that is close to the median system profit (low standard deviation)

✔ Sustains manageable drawdowns

✔ Does not rely on a handful of trades for profitability

Note that a system doesn't have to have more winning trades than losing trades. Many trending systems rely on letting profits run for a smaller number of trades while cutting losses quickly on the losing trades.

After creating a system that performs reasonably in backtests, you complete forward testing by running the rules on a shorter period of time. Generally you start the test at the latest backtest date and run it to some point in time before implementation. Expect diminishing returns during forward testing. System trading is not a secret key that unlocks profits. It is a way you can minimize harmful trading emotions. Consider it an approach that merits your attention if you're willing to roll up your sleeves and do some exploring.

Following the right steps

Here are the steps you should take when backtesting a system:

1. **Identify basis of strategy (i.e. capture trending conditions).**

2. **Identify trade entry and exit rules.**

3. **Identify market traded and period backtest.**

4. **Identify account assumptions (system and trade allocations).**

5. **Test system; evaluate results.**

6. **Identify reasonable filters to minimize losing trades (number and/or size of such trades)**

7. **Add filter based on conclusions from step 6; test system; and then evaluate results.**

8. **Add risk-management component.**

9. **Test system; evaluate results.**

Although I don't detail each step with a figure, you will see figures in this chapter that highlight some of these steps to give you a feel for what you'll be doing when you perform your own backtest.

Check the average value of losing trades, as well as maximum and consecutive losses to determine if a system is suitable.

A long only, rate of change (ROC) momentum system was tested using a simple moving average (SMA) crossover to signal trade entry[ROC: 34, SMA: 13] and exit [ROC: 21, SMA: 8]. Because a faster signal was used for trade exit, a second parameter had to be added to trade entry requiring the 21-day ROC to be higher than its 13-day SMA. Otherwise the appropriate trade exit may never be signaled. This is a trending system that seeks to capitalize on a longer- term momentum push upward. To limit losses and profit erosion a faster momentum signal is used to exit the position.

The backtest was performed over a six year period that included bullish and bearish periods (1999 to 2005)on a group of six semiconductor stocks including SMH, an ETF for the sector. $20,000 was used for the system with 50% of the cash available used for each trade. A $10 per trade commission was added to the costs. No stops were part of the initial system test.

Figure 7-4 displays side-by-side charts for a trade generated by the system.

Figure 7-4:
ROC trending system sample trade (INTC 12/30/1999–1/5/2000).

The image provides two charts for Intel Corporation (INTC) showing trade entry and trade exit conditions. The position was entered on 12/29/1999 and exited six calendar days later for a gain of 3%.

A system does not have to be robust to be effective. Because volatility and trending characteristics vary for different securities, some are better suited to certain types of systems.

Reviewing system results

Because managing risk is a main theme throughout this book, evaluating a system with no stops may seem counter-intuitive. When you think about it though, stop levels are pretty arbitrary — the market doesn't really care if you entered a position at $45. It may or may not have support 5% or 10% below that amount. Allow the system to identify a viable stop-loss point when backtesting it, then decide if it represents suitable risk for you.

System results were very favorable on a variety of measures for the initial run, so no filter was added. The Max Adverse Excursion% was reviewed to determine if a reasonable stop level could be added. A 15% stop was included and the system test run once again. Results were only slightly less favorable so the stop was incorporated.

Charting packages may use different calculations for the same indicator. If changing systems, be sure to compare indicator values that provide signals so you're trading the same system tested. Always consider re-testing the system on the new platform.

Two forward tests were also run, with and without the stop. A two year period was used for each and the system remained viable, with much lower profitability. Expect this to happen with forward tests and actual system performance. This is due to changing conditions and inefficiencies that get worked out of the markets. That's one of the reasons why you need to periodically review system performance and incorporate reasonable stops whenever possible.

Table 7-2 provides system results for the four different runs.

Table 7-2			ROC System Review			
System Run	Average Return	Median Return	Gain: Loss (number)	Average Gain	Average Loss	Max Loss
Test1	4.7	3.0	1.96	10.1	5.8	35%
Test2	4.6	3.0	1.91	10.0	5.9	16%
FTest1	1.6	1.0	1.56	4.0	2.3	10%
FTest2	1.6	1.0	1.56	4.1	2.3	10%

A lower percentage stop can be considered to bring the average and median return closer, but because average gains are outpacing average losses (letting profits run) you want to first compare the average and median for winning trades and losing trades separately.

You can use a standard deviation calculation to assess the stability of profits for any market approach.

Adding risk management to a backtest

All trade approaches need to take risk management into account. Focus on larget adverse moves for a strategy when trying to identify stops that still allow the strategy to work. If adding this stop maintains profitability and stability of the system *and* is consistent with your risk tolerance, you can consider implementing the strategy or system.

Cutting losses

An approach that is systematic, but not mechanical, can still be backtested. Regardless of how you go about performing that backtest, you should keep an eye on large adverse moves that occurred for the trades generated. This allows you to identify reasonable, systematic filters and stops geared toward minimizing losses.

A stop-loss order can result in a larger percentage loss by the time a trade is executed. A worst-case scenario occurs when a signal is generated at the close of trading one day and the security has a price gap at the open the next day.

Taking profits

Identifying stop-loss points that manage risk is probably secondhand to you by now. On the other end of the spectrum, have you ever been in a profitable trade that starts moving the wrong way? Right around that point you realize you don't have a specific exit plan for taking profits. Sometimes you focus so much on risk that you forget to identify favorable price targets. Or maybe you did identify a profitable exit point, but conditions start to deteriorate before that price level is reached.

In addition to identifying a stop-loss level, identify a trailing stop percentage or dollar amount to minimize the number of profitable trades that turn into losses. The trailing stop should be incorporated into your system or strategy and tested. If you want the system to generate the trailing amount, evaluate trades with large favorable moves that yielded significantly less in the way of profits (or turned into losses). After completing your review, you may do as follows:

- ✔ Add a filter that accelerates your exits
- ✔ Generate a trailing percentage using max favorable excursion % data

Letting profits run

An effective trading approach doesn't necessarily have to have more winning trades than losing trades. It just needs profits to outpace declines. That's actually the case for many trend-oriented systems. You end up with more losing trades, but the average value of the loss is much smaller than the average value of gaining trades. And so goes the mantra, "be sure to cut your losses while letting profits run."

Sorting trades by greatest lost to greatest profit allows you to more easily review statistics for both.

Although you need to identify a method for taking profits, you also have to avoid cutting profit levels in such a way that they no longer outpace losses. Trading successfully requires quite a bit of pre-work. You'll see your trading evolve by focusing on the following:

1. **Cutting losses.**
2. **Preventing profits from turning into losses.**
3. **Letting profits run . . .**

Shifting from Knowledge to Mastery

Strategy mastery doesn't mean that every trade you place for a given strategy is profitable — it means that the appropriate conditions were in place when placing a particular trade, putting the odds in your favor for a profitable trade. Managing the position correctly is also another component that highlights discipline by exiting a trade if conditions change. It sounds pretty easy, but strategy mastery can take years to evolve. Your goal is to stay in the trading game long enough to achieve this mastery.

By focusing first on basic concepts and mechanics, you create a strong foundation that allows you to grasp advanced techniques more quickly. You implement new strategies via paper trading to avoid the most costly mistakes. When you're ready to take the new strategy live, you can further minimize the cost of mistakes by reducing your position size and remembering to take profits. This approach keeps you in the markets longer, allowing you to find and develop strategies that are best suited to your style.

Setting the right pace

There are a ton of great option strategies in this book, with some that probably pique your interest more than others. Start out paper trading a couple of the more straightforward approaches, then transition to live trading with them. After that check out the strategy that has the most appeal to you, again by paper trading. There's no guarantee that market conditions will be conducive to that strategy, so you may prolong your paper trading days until the market changes or you're ready to explore a new strategy. But . . . it's really important to keep this in mind. You want to focus on strategies that make sense to you and better suit your style. That's how you'll ultimately develop mastery.

Starting with a few strategies

Learning new strategies is hopefully something you enjoy. It's amazing to find out about all the different ways you can make money in the markets. But not all strategies work in all market conditions. More importantly, they won't all suit your style. If you're new to option trading, stick with one or two basic strategies to develop a really good understanding of premium changes and mechanics.

There are a variety of strategies available to you that allow you to make money in the markets. Just like your preferred method of analysis, you'll find you develop a preferred list of strategies that work for you.

Experienced option traders should identify current market conditions, then explore one, maybe two strategies that excel given those conditions. Start by paper trading and progress from there. If there's a specific strategy that really intrigues or speaks to you, but conditions aren't quite right, just paper trade it. In the long run, it's better to focus on market approaches that make sense to you.

Adding strategies as market conditions change

I look at the markets as a lifelong pursuit because conditions are always changing. Although there's a continuous cycle of bullish and bearish phases, the market is never exactly the same. It seems you already recognize this by purchasing the book in the first place.

When strategies that typically work well for you start weakening, take some time over the weekend to complete a comprehensive market assessment. You may detect early signs of a change in conditions.

Option trading allows you to implement strategies that can be profitable regardless of market conditions. A sampling includes:

- ✔ Bullish, low volatility (basic long call, married puts)
- ✔ Bullish, high volatility (covered calls, credit spreads — Chapter 11)

> ✔ Bearish, low volatility (basic long put, debit spreads — Chapter 11)
>
> ✔ Bearish, high volatility (collars, credit spreads — Chapter 11)
>
> ✔ Range-bound, low volatility (butterfly, condor — Chapter 16)

The combination of stock with options or options with options really provide you with great choices. That can be good and bad news because each approach requires some time to master. Be careful about checking out a strategy haphazardly, then discarding it because "it doesn't work."

Chances are you won't be trading every strategy available. Most traders try different ones along the way, then master a smaller number of them. The experience gained allows them to maximize profits on their favored strategies (knowing when to hold them), while minimizing their losses (knowing when to fold them).

Deciding which option strategies to use is just like market analysis — there are a variety of ways to approach it, none of which represent the one 'right' way. The best approach for you is the one that intuitively makes the most sense so that when conditions change and things get tougher (and they will), you have the confidence to stick to your plan.

Achieving mastery through longevity

Experiencing different markets and exploring suitable strategies requires you to have longevity in the markets. Bull markets can run for years and volatility conditions can remain stable too. Expect to incur additional losses when markets transition or when implementing a new strategy. Managing risk by using limited loss, unlimited gain strategies whenever possible sets a foundation for longevity.

Paper trading provides a technique to minimize learning curve losses. A second method is through proper position sizing. By starting out with smaller initial positions, potential losses are manageable. Adding rules that include profit-taking is the icing on the cake.

Successful trading does not happen overnight. Be prepared to spend time making low-cost mistakes, observing different market conditions, experiencing varying levels of emotion, and developing your trading skills.

Determining appropriate trade sizes

There are different techniques available to identify proper trade sizes. Many are beyond the scope of this book simply due to space constraints. Two easily incorporated ones include the following:

- ✔ Identifying a maximum dollar amount allocated per trade
- ✔ Identifying a maximum percentage amount allocated per trade

I prefer the latter because it automatically changes as your account size changes.

Options represent a leveraged position (see Chapter 3) so you don't need to allocate the same amount to option positions as you do for stocks. In fact, it's probably not a good idea to do that at all. Using your stock allocation plan as a base, you can estimate an initial allocation amount by identifying an option position that controls the same amount of stock. This serves as a starting point that should be tested and reviewed.

Establish trade allocation amounts prior to analyzing a specific trade. You need to know in advance the maximum amount available for an individual trade so that you minimize your account risk.

When trying a new strategy (after paper trading), further reduce trade sizes so mistakes are more forgiving. If that means trading in one option contract sizes, so be it. Remember, you're not out there to impress Wall Street with your trade sizes — you're out there to make money in the markets.

As your skills develop, increase position sizes to those tested allocations. This will improve profits because option trading costs are often higher than stock trading costs from a percentage standpoint. If you've properly prepared and continue to manage your risk, increasing position sizes shouldn't be a problem. In fact, it should improve results because you'll realize economies of scale with trading costs.

Emphasizing profit-taking

Throughout this book there's an emphasis on managing risk. In this chapter though there's an additional emphasis — that's on profit-taking. It's not enough to simply have a high number of profitable trades. Your profits must include the following:

- ✔ Exceed trading costs
- ✔ Exceed conservative investment approaches
- ✔ Exceed your losses

This doesn't just happen out of the blue, you have to have a plan that includes reviewing strategy and trade results to put the best profit-taking rules in place. Such rules should minimize the number of profitable trades that turn into losses and allow profits to run. Developing these skills means you're evolving as a trader.

There are a lot of different price points that can invoke an emotional response while in a trade. Be sure to identify exit points for a loss as well as exit points for profits.

Chapter 8

Mapping Out Your Plan of Attack

*T*rading is a business and developing as a trader means evolving as a business manager. Understanding the costs associated with the business helps you budget accordingly. Initially certain costs will be higher and others will be lower. You'll likely be paying more for education and your learning curve (a.k.a. losses) when you start out. As your trading evolves, those costs will go down while subscriptions to analysis platforms and data services will go up.

Always keep in mind that losses are part of operating expenses. Minimizing them by managing risk is your goal — not eliminating them. This is done by determining proper trade allocation amounts and maximum loss per trade. Effectively executing trades is another step toward minimizing losses. I cover all these topics in this chapter.

Managing Your Costs

There are a variety of costs to consider with your trading — some are higher when you first start and many continue throughout your career. You need to think of trading as a business and manage these expenses so you can minimize them as your business matures. The expense categories included in the following list will all continue throughout your trading career, but some will begin higher than others:

> ✔ **Education:** Education expenses include materials, courses, and learning curve costs for new markets and strategies. These costs will decrease as time progresses, but will remain on-going as stay current with market conditions (books, periodicals) and continue to develop new strategies.

One of the largest education costs is your learning curve. These decline as you figure out how to:

- Trade under best conditions for the strategy
- Use options with the appropriate liquidity
- Develop paper-trading skills
- Allocate the appropriate amount to the trade
- Effectively enter orders for the best exit
- Take profits

✓ **Analysis costs:** As your skills progress and your trading generates regular profits, you may add analytical tools to your business costs. Talking to fellow traders that use such tools and finding out which ones you may be able to take for a spin using free trials are good places to start. Such costs represent one of the few that may increase over time. Be sure to only subscribe to a limited number of services so you can make the most out of them.

✓ **Trading costs:** You have to not only have to account for commission but also for slippage. *Slippage* is the cost associated with the market spread — the difference between the bid and the ask. A good exercise is to calculate commission and slippage percentages for different size option positions (i.e. 1, 5, 10 contracts) established at different price points (i.e. $1, $5, $10).

Taxes are another consideration, so you need to identify what types of trading will be completed in different accounts. In addition, when establishing certain option positions, you may trigger a tax event in the underlying. Be sure to contact your accountant about option trading tax considerations. The bottom line for these cumulative costs is that in the long-term, they must outpace a buy and hold approach.

If you borrow from your broker via trading on margin, you need to add monthly margin interest charges to your trading costs as well. Short option positions have margin requirements that can get complicated. The main consideration for this margin is whether the option is covered or naked. If you decide to move forward with strategies requiring margin, be sure to contact your broker so you fully understand all of the calculations and account requirements. Then add these costs to your expenses.

Losses are another trading cost that should be considered part of doing business. They will likely be higher at first, but reduced with time and experience. Following these trading plan guidelines should help keep these initial costs to a minimum:

✔ **Determining the trading allocations:** As part of an overall trading plan you should identify both your total trading assets and your maximum allocations for different assets and strategies. Stock and ETF trading will require larger allocations than option positions. You may even want to break this down further to include a maximum allocation amount for new strategies based on paper trading results.

✔ **Calculating trade size:** You must also determine guidelines for maximum position size prior to entering any trade. Once these are set, identifying the maximum number of contracts you can allocate to a position is pretty straightforward. Divide the option price by an allocation amount below your maximum and you're all set. Don't anticipate using the max allocation.

✔ **Identifying maximum acceptable loss on trades:** Your maximum acceptable loss can be defined as a dollar value or a percentage. I prefer the latter because a fixed dollar amount can be significant with smaller trades or if your trading assets decrease. Periodically perform an analysis on your trade results to determine if your losses remain at reasonable and sustainable levels.

✔ **Focusing on entry and exit rules:** Option entries are often driven by trending and volatility conditions, but may also be time oriented with positions created prior to specific scheduled event. Option exists can also be time driven (post-event or pre-expiration) or may be triggered by movement in the underlying security. Regardless, these methods must be focused on supporting your risk management and maximum allowable loss.

Exiting with technical indicators typically does not provide you with a price for use with risk calculations. A maximum loss price should also be identified.

Optimizing Order Execution

Successfully trading options means gaining proficiency with order execution. A variety of factors come into the mix here including:

✔ Understanding order placement rules unique to options

✔ Knowing how different order types work

✔ Learning how to use combination orders for multi-leg positions

✔ Gaining skill while using the underlying to identify option exits

✔ Recognizing your broker's role in execution quality

There is also a learning curve for executing option trades, but for the most part these are mechanical steps that can be easily mastered with some practice. This will go a long way toward successful strategy implementation.

The *ask,* or best price available from sellers, is also referred to as the *offer.*

Understanding option orders

Options are not limited to a certain number of contracts the way stock is constrained by its float. Contracts are created by the marketplace, so they have some unique considerations when placing orders for them. An option is created when two traders create a new position; or *open* a trade. This increases open interest for that specific option. Open interest decreases when traders close existing positions.

Float is the term used to describe the number of shares outstanding and available to trade for a stock.

Open interest doesn't get updated on a trade by trade basis, it's more an end of day reconciliation through the Options Clearing Corporation (OCC). That explains why option orders are placed in a specific manner — the OCC needs to keep the accounting straight. It also means you'll be communicating a little more information when placing option orders.

Knowing basic option order rules

Buying or selling options can be done in any order. Choosing whether you want to be long (buy) or short (sell) a contract depends on your strategy and the option approval level for your account. You can't jump out of the gate creating unlimited risk, short option positions until your broker approves you for it — after checking your temperature of course.

The current bid and ask price for a security is referred to as its *current market.*

Because contracts are created and retired, you need to enter orders in a way that supports this end of day reconciliation by the options markets. You need to identify:

- ✔ A new position you're creating as an *opening order*
- ✔ An existing position you're exiting as a *closing order*

Using a call option as an example, Table 8-1 provides you with the transactions required to enter and exit a long call or short call position.

Table 8-1	Option Order Entry Process			
Position	*Entry*	*Also*	*Exit*	*Also*
Long Call	Buy Call to Open	BCO	Sell Call to Close	SCC
Short Call	Sell Call to Open	SCO	Buy Call to Close	BCC

When exercising or getting assigned on an option contract, there is no closing transaction. The same holds true for options expiring worthless. In each case the appropriate amount of contracts are removed from your account after the transaction completes or expiration weekend comes to an end.

Reviewing order types

You have a variety of different order types available to you, some guarantee executions (i.e. market order) while others guarantee price (i.e. limit orders). Although there are unique considerations for option orders, this execution versus price distinction remains the same. Effectively managing order execution means knowing when it's more important to get the order executed versus the price where it's executed. When in doubt, consider what limits your risk.

Table 8-2, which you a quick glance at popular order types and which guarantee execution or price.

Table 8-2	Order Types by Guarantee
Order	*Guarantees*
Market order	Execution
Limit order	Price
Stop order or stop-loss order	Execution
Stop-limit order	Price

Generally, limit orders are good for entering a position so you only establish those that are within your trading allocations. If you need to guarantee an exit only a market order accomplishes this for you.

A stop order is your risk management tool for trading with discipline. The stop level triggers a market order if the option trades or moves to that level. The stop represents a price less favorable than the current market and is typically used to minimize losses for an existing position when emotions run high. Placing a stop order is similar to monitoring a security and placing a market order when certain market conditions are met.

Stops are superior to stop limit orders for managing risk because they guarantee an execution if the stop condition is met.

In terms of duration, the two primary periods of time your order will be in place are:

- ✔ The current trading session or following session if the market is closed
- ✔ Until the order is cancelled by you or the broker clears the order (possibly in 60 days — check with your broker)

Order duration is identified by adding Day or good 'til canceled (GTC). Market orders guarantee execution so they are good for the day only.

If you want to cancel an active order, you do so by submitting a Cancel Order. After the instructions are completed, you receive a report back notifying you the order was successfully canceled. It is possible for the order to already have been executed, in which case you receive a report back indicating, too late to cancel, filled with the execution details. Needless to say, you can't cancel a market order.

Changing an order is a little different than canceling one because you can change an order one of two ways:

- ✔ Cancel the original order, wait for the report confirming the cancellation, and then enter a new order
- ✔ Submit a Cancel/Change or Replace Order which replaces the existing order with the revised qualifiers unless the original order was already executed. If that happens, the replacement order is canceled.

Even though the order process is incredibly fast, when replacing an order it's better to use the Change/Cancel approach. Otherwise you must wait for the cancellation confirmation to avoid duplicating an executed order.

There are other less widely used order types available. Check with your broker if you need additional information about them or if you need help placing a new order type. For the most part, they'd much rather be on the phone helping you place an order than explaining to you why the trade wasn't executed as you expected.

It is absolutely, positively your responsibility to understand order types and how they are executed (or not) in the market. Do I sound wishy-washy on this?

Identifying option stop order challenges

Just in case your eyes haven't glazed over yet, there are a few additional considerations specific to option stop orders. Maybe more than a few, but I'll try to focus on couple of the major ones. An option stop order can be triggered in two ways:

- ✔ If a trade is executed at the stop price
- ✔ If the bid or ask moves to the stop price

Because option contract volume is much lower than stocks, the quote frequently is the trigger for a stop order. Otherwise it's possible for hours to pass before an actual trade triggers the stop. At that point, who knows where the underlying would be trading and what the quote would be when your market order got triggered.

Typically when placing a stop order on an option you use a maximum risk amount to target an exit price for the option. It's an estimated amount since the order may be triggered by the option quote and you won't know in advance the spread amount when it's triggered.

The worst-case scenario for this type of order is to have the underlying security gap up or down (against you) at the open, causing the order to be triggered well below your risk target. Actually, the only thing worse than that is to have no order in place and be left with a position that keeps declining.

Some systems allow you to have two standing orders for the same underlying. They include a stop loss order (risk management) and a limit order (profit-taking). If your platform allows a "one cancels other" trade type, then enter such orders using that feature. If not, be extremely careful about entering two orders — they both may be filled.

A *one cancels other order* allows you to enter two different orders that are active in the market. If and when one of those orders is executed, the system automatically cancels the other order. If this order set-up is not available to you, having two live orders for the same position is pretty dangerous. A strong swing in the position can result in both orders being executed, possibly leaving you with an unlimited risk position.

The best market for bidding and asking (offering) prices are referred to as the *NBBO*, which stands for the National Best Bid-Offer. The NBBO represents composite information from the various option exchanges.

A sell stop order gets triggered when the option trades at or below your stop price *or* if the ask reaches your stop. A buy stop order gets triggered when the option trades at or above your stop *or* the bid reaches your stop. Because you sell on the bid and buy on the ask, you need to account for the bid-ask spread when determining an option stop level.

A second issue with option stop orders is duration. The option contract you're trading may only allow day stop orders. If this is the case, you'll need to enter a new stop order each evening after the market closes.

If you're used to trading stock, don't assume option orders work the same exact way. Be sure you know the implications of all orders you place.

Entering a new position

Okay getting ready to enter an option order? Just a few more points ahead. Option positions can include:

- ✔ Single option contracts
- ✔ Options contracts and stock
- ✔ Multiple option contracts

A quick review of single contract order entry is provided, followed by combination orders.

Creating a single option position

A single contract option order entry requires information about:

- ✔ The transaction type (buy or sell)
- ✔ Position information (open or close)
- ✔ Contract specifics (underlying, month, strike price and option type)
- ✔ Order type (market, limit, . . .)
- ✔ Order duration (day, good 'til canceled, . . .)

After entering your order, it goes from broker's system to one of six option exchanges. The exchanges are linked so your order can be executed on the exchange receiving the order or it can be forwarded to the exchange with the best market. Technology makes the process is seamless and speedy. Some brokers also allow you to direct the order to the exchange of your choice.

Option exchange linkage and the introduction of penny increment trading has minimized the benefit to direct access trading.

Creating a combination position

Combination positions can be entered as a single combined order or individual orders for each portion of it (a.k.a. *legging in*). An advantage to combining the order is that you have a better chance of having the trade executed between the bid-ask spread. This applies to both option-stock combinations as well as option-option combinations.

Assuming ABC is trading at 33.12 by 33.14 and the ABC Jan 30 put is trading at 1.00 by 1.05. You wish to place a limit order for a married put position that is good for the current market day, so the combination is entered as follows:

- ✔ Buy 100 shares of ABC

- ✔ Simultaneously Buy to Open 1 ABC Jan 30 put

- ✔ For a limit (net debit) of $34.17, good for the day

All legs for a combination order will either be executed or not executed.

The qualifiers for a combination order are the same for each leg and you can only get filled on both portions of the order. Chapter 11 introduces spread trades including a Bull Call Spread which is a debit position that combines two calls. A long call is purchased at the same time a less expensive call expiring the same month is sold.

Using ABC, you create a Bull Call Spread by purchasing a $30 call and selling a $35 call. The quotes for the two options follow:

- ✔ Mar 30.00 Call: Bid $3.10 by Ask $3.30

- ✔ Mar 35.00 Call: Bid $1.00 by Ask $1.05

Because you're buying the 30 strike call (Ask $3.30) and selling the 35 strike call (Bid $1.00), the net debit at the quote is $2.30. You can identify this net debit as a limit amount for the spread order or can try to reduce the cost by reducing the debit slightly. Entering an order slightly lower than the market is accomplished as follows:

- ✔ Buy to Open 1 ABC Mar 30 call and

- ✔ Simultaneously Sell to Open 1 ABC Mar 35 call

- ✔ For a limit (net debit) of $2.25, good for the day

Again, the qualifiers for a combination order are the same for each leg and you can only get filled on both portions of the order.

Fill is another term for order execution.

Exchange traders agree to make a market on the list of securities they handle which subjects them to risk that they must manage constantly. They do this for single option orders by buying and selling the underlying stock or other options to hedge the risk (see Chapter 12).

Spread trades are different — they represent a naturally hedged position and are appealing to the trader regardless of whether it creates a debit or credit in their account. When trading spreads you should:

- ✔ Moderately reduce the limit below the market on a spread debit order
- ✔ Moderately increase the limit above the market on a spread credit order

Spreads have high appeal on the trading floor; try to shave a little off the market price for these orders.

Spread orders are less automated on the exchanges, which means it can take a little more time to receive an execution report. With this in mind, expect the process of replacing an order to really take some time if you've shaved too much off the price. If executing the spread is more important than shaving some money from the current quote, stay closer to the current market. Prices can move significantly in the time it takes you to receive a confirmed cancellation report for an unexecuted order.

Executing a quality trade

Execution quality describes a broker's ability to provide speedy order executions at or better than the current market for the security. This means if you have an order to buy a security with a bid of $22.95 and an ask of $22.98, your order will be filled in a timely manner at $22.98 or better. When considering brokers, good execution quality is as important as reasonable commission costs.

Trading platforms are so fast these days and a lot of orders never even touch an exchange trader's hands — it's all about the technology. If you're having significant option execution problems it's possible your broker does not handle many option trading accounts and you should consider using a different broker for the option trading portion of your assets.

A variety of factors can impact your execution quality and are generally good for you to know about when trading. I discuss a few of these in the sections that follow.

Fast markets

A security is in a *fast market* when a very large volume of orders is flowing to the market and it's difficult for the market maker or specialist to maintain an orderly market for the security. Volume is high and quotes and execution reports are delayed. Although technology has reduced the number of securities placed in Fast Markets by the exchange, traders must be aware that standard rules for execution are waived at this time.

When a stock goes into a fast market, so do the options derived from it.

If you place a market order when fast markets are declared, the trade may end up getting executed minutes after the order is placed when the price is significantly different. The trade could cost you much more than anticipated.

If you must exit a position, you may have no choice but to trade under these conditions, but consider entering a marketable limit order that provides you with a cushion because it's not uncommon for movements to occur quickly in both directions. As always though, managing your risk comes first.

Trader-driven conditions

Consider your trading platform and connectivity when identifying factors that impact order execution. If the time it takes to get a quote and submit an order is lengthy, the delay in obtaining an order execution may be on your end and not the broker's or exchange's. Given the amount of bandwidth required for trading platforms, a slow computer or connection could put you behind the trading curve.

If you're trading this way and can't upgrade, keep the real short-term trading to a minimum and consider using marketable limit orders instead of a market order any time you enter a new position so you can control your costs.

Execution delays may not be a broker or exchange issue — it may be your system.

Booked order

When an order that is better than the current bid or ask enters the option market, the exchange can fill it or post it as the current best bid or best ask. If this is done the order is considered a *booked order.* The impact to you is that the depth of the market at this price may be pretty small — the order may represent just one or two contracts. Execution quality rules don't apply to such quotes.

Electronic review

Your broker may have an electronic order review process that delays routing your orders to an exchange. This delay can be several minutes. You may trade actively and never encounter such a delay or experience such a quick review that order routing appears to be seamless. Only a very small fraction of retail orders are reviewed during any given trading day. Check with your broker if it appears to be an issue.

Exiting an existing position

The order platforms and trading screens available today also provide you with a variety of approaches to exit an option position. In addition to placing an order for the specific option contract, you can place contingent orders based on the movement of the underlying security. This is extremely helpful in protecting your downside and establishing exits based on technical levels.

Understanding what to expect in actual trading is pretty important. There are times when different types of orders are appropriate, but without a lot of experience using them, you're not sure how to proceed. Your broker should always welcome your call when clarifying exchange rules or proper order entry for their trade platforms.

There are SEC rules in place requiring brokers to provide execution statistics on different orders. The regulation primarily covers market and marketable limit stock orders, but also include some reporting for options.

Managing risk with single options

There are a couple of different ways to manage risk when you hold a single option position. The first includes using a stop order on the option itself and was discussed earlier. The second involves placing a conditional or contingent order on the underlying stock.

Conditional or *contingent orders* refer to those that rely on movement in the underlying or an index to trigger an option order. There are a variety of criteria that can be established on the underlying or index, including

- ✔ Closing price equal to, greater than or less than a certain value

- ✔ Intraday price equal to, greater than or less than a certain value

- ✔ Percentage changes in price

- ✔ Quote levels equal to, greater than or less than a certain value

After setting the criteria for the trigger, you enter the specifics for the option order, which has the standard qualifiers available. A big distinction between a stop order and a contingent order is that a stop order is active on the exchange while a contingent order is active on your broker's system. The market doesn't have a view of your contingent order.

An advantage to placing stop orders to exit a position versus contingent orders on the underlying stock is that you can better estimate the trade value with the option order.

Some of the triggers appear similar to a stop order for the option, but remember the contingent order generates an option order when you have much less of a handle on where the option is trading. You can estimate the expected option value using the price of the underlying and the option Greeks.

The absolute best reason to use contingent orders is they allow you to identify technical (or fundamental) exit points for the stock. Since managing risk is critical, this approach allows you to exit the option when conditions in the underlying have changed.

Consider using an option calculator to estimate an option's value when a contingent order is triggered.

Be aware of all active orders with your broker, there is a potential to duplicate them if your platform doesn't have safeguards. Having triggers set above the market and below the market at the same time can be dangerous. The best way to manage this is by using the one cancels other (OCO) order type which can be discussed with your broker.

Exiting a combination

Combination orders are exited in the same way they are created — either by legging out of the position or by entering a combination order for a credit or debit. When presenting a hedged position to the floor, consider shaving off a little from the debit or adding a bit to the credit. Unless you're very close to expiration for the position, you'll likely have the order executed at the more favorable limit.

Rolling an option position

You may hear people talk about rolling an option and wonder what exactly is involved in this process. *Roll* is used to describe an option transaction that involves closing one position and opening a similar one for the same stock. It's common for this process to occur near expiration as protective or income positions are pushed further out in time.

Rolling out involves pushing back expiration for a strategy. When rolling an option, you place a combination order similar to the any other combination. Because the expiration date is so close, you may not be able to get a more favorable execution for the combination.

You end up paying an extra commission to close the original option, which probably would have expired worthless, but you are also gaining some time value for the new option sold.

Instead of rolling the option out in time, you can *roll up* in price to avoid assignment risk or capitalize on atypically high implied volatility for a higher strike option.

A third alternative to rolling out or rolling up is *rolling down* the strike price. Again, you may elect to do this to avoid assignment risk or capitalize on atypically high implied volatility for a lower strike option.

These rolling combinations can also be combined so that you can roll out and up or roll out and down, depending on the price for the underlying, you're market outlook for it, and implied volatility conditions.

Part III:
What Every Trader Needs to Know About Options

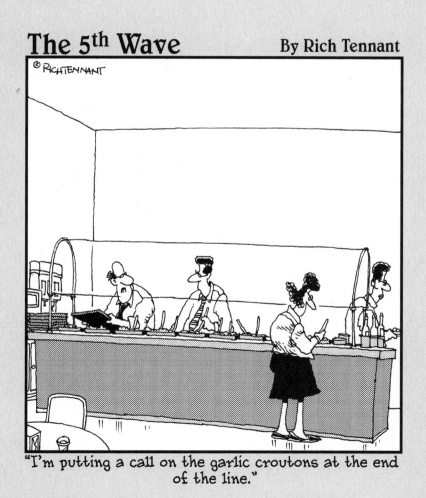

The 5th Wave — By Rich Tennant

"I'm putting a call on the garlic croutons at the end of the line."

In this part . . .

Options provide you with some distinct trading advantages, but like other types of securities, they are not without risk. In fact, used the wrong way, they can be very risky. By understanding option styles and the risks associated with each you can manage that risk. Even if you chose to use options on a limited basis, you can consider a few core strategies to limit your overall market risk. These can be implemented with existing stock positions, single option positions, or through combination option positions.

All of the strategies provided in this part focus on alternative, reduced risk approaches to stock positions. Exchange-traded funds (ETFs) and option strategies using ETFs are also discussed here to provide some insights on ways to reduce portfolio volatility as well as single stock risk.

Chapter 9

Getting a Handle on Option Styles

Knowing your risk as a trader means you really understand the market mechanics for the securities you use, as well as the different ways it can hit you with losses. Options present you with a unique challenge because they come with an expiration date — you need to know how to handle a security that eventually "goes away." In this chapter, I focus on key points about indexes and index options that impact trading. I also address exercise style exercise, and assignment issues, as well as other things you need to be wary of going into expiration.

Nailing Down Index Options

You can group most monthly listed stock options together when applying strategies or managing a position because their basic features match. For instance, the last trading date and exercise cutoff time for each are the same for all monthly stock options. Index options are slightly more challenging because those things can vary by contract. Here's a primer on index and index options to help you avoid some unpleasant surprises.

Getting to the nitty-gritty of indexes

An *index* is a tool that combines individual stocks, bonds, or commodities into one value so you can track the health of a particular market. This helps you target your trading on broad, diversified markets or narrower, focused ones.

Taking a peek at popular indexes

You're probably familiar with indexes, by name at least. The refresher on the next page shows you a few of the most popular indexes Wall Street has to offer and what they do:

- ✔ **S&P 500 (SPX):** If you want to get a feel for the health of a diverse group of U.S. large-cap stocks, the S&P 500 Index (SPX) is the one to do just that. It is used by professional money managers and individual investors all over the globe to check the pulse of the U.S. stock market.

- ✔ **The Dow (a.k.a. the Dow Jones Industrial Average):** To gain insight on how 30 select manufacturers in the U.S. stock market are doing, use another widely followed index, the Dow.

- ✔ **Nasdaq-100 (NDX):** If you like a faster pace, the Nasdaq-100 Index (NDX) is made up of the 100 largest, nonfinancial companies trading on the Nasdaq exchange. The index is made up primarily with stocks in the technology industry and is most frequently used to measure this sector. It usually swings up and down more widely than the S&P 500 or the Dow.

The market capitalization or cap of a company is calculated by multiplying the current stock price by the total number of shares outstanding. Market cap sizes include small-, mid-, and large.

Shifting to a more specific focus and showcasing variety

If you wish to focus on a more specific group of stocks, this list shows you the wide variety of indexes available:

- ✔ **PHLX Semiconductor Sector Index (SOX):** If you want to concentrate on just semiconductor stocks rather than all technology stocks, one index you may want to track is the SOX. It's made up of 19 different companies in the semiconductor industry.

- ✔ **AMEX Select Utility Index (UUO):** In addition to choosing stocks in one sector, the Select Utility Index ranks the group by dividend payments and uses the top 20 ranked companies to create the index. The names in the group are updated quarterly.

- ✔ **Russell 2000 Growth Index:** This index allows you to narrow your focus on two levels — it tracks stocks that are both small-cap and growth oriented. Expect big moves in both directions because small-cap names take less volume than large-cap names to impact where the stock trades.

Because an index is made up of a group of stocks, declines in one stock can be off-set by increases in another stock. As a result, you'll find that indexes tend to be less volatile than individual stocks.

Creating indexes and creating change in stocks

It's important to understand that not all indexes are created equally (well . . . one is). The three ways to construct an index are as follows:

- ✔ **Price-weighted:** Favors higher priced stocks
- ✔ **Market cap-weighted:** Favors higher cap stocks
- ✔ **Equal dollar-weighted:** Each stock has same impact

By having a basic handle on the different methods, you gain a much better feel for how changes in one stock translate into changes for the index. The construction names should help. The following examples show you what I mean:

- ✔ **When a high-priced stock declines in a price-weighted index, it leads to bigger moves down in an index compared to declines in a lower priced stock.** The Dow is an example of a price-weighted index that is affected more by Boeing (trading near $100) than Pfizer (trading near $25).

- ✔ **A market-cap weighted index such as the S&P 500 is impacted more by higher market capitalization stocks regardless of price.** Even though Microsoft may only be trading at $30 per share, its market cap is huge — about $290 billion. When it moves up or down it creates a greater change in the S&P 500 than say, Amgen which trades at $55 per share, but only has a market cap of approximately $64 billion.

- ✔ **All the stocks in an equal-dollar weighted index should have the same impact on the index value.** To keep the index balance, a quarterly adjustment of the stocks is required. This prevents a stock that has seen large gains during the last three months from having too much weight on the index.

The best way to obtain specific construction information for an index is by accessing the Web site of the company that created the index. You can often bring up a list of component stocks, bonds, or commodities for the index, along with other useful information. For instance, you can access index levels, charts, construction approach and component lists for Dow Jones indexes when you access: www.djindexes.com.

So who creates these indexes and why should you care? Different groups construct them, including financial information companies, exchanges, or brokerage firms. By knowing the company that creates them, you know how to get the index detail you need for different strategies. Table 9-1 provides sample indexes that include the company that constructs them and how you can use them.

Table 9-1		Sample Index List	
Name	*Symbol*	*Company*	*Generally Used For:*
S&P 500	SPX	Standard and Poors	Trading or hedging a diverse U.S. large-cap stock portfolio
S&P Midcap 400	MDY	Standard and Poors	Trading or hedging a U.S. mid-cap stock portfolio
MSCI EAFE	MSCIEA	Morgan Stanley Capital International	Trading or hedging a diverse global stock portfolio
Footsie-100	FTSE 100	FTSE Group	Trading a narrow international stock group (UK blue chip)
AMEX Biotech	BTK	American Stock Exchange	Trading focused on a narrow industry stock group (biotechnology)
CRB Index	CRBI	Commodity Research Bureau	Trading or hedging a diverse, commodity portfolio
Goldman Commodity Index	GSCI	Goldman Sachs Group	Trading more narrow commodity group that over-weights energy
Aggregate Bond Fund	LEHM or AGG	Lehman Brothers	Trading or hedging a diverse U.S. govt. and corporate investment grade bonds portfolio
CBOE 30-year Yields	TYX	Chicago Board Options Exchange	Trading focused on U.S. 30-year treasury yields

Capitalizing on an index with options

In addition to options whose value is derived from an individual stock, you can also find many options that are based on index levels. In fact, the S&P 500 (SPX) is one of the most widely traded option series for all stock and index options, so it's very easy to create and exit a position. But because you can't actually own an index, how can you deliver one if you chose to exercise an index put?

The answer is . . . you can't. Index options don't actually involve the exchange of an asset. Index options are referred to as *cash-settled* because the exercise and assignment process involves the transfer of cash instead of a security. The amount of cash is determined by the intrinsic value of the option. (See Chapter 3 for more detail on intrinsic value.)

Determining value

Options on an index are very similar to options on a stock. There are calls and puts with different expiration months and strike prices available. This list identifies factors that determine the option's value:

- **Its type (call or put):** Calls increase in value as the index increases while puts increase in value when the index decreases.

- **The value of the index level relative to the option's strike price:** A call has intrinsic value when the strike price is below the index level. When the index is trading below the call strike price, the option only has time value. On the other hand, a put has intrinsic value when the index is trading below the put strike price.

- **Time to expiration:** The more time until expiration, the greater the chance an option will have value at expiration. So you pay more money for options with more time until expiration, regardless of type.

- **Historical volatility:** An index that has made bigger moves in the past will have options that are more expensive than an index that historically moves less because there is more uncertainty about where it will be at expiration. Index gains or losses can be significant.

- **Volatility expected in the future:** The expected future movement affects an option's value in the same way its past movement does — in fact, it's partially based on it. The greater the potential move, the more expensive the option.

Detailing option components

The main components of an index option are basically the same as those for a stock option. (See Chapter 2 for more detail.) The main difference is that an index isn't a physical asset — this affects the exercise or assignment process though.

Here's a list of index option components similar to stock options:

- **Underlying:** Name of the index the option is based on.

- **Strike Price:** Level that determines where the owner has rights and the seller has obligations.

- **Premium:** Total cost of the option based on the current market price and the option multiplier.

- **Multiplier:** Number used to determine the total value of the option premium and the exercise value.

- **Exercise/Assignment Value:** Amount credited to the option owner and debited from the option owner seller. It is determined by multiplying the strike price by the option multiplier.

- **Settlement Value:** Index closing value used to determine intrinsic value.

Moneyness is another term used to describe the option's intrinsic value. It is the amount an index closes above a call option strike price or below a put option strike price. Moneyness is zero for out-of-the-money options at expiration.

Suppose the SPX closes at 1,523 at June expiration and you own one June 1,520 call. Since a short option holder can't deliver the SPX to you, they satisfy their obligation in cash. You receive a $300 credit in your account and the short contract holder is debited the same amount. This is how the cash amount is determined:

(Index Settlement Value – Call Strike Price) × Multiplier

(1,523 – 1,520) × 100 = $300

You probably noticed the cash settlement amount at expiration is similar to the intrinsic value calculation for a stock option. The two types of options do have many similarities, as well as important distinctions. In the next section I provide you with some differences between stock and index options.

Watching Out for Style Risk

I'm not worried about you trading last year's big fad — I want to make sure that you know options have style. An option's *style* primarily refers to the way the contract is exercised, but it also impacts the end of trading for the option. You have to know where to look to find an index option's style and how it affects you.

If you don't know the style for a particular option, you could end up with an unpleasant surprise . . . such as missing an opportunity to sell an index call contract before it takes a tumble on the settlement value day.

The U.S. markets trade two styles for option contracts:

- ✔ **American style:** If you own an American-style option you can exercise your rights *at any point up to* the exercise cutoff time.

- ✔ **European style:** If you own a European-style option you can only exercise your rights on a designated date.

American-style options

Options that use stock for the deliverable package are American style. Unless stated otherwise, I refer to American-style stock options whenever I use the general term "option contract" in this book. You can determine an option's style by checking out its product specification sheet available from the Options Clearing Corporation (OCC) or the different option exchanges. The OCC Web site (www.optionsclearing.com) and exchange Web sites serve as excellent resources for this information.

Here are instructions for accessing some popular index options:

- ✔ **CBOE:** www.cboe.com/products/IndexOptions.aspx
- ✔ **PHLX:** www.phlx.com/products/index.html
- ✔ **AMEX:** www.amex.com, select "Index" from the "Other Products" menu
- ✔ **ISE:** www.iseoptions.com, select "Index Options" from "Products Traded"

American-style stock options have these characteristics:

- ✔ When initiated by the OCC, the option contract trades from that point in time until the last trading day prior to option expiration. Recall that option expiration is the Saturday following the third Friday of the month.

- ✔ After purchased, these contracts can be exercised by the holder at any point during the life of the contract. Retail brokers have different requirements for submitting exercise instructions — find out your broker's specific rules. In most cases, you can exercise a long contract at least an hour after the close on the last trading day prior to expiration.

- ✔ After assigned the option seller must fulfill their obligation under the contract by delivering or taking delivery of the option package (usually 100 shares of stock for a stock option).

- ✔ The option seller can "buy to close" the option in the market prior to the close on the last day of trading to offset the position and alleviate the obligation.

European-style options

Options that use an index to derive its value are *often, but not always* European style. This type of option has a specified exercise date if you are long the contract. So you can't exercise the option prior to that date the way you can with American-style options. Not only is there a specified exercise date for an index option, but this date also varies by index — there's not one common index exercise day each month.

With this in mind, it's extremely important for you to check the product specification sheet prior to trading one of these contracts. Key dates for you to note for European-style index options include:

- ✔ **Last trading date:** The last date the contract can be traded in the market — it may be two days prior to expiration.

- ✔ **Settlement date:** The date (and time) used to determine the index closing value at expiration.

- ✔ **Exercise date:** The date in which a long contract holder can exercise their rights under the contract.

Some index options stop trading on a Thursday rather than a Friday so you need to know the specifics to properly manage your position. The style designation, expiration, and exercise dates, and other critical trading details are all included in the option contract specifications available from the OCC or different exchanges that trade the ocntract.

The stock option package identifies the deliverable asset(s) for a contract. Although there are securities that track an index, indexes themselves are not physical securities. As a result, index options settle in cash rather than a physical asset because a trader can't deliver an index. This cash-settlement approach applies to index options regardless of exercise style.

European-style index options have these characteristics:

- ✔ When initiated by the OCC, the option contract trades from that point in time until the specified Last Trading Date which is usually two trading days prior to option expiration. Check the contract specifications to determine the last trading date for each index option.

- ✔ After purchased, these contracts can only be exercised by the holder on the exercise date which is *usually* the last business day before options expiration. Retail brokers have different requirements for submitting exercise instructions so you need to contact your broker to get their specific rules — which may be different than stock option exercise.

- ✔ When assigned, the index option seller must fulfill their obligation under the contract with a cash settlement. The appropriate amount of money is debited from the account.

- ✔ The option seller can "buy to close" the option in the market prior to the exercise date and close of trading for the contract to offset the position and alleviate the obligation.

You should note that not all index options are European style. The S&P 100 Index (OEX) includes the top-100 stocks in the SPX and is an example of an American-style index option. These contracts can be exercised at any time during the life of the option.

Indexes are generally less volatile than stock and a diverse index such as the S&P 100 is generally less volatile than a sector-oriented index. That's because a group of stocks in the same industry tends to respond the same way to news, pushing the index in one direction. That won't necessarily happen with a diverse index because some news can be bullish for one industry and bearish for another.

The S&P 500 Index is one of the most widely followed indexes and options on the index are offered by the CBOE as a proprietary product. They are high-volume contracts used by many institutional traders, so they are very liquid. Using this option contract as an example, here are some things to note from the specification available at www.cboe.com:

- **Underlying symbol:** SPX
- **Multiplier:** 100
- **Premium:** Quote x Multiplier, so 1 point is equal to $100
- **Expiration date:** Saturday following the third Friday of the expiration month
- **Exercise style:** European — options generally may be exercised on the last business day before expiration, usually a Friday.
- **Last trading day:** Trading usually stops on the business day (usually a Thursday) prior to the day the exercise-settlement value is calculated.
- **Settlement of option exercise:** The exercise-settlement value (SET) is calculated on the last business day before expiration using the first reported sales price for each component stock from the market where the stock is listed. This day is usually a Friday.
- **Margin:** Check the specification margin rules and then check your broker's rules which may be more stringent.
- **Trading hours:** 8:30 a.m. – 3:15 p.m. Central Time.

Additional information is available, but key elements are previously listed.

Not all European-style options have the same specifications — one may calculate the settlement value using an opening price while another may use closing values from the previous day. To trade an index option, first check the specs!

Exercising Your Options American Style

How you exercise an option is much more straightforward than whether or not to exercise, so I cover mechanics first. As a retail trader, you provide exercise instructions to your broker who then provides these instructions to the OCC. The OCC randomly assigns a broker with accounts holding the same option short and the broker assigns one of those accounts.

When you own an American-style call or put, you have the right to exercise the contract at any point up until your broker's exercise cutoff time. You exercise the contract by submitting *exercise instructions* to the broker either by phone or electronically.

It can't be stressed enough: do not assume that you have the same exercise cutoff time as your trading partner, a clearing firm, or anyone else. Always check the specific cut-off time and exercise process with your broker. Be sure to leave sufficient time to reach them and provide instructions.

Mechanically speaking

I recommend contacting your broker ahead of time to check their exercise process — you want this information in advance so everything goes smoothly when you actually need to submit instructions. Prior to exercising a stock option contract, be sure to check the following:

- ✔ For calls, that sufficient money is in the account to pay for the stock purchased

- ✔ For puts, that shares are in the account or that you are able (and wish to) create a short stock position. This would be prohibited in a retirement account.

Definitely ask any questions you may have during the broker discussion.

Even if you can submit exercise instructions electronically, you may want to contact your broker directly the first few times you complete the process.

What you see is what you get

Although clearing and brokerage systems are getting more efficient all the time, you may not immediately see the exercise take place when you submit instructions. Typically you'll see the appropriate transactions in your account by the next trading day.

When you exercise an option, the actual option position is reduced by the number of contracts exercised and a stock buy or sell transaction appears. After you submit exercise instructions to your broker the action is final. If you decide to exercise your call rights to purchase a stock at 10 a.m. on a certain day and by 2 p.m. that same day the stock drops dramatically due to bad news, you cannot cancel your exercise instructions.

When you exercise a put and do not have the underlying stock in your account, you create a short position. This means a previously limited risk position is now technically an unlimited risk position because a stock can just continue to rise. Be sure you consider the exercise ramifications before submitting instructions.

To exercise or not, that is the question

Before you exercise an option, there are a couple of calculations you need to complete to decide if it's the best approach. You want to make sure you maximize profits by checking two alternatives:

- ✔ Exercise the rights under the contract to buy or sell stock
- ✔ Sell the option, then buy or sell the stock in the market

As a basic rule of thumb, complete both of these calculations when the option contract has time value (premium greater than the intrinsic value). It's a good habit to always complete the checks when first using options. The last thing you want to do is walk away from money on the table . . . or in the market.

The option exercise decision is different than the stock ownership decision. You need to consider the most profitable way to execute your transaction in the market, which is why you want to calculate both alternatives provided in this section.

Here's an example to show you what I mean. Suppose you own 100 shares of ABC. You purchased the stock at $23 per share and at the same time purchased one 22.50 put for $0.50. Later the stock is at $27, but news just hit that ABC is under investigation for funny accounting practices. The price plummets to $21 per share and the 22.50 put immediately moves to $2.50. What should you do?

Assuming you no longer wish to own the stock, you need to calculate the net gains or losses for the two alternatives available:

- ✔ **Alternative 1: Exercise put**

    Buy 100 ABC @ $23 = Debit: $2,300

    Buy 1 ABC 22.50 put @ $0.50 = Debit: $50

    Exercise Right to Sell @ 22.50 = Credit: $2,250

    Net Loss = $100

> ✔ **Alternative 2: Sell put and sell stock in market**
>
>   Buy 100 ABC @ $23 = Debit: $2,300
>
>   Buy 1 ABC 22.50 put @ $0.50 = Debit: $50
>
>   Sell 100 ABC @ $21 = Credit: $2,100
>
>   Sell 1 ABC 22.50 put @ $2.50 = Credit: $250
>
>   Net Gain = $0

It makes more sense for you to sell both the option and stock in the market. After you add trading costs the difference narrows but will still likely favor the second alternative.

Generally when an option has more than $0.20 time value remaining the second alternative will result in a credit that exceeds the extra transaction. This includes commissions and the extra trading costs due to spreads in the market quote.

Exercising Your Options the Euro Way

When trading European-style index options, you need to be more familiar with the contract specifications. Here I cover what you should understand about the index settlement process which determines option moneyness at expiration. It is the index settlement value that you use for exercise decision-making.

Stock option moneyness is calculated using the closing value during regular market hours for the stock on the last trading day before expiration. Occasionally a late print gets posted by the exchanges that can confuse things a bit, but all stock options use this "last trade" rule.

Tracking index settlement (the "SET")

Because stock index values are calculated using a group of stocks, determining option moneyness at expiration is more complicated. Not all stocks have opening and closing trades at the exact same time, so the opening level for an index won't necessarily include the opening price for all components — some prices may include closes from the previous day.

You access the index settlement value to address this timing issue. This index level is calculated using only opening or closing values and is referred to as the *SET.* Check the option specification for more detail on how a particular settlement value is determined and the symbol used to access it.

Exercise instruction procedures can vary by broker and instrument. Even if you provided stock option exercise instructions with your broker in the past, you may find their index exercise process is different. Check with your broker about their exercise process for index options before you need to submit instructions.

Cashing in with exercise

Your window of opportunity to exercise a European-style option is much smaller than with American-style options — it's usually just a day. That day is very close to the Saturday of expiration and may or may not coincide with the last trading day for the option.

Because European-style index options are based on something that can't be traded, these options are referred to as *cash-settled*. That means no securities change hands during exercise or assignment — just cold hard cash. The amount of cash for this option is determined by the option moneyness and option multiplier.

You calculate European-style option moneyness using the SET as follows:

Index SET – Option Strike Price = Call Moneyness

Option Strike Price – Index SET = Put Moneyness

So you determine the exercise cash amount this way:

Option Moneyness × Option Multiplier = Cash Settlement Amount

When moneyness falls below zero an option has no intrinsic value. In this case no cash would change hands.

Even though there is just one day to exercise cash-settled European-style options, they can be traded any time up to the close on the last day of trading for the contract.

Assuming a SET value of 1523 for SPX and a multiplier of 100, the exercise and assignment amount for expiring call and put options with a 1520 strike price is:

✓ Call Moneyness: 1523 – 1520 = 3

✓ Call Exercise Amount: 3 × 100 = $300 credit

✓ Call Assignment Amount: $300 debit

✔ Put Moneyness: 1520 − 1523 < 0

✔ Put Exercise Amount: 0 × 100 = $0 credit

✔ Put Assignment Amount: $0 debit

Because no asset changes hands during this process, your market risk over the weekend due to good or bad news is nonexistent.

Satisfying Option Obligations

When you sell an option short, you have an obligation not a right. This makes your decision-making about whether or not you wish to be assigned really easy — you have no choice. The only way you can avoid assignment is by purchasing the option back to off-set your position. This is the same for both option styles.

Although all stock options are American-style contracts, not all American-style contracts are stock options. There are also American-style index options that settle in cash.

American-style stock options

Assignments usually occur over expiration weekend, but because we're talking about American-style stock options, it could occur anytime after you create the short option position. In either case, you satisfy the assignment through the transfer of shares into or out of your account.

There are a couple of nuances for you to consider regarding assignment, but first I provide information about basic mechanics. When you are assigned on a stock option, two transactions appear in your account:

✔ **Assigned:** The short option is removed from your account and the term Assigned or abbreviation "ASG" appears.

✔ **Buy/Sell:** The stock transfer appears the same as a regular stock order.

The assigned contract(s) is no longer in your account; *however*, you may not have been assigned on all contracts. Be sure to check your positions to see if there are any short contracts remaining. Also, a commission is usually applied to the buy/sell transaction.

You usually get assigned when your short option no longer has time value. Puts generally have a better chance of being assigned early because the person exercising the right will be bringing in money. The risk of you being assigned early on a call jumps significantly when certain corporate actions are pending and the option holder wants to own the stock by the record date. Such actions include the distribution of large cash dividends.

Most short in-the-money (ITM) options get assigned over expiration weekend. Early assignment of puts usually increases when strong market declines drop stock values significantly.

Now for those nuances I mentioned . . .

Short put assignment

Assuming you were assigned on a short put, you are now the proud owner of ABC stock at a cost that is likely higher than the current market.

You need to decide whether or not you wish to keep the assigned shares and how it impacts your account. If you didn't have enough money for the transaction, you can either bring in more cash before stock settlement or you may be able to buy the shares on margin. When you buy shares on margin you are borrowing money from your broker. This can only be done in certain accounts and the borrowing terms are determined by the following:

✔ The cost and margin requirements for the stock

✔ The cash in your account before the assignment

✔ Your broker's rules and rates

When buying on margin, your expected returns should exceed the risk-free rate associated with US Treasuries plus the interest rate charged by your broker for using margin. Because the market value of an assigned position is likely below what you paid, you need to consider cutting your losses and selling the position.

Short call assignment

If you were assigned on a short call, things get trickier unless you already owned the stock. Then it simply is sold at the option strike price, which is likely below the current market price.

When you don't own the stock, assignment of the short call results in a short stock position. This exposes you to significant risk because the stock can keep going up. Even if you want to hold the short position, your broker may not have access to shares for lending. If that happens, the stock is bought at whatever price it's trading in the market to close the short position. This can be done with or without your knowledge.

The only thing worse than shares bought back without your knowledge is being short the stock without knowing it! Be sure to always monitor your accounts regularly when holding short option or stock positions. Beware of conditions that may trigger assignments, such as deep in-the-money options or news events that significantly impact the value of the underlying.

To create a short position, your broker must go out and borrow the shares. These may or may not be available. As a result, even if you have enough money and want to hold a short position, it may not be an option.

Expiring uninspiring options

Because it's always best to actively manage your account, ideally expiration will come and go without incident. That said, I'm sure there will be a time when you end up holding a position at expiration. Here's what to expect when you are long or short an option going into expiration weekend.

Long option positions

Before you buy an option you should know how you will close it. As you near expiration, here is what you need to consider:

- If the option is out-of-the-money (OTM) or roughly at-the-money (ATM) and you don't want to exercise the contract rights, try to sell it when the credit you receive exceeds your commission for the transaction.

- If you want to buy or sell the stock, calculate whether selling the contract or exercising it is more cost effective.

Never assume a slightly OTM or ATM option will expire worthless. It's possible for the stock's last trade to get reported late, resulting in an in-the-money (ITM) option. Even if the stock closes exactly at the strike price or is OTM, monitor the news after the close. You may decide to exercise the option if you expect a big change in the company's value over the weekend.

When you hold an ITM option into expiration, here's what will happen:

Exercise by exception (auto-exercise)

Currently, when a stock option is ITM by $0.05 or more at expiration, the Options Clearing Corporation (OCC) assumes you did not want an option with value to expire worthless. They exercise it on your behalf over expiration weekend. So even without specific instructions, stock shares are bought or sold for you. This may create a short position in your account without your knowledge.

You can instruct your broker to not allow auto-exercise for specific contracts, but you must do so within their cutoff times. Specific instructions are required for each long option position you hold through expiration. Note that the OCC trigger levels for auto-exercise has declined over the years.

Short option positions

A short stock option obligates you to buy or sell shares of the underlying stock. As a result, you're more reactive at expiration than active. Short options are usually assigned when market conditions are against you. The only way to prevent assignment is to exit that position before the market closes on the last trading day.

Stock price can change significantly over the weekend if important news is released. A stock's value will shoot through the roof if they just discovered cures for five major diseases or would drop like a brick if they disclosed they were just kidding about their profits for the last three years. Monitor news after the close to see if you can benefit from exercising expiring options.

If your short option is OTM, there is a good chance that it will expire worthless. However, traders long the option will monitor conditions after the close. If big news comes out about the company, you still may be assigned over expiration weekend on the OTM option. Table 9-2 summarizes what you should expect heading into expiration weekend.

Table 9-2	Stock Option Expiration Summary	
Option Type	*Typical Action*	*What You Should Consider*
Long: OTM	Expires worthless	If the OTM option has value on the last trading day, don't let it expire worthless when you can close it for a credit greater than the commission. Monitor trading at the close to be sure the option is truly OTM.
Long: ATM	??	Manage an ATM option similar to OTM and ITM options. Either close it for a credit greater than the commission or submit specific exercise instructions. Don't leave the result to chance.

(continued)

Table 9-2 *(continued)*

Option Type	Typical Action	What You Should Consider
Long: ITM	Auto-Exercised when ITM > $0.05	Don't passively manage ITM options through auto-exercise. Either send specific exercise instructions to your broker or exit the position for a credit.
Short: OTM	Usually expires worthless	Monitor news and the account after the close. Even when the option closes OTM, anyone can choose to exercise their rights resulting in an assignment for you. Consider closing the position.
Short: ATM	??	Monitor news and the account after the close. Once the option is ITM by even $0.01 assignment risk increases exponentially. To avoid assignment, close the short position on the last day of trading.
Short: ITM	Assigned	Monitor market news and your account over expiration. Since auto-exercise occurs when an option is ITM > $0.05, you should expect assignment at this level. Close the short position on the last day of trading if you want to avoid assignment.

Whether you hold a long or short option position, it's best to actively manage the position. This usually means exiting it before the close on the last trading day, but can include providing specific instructions to your broker.

After an option closes even a penny ITM, expect it to be assigned. Currently, if it's ITM by $0.05 or more, auto-execution kicks in for long contract holders. At that point you can forget about dodging the assignment bullet.

When you hold a stock position that meets the short option obligation, you'll be less stressed over expiration. But when the assignment creates a new position in your account, you have two choices:

- ✓ Exit the position in the market Monday morning, or
- ✓ Hold the position, if you have sufficient funds.

Your broker may or may not have shares available for a short stock position, so exiting the position could be your only choice.

When trading a European-style option, you must know the option's last trading and exercise days, as well as how the SET is determined.

When you manage risk it means you manage your positions, long and short. Although you don't typically consider a long option very dangerous, there are times when it can catch you off-guard. A perfect example is when a long put is auto-exercised.

European-style options

European-style options provide you with an advantage over American-style options if you are short the option contract. That's because you don't have to worry about early assignment. You can completely avoid assignment when you buy the option back by a specific date to off-set the short position.

Other than covering a short position, you don't have much to decide heading into expiration weekend. If the option is in-the-money (ITM) at expiration your account will be debited the settlement value for the assignment.

Note there may be a period of time when news affects an index SET, but you are past the last trading day for a European-style option. If you are short OTM SPX puts at the end of trading on Thursday, bad news overnight could result in a strong drop in the morning when the SET is determined. This may result in OTM puts becoming ITM.

Breaking It Down: American-Style Index Options

One of the most popular American-style index options is the S&P 100 Index (OEX) contract. You can exercise your rights anytime you own a long contract or be assigned whenever you hold a short contract. American-style index options settle in cash because an index can't be bought or sold.

Because these contracts can be exercised any time, you have to know how the settlement value is determined prior to expiration. You can find these details in the contract specification.

Using the OEX specification from the CBOE as an example, here's how it works:

- ✔ **OEX SET at expiration:** Uses primary market closing prices on the last day business day before expiration (usually a Friday).
- ✔ **OEX settlement for early exercise:** Uses primary market closing prices for the day the exercise instructions are submitted.

Exercising rights

You need to contact your broker to find out the exercise cut-off time for American-style options since the settlement value for the index option you trade may be determined by closing values. You should consider time value when deciding whether to sell the index option in the market or exercise your contract rights. If you decide to exercise the contract, the amount credited to your account is determined using the option strike price, the index settlement value and the multiplier, as outlined in the contract specification.

One reason you may decide to exercise your rights even when time value remains in the option is if there is a news event that could significantly impact the index value the next day. Consider the type of rights you own and the likely impact the news will have on index trading levels.

Meeting obligations

The only decision you have as a short contract holder for American-style index options is whether or not to buy back the option to avoid assignment. Because early assignment is possible, you need consider this each day you hold the position, rather than just on the last trading day. If assigned, your obligation is met in a cash amount using the option strike price, the index settlement value and the multiplier.

Always, always check contract specifications prior to trading both European-style and American-style index options.

Chapter 10

Guarding Your Assets with Options

In This Chapter

▶ Protecting assets with options

▶ Hedging a portfolio using options

▶ Watching out for nonstandard options

*B*y adding option strategies to both your investment and trading portfolios, you minimize trading stress. Trading is challenging enough, but when market conditions threaten your long-term holdings, the distraction can be downright destructive. Reducing stress is one key to better decision-making for both aspects of your portfolio.

Options offer protection for both portfolios and trading positions. Because there are a variety of strategies available to you, you need to have a plan for implementation. In this chapter I discuss a few protective strategies and some things to consider when putting them into practice.

The last portion of the chapter addresses a unique risk that adjusted options pose to investors and traders alike. Adjusted options are those contracts with a non-standard deliverable package due to corporate actions that occurred during the option's life. I cover adjusted options here because they can add risk to even conservative, protective strategies included in this chapter.

Putting Protection on Long Stock

I generally focus on shorter term option trading strategies in this book, but options are definitely well suited for longer term holdings as well. Applying protective strategies to your existing holdings can turn anxious, sleepless nights into restful ones during market downturns. Since no one knows when these downturns will occur, incorporating protective strategies as a regular consideration in your investment planning could be the difference between meeting your financial goals on time or waiting for the next bull run to get you there.

Combining puts with long stock

Purchasing puts on your existing stock investments provides insurance against significant losses when a major downturn occurs. Like other forms of insurance, it's frustrating to write a check for something you may not need, but it's really nice to have when the time comes. Two strategies that combine long stock with a long put are:

- ✔ Married put (stock and put purchased together)
- ✔ Protective put (stock and put purchased separately)

The two positions are essentially the same, but differ in the timing of purchases. Each consists of one long put for every 100 shares of stock held. There's no need for you to distinguish between the terms. What is important for you is understanding why and how you protect your assets. I use the term protective put for the remainder of this chapter.

A put option gives you the right, but not the obligation, to sell the underlying stock at the contract strike price until the trading day prior to the option's expiration date. You can also sell this right in the market up until this time.

Protection considerations

The expression, "A rising tide lifts all boats" is sometimes used to describe the stock market and its tendency for all stocks to rise together during a bullish run. Unfortunately the reverse is also true. Regardless of the merits of an individual stock, when a bear market hits it takes no prisoners — even quality stocks decline.

Trying to anticipate swings in the market is almost impossible, so the next best thing is protecting stock earmarked for the long-term. Suppose you bought stock ABC a few months ago at $34.00 and wish to hold it for the long-term. You can lock in a sell price for that stock at anytime by purchasing a put. It doesn't matter whether it's your intention to exercise your right or simply off-set losses with option gains.

When considering two different stock investments with equal growth potential and prospects, check to see which has options available. This may make your investment decision easier if one allows you to purchase protection on it while the other doesn't.

Rather than an all-or-nothing approach that includes selling ABC and trying to buy it back if the market declines, the position can be protected over the short-term or long-term using puts. Before analyzing specific options, you need to decide whether you will continually protect a position or if you will do so intermittently according to your market outlook.

Suppose you seek temporary protection for ABC (30 to 60 days) When looking at option chains, you'll then need to evaluate options with 60 to 90 days to expiration. This gives you the flexibility to exit the position prior the acceleration of time decay 30 days prior to expiration. The next thing to consider is how much protection you want to have. Table 10-1 provides partial put option chain data for ABC to help with this decision.

Open interest is the total number of contracts outstanding for a specific option contract. Since option contracts are created by demand, it reflects information from the previous day's trading activity.

One size does not fit all

Since you're concerned with market action in Sep and Oct, it's reasonable to focus on options for Oct and Jan to cover the bearish period. Next you have to identify the losses, if any, you're willing to accept. You purchased the stock at $34 and it's currently trading at $37.50. Do you want protection ABC at the current price or the level where you purchased it? These are questions you face each time you consider protecting a position.

The more time remaining until expiration, the more uncertainty there is regarding the price of the stock at expiration. An in-the-money (ITM) has more time of becoming an out-of-the-money (OTM) and vice versa. Option pricing uses past movement in the stock to value different probabilities for future price movement. Use delta as a resource to check the probability the option will be ITM at expiration, given its movement in the past.

Table 10-1	Put Option Chain Data for ABC on Aug 22nd			
Month	*Strike Price*	*Bid*	*Ask*	*OI**
Oct	30.00	0.20	0.25	36,287
	32.50	0.30	0.35	1,965
	35.00	0.60	0.70	24,641

(continued)

Table 10-1 *(continued)*				
Month	**Strike Price**	**Bid**	**Ask**	**OI***
	37.50	1.25	1.45	1,338
Jan	30.00	0.50	0.60	45,795
	32.50	0.75	0.85	156,657
	35.00	1.25	1.35	52,734
	37.50	2.00	2.15	24,225

* OI = Open Interest

Although the protective put is a relatively simple strategy, the number of ways that protection can be provided is numerous. To help with your analysis, identify your protection time horizon along with the maximum loss you seek prior to viewing option chains. This will aide your decision-making.

Assuming you seek protection above the stock purchase price, you then have limited your analysis to the 35 and 37.50 strike prices. Table 10-2 provides an analysis of the protection provided by select puts if you choose to exercise them.

Table 10-2		Put Short List for ABC on Aug 22nd			
Month	**Days to Exp**	**Strike Price**	**Ask**	**Delta**	**Exercise**
Oct	60	35.00	0.35	−0.186	$65
	60	37.50	1.05	−0.460	$245
Jan	150	35.00	1.35	−0.291	($35)
	150	37.50	2.15	−0.440	$135

The exercise column is calculated by subtracting your purchase price from the option breakeven. From Chapter 4, the breakeven for a put option is:

Put Strike Price – Put Purchase Premium = Put Breakeven

(Put Breakeven – Purchase Price) × 100 = Net Profit/Loss

Unless otherwise stated, the multiplier for a stock option is 100. When working with a combined position that includes 100 shares of stock, be sure to remember to incorporate this value in the formulas.

From this point, the actual option selected for the strategy is definitely a personal decision. You may prefer longer term protection and include April put options in your review. You may only seek catastrophic coverage in which case you may add strike prices below 35.00 as well.

To wrap up the example, the 37.50 strike should be selected if you don't want to see a profitable position turn into a loss when exercised. If you're bearish through the entire month of October, the ABC Jan 37.50 put option provides you with protection for the full time period.

There are a variety of things to consider when seeking protection for an existing stock position including:

✔ Term for the protection (expiration month)

✔ Level of protection (strike price and option price)

You could also consider the likelihood an option will be ITM at expiration by referencing delta. By making use of options that have a greater chance of being ITM at expiration, you may find you can trade out of the protective position and use the proceeds to help finance a new protective put. The more experience you gain, the more you'll find an approach that suits your style.

You can always sell a protective put before it expires if you feel the markets have stabilized and the intermediate outlook for your stock turns bullish again.

Since no one knows what the next day in the markets will bring, an investor may decide to maintain some level of protection on stock positions regardless of the short-term or intermediate outlook. To minimize expenses, lower strikes may be considered as part of a plan that provides catastrophic coverage — kind of a crash protection approach.

Accelerated time decay

When trading options for this strategy or others, you need to consider the impact of time decay on the option position. Theta is the option Greek that identifies the daily loss of option value associated with the current price of the option.

Using an ABC Oct 37.50 put option with 60 days to expiration, you can obtain theta by accessing an option calculator such as the on located on the OIC Web site (www.optionscentral.com).

The theta value for the option trading at $1.05 is –0.0078. That means if every-thing stays the same tomorrow, the option quote will lose 0.0078 in value. It may not sound like much, but it can add up.

In addition to the cumulative impact of time decay, this rate of decay acceler-ates as expiration approaches particularly within the last 30 days of an option's life.

The impact of time decay accelerates the last 30 days of an option's life. This means extrinsic value will decline more quickly along with the value of the option — assuming all other conditions remain the same.

To minimize the impact time decay within 30 days of expiration, trading strategies that make use of long options should incorporate an exit plan that addresses the issue. I generally exit a long option position 30 days prior to expiration to avoid accelerating losses to its extrinsic value.

Table 10-3 provides theta values for the ABC Oct 37.50 put for various days to expiration, assuming all other factors remain the same.

Table 10-3	Theta Values for ABC Oct 37.50 Put	
Days to Expire	**Ask**	**Theta**
60	0.35	–0.0078
30	0.75	–0.0117
10	0.45	–0.0216
5	0.30	–0.0314

If you think $0.02/day is manageable, consider what this represents in terms of percentages. With ten days to go until expiration, 0.0216 is 4.8% of the con-tract's value.

The way you go about protecting positions is similar to any other investment decision — it depends on your risk tolerance and personal preferences. Find an approach that suits your style.

Before moving on to the cost of a protective put relative to the stock, the risk graph in Figure 10-1 displays the improved risk-reward profile that results when you add a put to long stock. Losses are now capped.

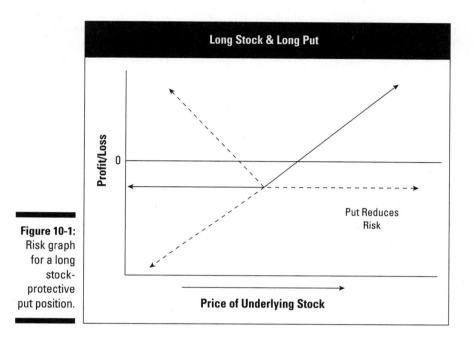

Long Stock & Long Put

Profit/Loss

0

Put Reduces Risk

Price of Underlying Stock

Figure 10-1:
Risk graph
for a long
stock-
protective
put position.

Weighing protection cost versus time

When you have a specific, reasonably short time horizon to protect a position, selecting the expiration month is pretty straightforward. Once you seek longer term protection the analysis requires a bit more effort. Since you expect the security to move upward on a longer-term basis, ATM options should be OTM by expiration and may be minimally effective. You need to weigh the cost of protection against the amount of time the protection is in place.

The investment process requires you to balance risk and reward. Without risk there is no reward, but it doesn't mean you have to risk it all. Consider protective positions as a means of limiting your losses while letting your profits run.

Long-term protection

Suppose you noted that stock XYZ has consistently realized annual gains of 8%, even during years with a 2% decline along the way. How do you go about protecting such a position? A $2.15 ATM put that provided five months of protection was used in the ABC example. Since ABC was at $37.50, the put premium represents 5.7% of its value.

Balancing the cost of protection versus returns is difficult and requires a game plan. Again, it's not a one size fits all proposition. If you buy puts on a regular basis you could be sacrificing stock returns and then some. On the other hand, ignoring protection completely could cost you a big chunk of your initial investment.

The short answer to this problem is that you pretty much have to find the balance that is right for you. You may decide to intermittently use puts when bearish periods arise, but if you could time the markets that well you probably wouldn't need protection. Give the issue some thought.

When purchasing puts to protect your investments, be sure to balance the cost of protection versus net returns for the protective put position.

By carefully evaluating different options rather than just looking for the cheapest alternative, there is a better chance the option will have some value 30 days prior to expiration. As part of your plan consider:

- ✔ The net exercise value and level of protection provided
- ✔ The statistical chance the option will be ITM at expiration (delta)
- ✔ The cost of protection versus the net impact on returns

Being clear about your strategy goals from the start should definitely help.

Cost per day calculations

As a last consideration, when selecting protective puts:

- ✔ Be careful about buying seemingly cheap puts that don't offer adequate protection and will likely expire worthless
- ✔ Consider the cost of protection over your stock holding period

Using the 37.50 strike price put for ABC, you can calculate the daily cost of protection for the two options. This is accomplished by dividing the option premium by the number of days to expiration:

- ✔ ABC Oct 37.50 put @ $1.05 = $1.05 × 100 = $105
- ✔ $105 ÷ 60 days = $1.75 per day
- ✔ ABC Jan 37.50 put @ $2.15 = $2.15 × 100 = $215
- ✔ $215 ÷ 150 days = $1.43 per day

The ABC Jan 37.50 put translates to a cost of approximately $0.014 per share for the option if held to expiration.

Do what you can to manage your positions by responding to market conditions, not over-reacting to them. No one can completely control their emotions when markets race up or come tumbling down. Do your best to manage them by completing your analysis when the markets are closed whenever possible.

Limiting Short Stock Risk with Calls

Long puts provide you with a means of protecting your investments for a specific period of time. Although you probably don't hold any short stock positions in your investment portfolio, you may periodically trade strategies that use short stock position that are held overnight. A long call can protect you from losses due to overnight gaps upward.

Protecting a short stock position

In the same way a long put protects a long stock position, a long call protects a short stock position. A call gives you the right, but not the obligation, to buy stock at a specific strike price by the expiration date. You can exercise your call rights to close out a short position if the stock rises quickly.

Since a short stock position is generally held for less time, protective call option selection is much easier. Typically you can evaluate options with the least amount of time to expiration or those in the following month. Stocks with options will have both months available.

Option months that are closest to expiration are generally referred to as *near month options* and those that expire right after that are referred to as *next month options*.

In addition to paying less for time for the protective call, strike price selection should be easier since there is less of a chance the stock will move far away from the entry price in the relatively short period of time the position is held. Try to use options that matches your maximum loss criteria.

Further reducing short stock risk

If you're really committed to reducing short stock risk, why not just consider implementing a long put strategy to capitalize on your bearish view for a particular stock? Suppose you didn't own stock ABC and you are bearish on the stock instead. How does a long put position compare to a short stock position? Assuming ABC is trading at $37.50, Table 10-4 compares a $37.50 put to the stock position, including maximum risk and reward:

Table 10-4	Bearish Positions for ABC on Aug 22nd		
Position	**Entry Cost**	**Max Risk**	**Max Reward**
Long 1 Oct 37.50 Put	$105	$105	$3,645
Short 100 Shares ABC	$1,875	unlimited	$1,875

Here's what you need to consider:

✔ **Stock entry cost:** The initial cost for the short stock position is 50% of the current stock price because short selling has a 150% margin requirement. 100% is credited to the account from the stock sale and the remaining 50% is cash you need to have available for the position.

✔ **Stock maximum risk:** Since the stock can theoretically rise without limit, the risk to a short seller is also considered to be unlimited. You may try to limit this risk by having an order in place to buy the stock back if it rises past a certain price, but overnight gaps in the stock could result in this maximum risk stop level being exceeded.

✔ **Option maximum risk:** The maximum risk for a long option position is the premium paid. In this case, that's $105.

✔ **Option maximum reward:** If you own the right to sell a stock for $37.50 and it is currently trading at $0, the intrinsic value of the option will be $37.50. Theoretically you can buy the stock in the market for $0 and then exercise your right to sell it for $37.50. The $1.05 you paid for this right must be subtracted from the $37.50 per share gain for the stock transaction to determine the maximum reward for the option position.

✔ **Option breakeven level:** The breakeven point for the option position is the put strike price minus the option price, or $37.50 − 1.05 = $36.45.

Puts increase in value when a stock decreases and represent a bearish position. Although they are wasting assets that are negatively impacted by time decay, they have limited risk and limited, but high reward potential.

Looking at your risk first, the put position limits the maximum risk to $105. This is equivalent to a $1.05 per share amount that could easily be exceeded with an overnight gap in the stock. From a reward standpoint, you're reducing the maximum gain by the cost of the put ($105), but you have the potential to far exceed the short stock reward when comparing the gains on margin.

Hedging Your Bets with Options

You can use the following options to protect stock positions:

- ✔ A long put with a long stock position
- ✔ A long call with a short stock position

The option can be exercised to close the stock position or gains in the option can be used to off-set losses in the stock. The term *hedge* describes a position used to off-set losses in a security resulting from adverse market moves.

Protecting a position or portfolio with options is a form of hedging. But not all hedges are created equal . . . some are more perfect than others. A *perfect hedge* is a position that includes one security that gains the same value that is lost by a second security. The gain offsets the loss. So a $1 dollar move down in ABC coincides with a $1 move up in XYZ.

The option Greek delta obtained using an option calculator provides the expected change in the option's value given a $1 change in the underlying stock.

Protecting a portfolio . . . partially

You partially hedge a position when you own a security that gains value when the hedged position loses value. Usually, when you combine two securities that tend to move in opposite directions you find it's not always a one-to-one relationship. A $1 gain in one stock may correspond to a $0.75 loss in another security. Assuming the relationship between the two continues, combining them provides you with a partially hedged position.

Delta can be used to help construct partially or completely hedged positions.

Hedging stock with stock options

The ABC Oct 35.00 put option has a delta of -0.186. Assuming you own 100 shares of ABC and the Oct 35.00 put, the expected impact to your account with a $1 decline in ABC is calculated as follows:

(Change in Underlying) × (Delta) = Change in Option

(−1) × (−0.186) = +0.186

When the stock moves down to $36.50, the option should move up to approximately $0.54. The stock position lost $100 and the option position gained about $19. Because the Oct 35.00 put gained value when the stock lost value it provided a hedge for ABC. However, the option gain was smaller than the stock loss, so it's only a partial hedge for the position.

Listed index options have different characteristics than listed stock options. For instance, an index is not a security so its not something you can buy and sell. As a result, index options settle in cash rather than the transfer of a physical asset. See Chapter 9 for details on options characteristics.

Hedging a portfolio with index options

Because listed options are available for both stock and indexes, portfolios can be protected on an individual position basis or with index options, assuming the portfolio is well correlated to a specific index. Hedging your portfolio may actually require both an index option for a group of stocks and individual stock options for others that don't correlate well with a given index.

Correlation is a term used to describe the relationship between data sets. The values range from –1 to +1 and when applying to stocks provide you with the following information:

- ✔ Stocks with returns that move in the same direction, by the same magnitude are said to be perfectly positively correlated (+1)

- ✔ Stocks with returns that move in the opposite direction, by the same magnitude said to be perfectly negatively correlated (-1)

- ✔ Stocks with returns that do not move consistently in terms of direction and magnitude are considered not correlated (0)

As an example, suppose you have a $150,000 portfolio that is well correlated to the OEX, trading at approximately 680. One quick approach to partial hedging uses the portfolio value and index strike price to estimate the hedge. OEX index options are available for different months in five point strike price increments. When it is trading at 682, a 680 call will have $2 of intrinsic value since option moneyness is the same for index and stock options.

Using a short-term protection approach, Table 10-5 provides potential put candidates for next month options expiring in approximately 60 days. These options may seem pricey, but a five-point move in the index reflects less than 1% of the index value.

Table 10-5	Put Option Chain Data for the OEX				
Month	**Strike Price**	**Bid**	**Ask**	**Delta***	**OI**
Mar	665	8.60	9.30	-0.321	1,663
	670	10.00	10.50	-0.361	3,277
	675	11.30	12.10	-0.406	748
	680	13.20	13.90	-0.455	2,883

*Delta using the Ask value

A common multiplier value for an index is also 100, so the total option premium for March 670 put is $1,050 ($10.50 × 100). The option package is valued using the strike price and multiplier, or $67,000 for the March 670 put (670 × 100).

The option multiplier is the contract valued used to determine the net option premium (Option Market Price × Multiplier) and the deliverable value of the option package (Option Strike Price × Multiplier).

Suppose you decide you want to protect the portfolio against market declines greater than two percent. You can estimate the hedge by starting with the current index level (682) and subtracting the decline you're willing to accept to obtain a starting point for strike price selection as follows:

- 682 – (682 × 0.02) = 13.6
- 682 – 13.6 = 668.4

Both the 665 and 670 strike prices can be considered. Using the 665 put option:

- Protection Provided by 1 Put: 1 × 665 × 100 = $66,500
- Protection Provided by 2 Puts: 2 × 665 × 100 = $133,000
- Portfolio Protected: $133,000 ÷ $150,000 = 88.7%

If the OEX drops below 665, your puts gain intrinsic value at a pace that is equal to the put's delta. The further the OEX declines, the closer the puts get to a 1:1 move with the index. The time remaining until expiration will also affect the actual gains made by the hedge.

At-the-money (ATM) puts and calls have deltas that are approximately 0.50. Once an option moves from ATM to in-the-money (ITM) or out-of the-money (OTM), delta changes in value. The option Greek that provides you with a feel for just how much delta change is gamma.

A stock option package generally represents 100 shares of the underlying stock. When using the strike price and multiplier of 100 to value the option package, it's common to think your paying the strike price for each share of stock. That's okay when applying this to regular stock options, but it's not quite accurate when considering index options or adjusted stock options. In both of these cases, it's best to consider the option package value as simply:

Strike Price × Multiplier

A stock option package is typically 100 shares of stock. When put contract rights are exercised, the stock option owner receives the strike price times the option multiplier — usually 100. The amount the put option holder receives is also called the *option package exercise value*. Other terms you may see for this value include:

✔ Option package assignment value

✔ Option package deliverable value

It depends on what side of the option you're on. All of these terms refer to the same thing, the money that is exchanged when the rights of a call or put contract are actually exercised.

Protecting a portfolio . . . completely

Recall in Chapter 3, that delta was given the following ranges:

✔ Call: From 0 to +1 or 0 to +100

✔ Put: From 0 to -1 or 0 to -100

To better discuss hedging, it helps to use the alternate range of 0 to +100 and 0 to –100 for delta. That's because it turns out that one share of stock has a delta of 1. Using this information and the ABC example, the Oct 25 put with a delta of –0.186 provides a near perfect hedge for 19 shares of ABC stock.

ATM calls generally have deltas that are slightly greater than 0.50 while ATM puts are generally slightly less than 0.50. Using 0.50 as an approximation is usually fine for the initial strategy evaluation.

Stock hedge

Starting with a perfect stock hedge using ABC, assume you have allocated approximately $5,000 to a combined position (stock plus put). Since ABC is trading at $37.50, you anticipate owning about 100 shares Using the ABC option data from Table 10-1, you focus on the Jan 35 strike price option with five months to expiration. The put has a delta of –29.1. Since three puts won't quite hedge 100 shares of stock you evaluate a potential position using four puts. The delta for four Jan 35 puts is:

$$\text{Position Delta} = \text{\# of Contracts} \times \text{Delta} = 4 \times (-29.1) = -116.4$$

Given that 1 share of stock has +1 delta, a long position of 100 shares represents +100 deltas. A perfectly hedged position has a combined delta equal to zero, so 116 shares of ABC are required. You calculate the position delta as follows:

- 116 shares × +1 delta per share = +116 Deltas
- 4 puts × –29.1 delta per put = –116.4 Deltas
- Position delta = +116 + (–116.4) = –0.4 Deltas

The cost of the position is the following:

- 116 shares × $37.50 = $4,350
- 4 puts × $1.35 × 100 = $540
- Position cost = $4,350 + 540 = $4,890

This near perfect hedge will not stay intact long, every time ABC moves up or down $1, delta changes approximately by its gamma value. Part IV provides you with ways to profit from this changing situation.

Recall that the delta for an option changes by gamma for each $1 change in the underlying stock. Because of this, options are referred to as a *variable delta* security. The delta for one share of stock on the other hand stays constant. One long share of stock will also represent +1 delta so it is referred to as a *fixed delta* security.

Portfolio hedge

You approach a perfect portfolio hedge in a similar manner, but the fact that not all portfolios are perfectly correlated to an index causes problems. The perfect hedge becomes elusive because the option delta changes when the index value changes and there is inexact movement between the index and portfolio.

Using a delta approach to protect the $150,000 portfolio will get you closer to a perfect hedge than the strike price estimate. Using an index level of 682, the Mar 690 puts are ITM by 8 points. The market price for these puts is $20.85 which corresponds to a delta of –0.549. A goal is to get closer to 1:1 protection, so purchasing two Mar 690 puts results in the following:

- $2 \times 690 \times 100 = \$138,000$
- $2 \times -0.549 = -1.10$

In this case, for each 1 point decline in the OEX, the value of the combined puts increases by 1.1. For a short period of time, this results in 1.1 times the protection of a $138,000 portfolio. Multiplying $138,000 by 1.1 yields protection for a portfolio valued at $151,800. Given the variable nature of an option's delta, you'll likely be satisfied with portfolio protection that is a little less exact.

Avoiding Adjusted Option Risk

Adjusted options are those that existed when certain corporate actions took place. As a result of those actions, the contract terms required adjustment to reflect the action. Business activities that can prompt this include:

- Stock splits
- Large cash dividend distributions
- Mergers and acquisitions
- Spin-offs

Most dividends do not result in option contract adjustment.

Justifying option adjustments

The two main reasons options are adjusted after different corporate actions is:

- To ensure the existing contracts retain their proper value
- So the contract reflects the corporate action in its deliverable package.

Without adjustments, the stock option market could be more dangerous. Maybe exciting is the right word . . . imagine one of your calls losing all of its value after a stock split and a put option doubling after a big cash dividend is distributed.

Corporate action 1: Stock splits

Adjustments due to stock splits are the quickest to understand. When a stock you own splits two for one (2:1) you receive one additional share of stock for each share you own on the record date — the date used to identify existing stockholders. On the day you receive the additional share, there is nothing significantly different for the company in terms of its financial statement. To correctly value the stock, its price is divided by two in the market on the day of the split.

Option adjustments resulting from a 2:1 split are handled the same way the stock split is handled:

✔ The number of contracts held is adjusted (similar to shares)

✔ The price where the owner has rights (strike price) is adjusted

A new option contract is created to address this corporate action and it is provided a new symbol. When you own an option with the underlying stock going through a 2:1 split, you'll see 2 contracts of a new option in your account for each 1 contract you owned previously.

In the current option symbol nomenclature, adjusted options are almost indistinguishable from regular options. The problem arises when the option deliverable or multiplier must change to reflect the corporate action, which is the case for a 3:2 split. Adjusting an option after a 3:2 split requires a lot more tweaking to get the valuation right.

When you exercise a put without holding the underlying stock in your account, you create a short position. This is because the put rights allow you to sell the underlying stock at the contract strike price. Selling a stock you don't own reverses the typical order for a stock transaction and creates a short position.

Corporate action 2: Mergers, spin-offs, and dividends

Mergers, acquisitions, spin-offs and large cash dividends all change the underlying option package when an option contract is adjusted. This happens because the original 100 shares of stock may now represent owner-ship in:

✔ 100 shares of original stock + shares of acquired stock (merger)

✔ 100 shares of original stock + shares of new stock (spin-off)

✔ 100 shares of original stock + cash amount (large cash dividend)

✔ No original stock + shares of acquiring stock (acquired)

In the last case, the original underlying stock may not exist if the company was acquired by another company. The adjusted options are now based on some ratio of shares in the company that acquired it.

If you think you found an option deal that seems to good to be true, you may have very well stumbled upon an adjusted option. Traders on the exchanges who are very familiar with corporate actions completed by the stocks they trade and know how to value adjustments to them. There's no free money on Wall Street so don't jump in to these options without fully understanding them.

The way you value these type of contract adjustments is more complex and beyond the scope of this book. It is extremely important to understand your rights, obligations and position valuations if a contract you own gets adjusted. Contact your broker if this occurs. And never, never create a new position using an adjusted option contract you don't completely understand.

Whenever a combined position (stock plus option) you own is adjusted, be extremely careful about exiting the stock or option position separately. The combined position maintains the proper stock-option ratios initially created, but by selling any portion of the adjusted stock position, you may be creating high risk in the option position. Call your broker to discuss any position changes.

Adjusting from adjustments

It's all well and good that the options markets have a way to address contract valuations and deliverable packages for different corporate actions, but what does that mean for you? Two things:

- ✔ When you note any adjusted option in your account, be sure to check the contract specifications so you understand your new rights or obligations, as appropriate.

- ✔ More importantly, be aware of adjusted options when establishing new positions so you properly value securities you trade and know your rights and obligations.

Whenever an option quote doesn't seem quite right, be sure you take the time to check the contract details.

Avoid creating new option positions using adjusted options. There's no hidden money in these contracts, just extra effort to understand and value them.

Detecting an adjusted option

The Option Symbology Initiative provides a revised approach to option symbols that should more clearly identify adjusted options. Until all option chains are changed over to the proposed system, you must be aware of ways you can detect adjusted options. Here are some things to check:

- An abbreviation "ADJ" appearing after the symbol in a quote
- A different option root symbol than the standard root
- Option package details may be partially listed with the quote heading — check the full quote to see any changes to the deliverable package
- One strike price appears twice in one month with different symbols
- An atypical strike price appears for a stock (i.e. 46.375)
- The market price for the option seems way out of line, either high or low

These are primary ways to distinguish adjusted options in the market. As with any security, when something doesn't seem quite right in terms of a quote or volume, be sure to dig deeper so you know why this is the case.

Valuing your split-adjusted options

When an option is adjusted due to a 2:1 split, the new contracts are valued the same way regular options are. Atypical splits, such as a 3:2 split require a little more of your attention. To value an option after a 3:2 split:

1. **Use the adjusted strike price and multiplier to calculate the package value (JKL 60 call: 60 × 150 = 9,000).**

2. **Determine the value of the underlying package in the market using current quotes (150 shares JKL × $62 = $9,300).**

3. **Subtract the package value from the market value to obtain the option's intrinsic value ($9,300 – 9,000 = $300).**

4. **Assuming an option quote of $3, the extrinsic value is what remains after subtracting the intrinsic value ($3 × 150 = $450, $450 – 300 = $150).**

Chapter 11

Limiting Your Downside When Trading the Trend

*Y*ou have two basic choices when trading stocks — you can create a long position to benefit when a stock price goes up or you can create a short position to benefit when it goes down. Along the way you may receive or have to pay a dividend here and there, but that's pretty much it on the trading side. Options allow you to benefit from up and down stock movement, while also offering a few more ways for you to capitalize on changes in price.

By establishing a basic option position, you can gain from upward stock movement (call) and downward movement (put). In either case your initial investment is usually much smaller than a similar stock position. In addition to single option positions, these securities can be combined to further reduce cost. This chapter provides you with ways to trade for less money and less risk.

Leveraging Assets to Reduce Risk

Usually when you think of leveraging assets you think of increasing your risk — at least on the stock trading side. Options allow you to leverage your assets while also decreasing your investment at risk. That's a nice combination. With options the premium you pay allows you to lock in a price for a stock without putting up 100% of its value. Although there's no guarantee the stock will move in the direction you want, this is the case whether you're trading options or stocks. So why not do it for less?

Determining your total dollars at risk

Options reduce risk because less money is invested — that's the bottom line. Once you create a position anything can happen — the stock can sky rocket upwards, drop like brick or sit around making minimal movements while the rest of the market is active. You just don't know. Nobody knows what's going to happen next.

Any stock can drop to zero, so any long stock or call position you own can similarly go to zero. As a result, your initial investment is your maximum potential loss. Actually, I take that back — if you buy a stock using margin you can lose twice as much as your initial investment.

The risk for a long stock position is considered limited, but high. That's because a stock cannot fall below zero. Unfortunately, there's a lot of room for losses between zero and the price of some stocks.

There are lots of possibilities between total loss and no losses at all though. The main takeaway here is that when you invest with less money at the start, you usually have less to lose. It's rare to have such a distinct advantage without any disadvantages. The distinct disadvantage with options is that you can't wait around for the move you anticipate to happen your investment to rebound because there's a time constraint.

Calling risk out when bullish

When you're bullish on a stock you can either:

- ✔ Create a long stock position
- ✔ Create a long call position

If the stock goes up you can profit with either of these positions — the extent you benefit depends on the actual move. Your risk is reduced when you purchase a call option because you reduced the total investment.

Figure 11-1 presents this using risk graph overlays for the two positions.

Two main things for you to note from the risk graph are:

- ✔ The significant difference in losses
- ✔ Profits accrue faster with the stock position

Because there are a series of tradeoff in this business, I'll take the slower accrual of gains with less total risk. It is certainly possible for the stock to remain dormant for months, causing me to exit the position for a loss only to then have it begin a serious upward move. Again, it's a tradeoff I'm willing to take.

Figure 11-1:
Overlay risk
graph for
XYZ long
stock and
XYZ call
option
positions.

A risk graph provides a very efficient way for you to understand the risks, rewards and breakevens associated with a particular strategy.

When monitoring option values, you'll find that if the stock moves around a little bit over time, the option can gain and lose value as follows:

- Increases or decreases as the stock price increases or decreases
- Increases or decreases as the option's implied volatility increases or decreases
- Decreases as time passes

Price alone doesn't dictate an option's price. The contract's implied volatility (IV) also plays a role in its value with higher IVs resulting in higher contract values. On a daily basis time decay plays a smaller role, but the cumulative effect can eat away at the option's value.

Establish long option positions when implied volatility (IV) is relatively low to increase the probability for profits and minimize losses due to decreases in IV. Keep in mind that a relatively low IV environment does not guarantee IV will rise over the life of the option.

Using LEAPS for long-term option positions

A LEAPS contract is a Long-term Equity AnticiPation Security. This isn't a new type of trading instrument, it's just an option that has a long time to expiration — anywhere from more than six months to as much as 2½ years. Not all stocks with options have LEAPS available, but for those that do the expiration month is almost always January. You'll note different root symbols for these options.

LEAPS work something like this:

- ✔ LEAPS contracts are created in May, June, or July, depending on the option's cycle (see Chapter 3 for more information on Option Cycles).

- ✔ The new contracts expire in January approximately 2½ years from the creation date so by August 2008 there are options available for both January 2010 and January 2011. The 2011 are the newly created LEAPS.

- ✔ When new LEAPS are rolled out, the closest January LEAPS (expiring in 2009) becomes a regular option as the Options Clearing Corporation (OCC) revises the symbol to include the regular option root.

The root symbol for a LEAPS contract is different than the root symbol for a particular stock to distinguish it from other January options expiring in different years. This approach to naming LEAPS may become obsolete when the new option symbol program goes into effect in 2008.

The acronym for a LEAPS contract comes from Long-term Equity Anticipation Security. These contract are simply options with a lot of time until expiration.

The more time you have to expiration for an option, the more money you pay. So it follows that you should expect to pay more for LEAPS contracts. Your risk increases with this increased cost, but the additional time provides you with a greater chance of holding a contract that is in-the-money (ITM) at expiration. LEAPS are:

- ✔ Available for some stocks and indexes that have regular options

- ✔ An investment alternative, providing you up to 2½ years to benefit from your contract rights.

In addition to providing more time for investing strategies, LEAPS provide extended warranties on the asset protection side. Combining a LEAPS put with long stock significantly reduces the cost per day for protection. You do have to balance the reduced cost with your desired level of protection since ideally the stock will rise over the time as you hold it. If this happens, the put value decreases during this time while the strike price remains the same.

Stocks that are more volatile generally have a larger number of strike prices available each month because there is a greater chance the stock will reach a strike price that is farther away.

To provide you with some pricing perspective, a partial option chain for Microsoft Corporation (MSFT) is provided in Table 11-1. It includes regular calls and puts, along with LEAPS contracts. When reviewing the details, assume MSFT trades at $27.90 and is pretty quiet, making relatively gradual moves up and down.

Table 11-1		Partial Option Chain for MSFT with LEAPS			
Call Bid	*Ask*	*Month/ Year*	*Strike Price*	*Put Bid*	*Ask*
3.95	4.05	Jan 09	25.00	0.65	0.70
2.25	2.30		27.50	1.35	1.40
1.05	1.10		30.00	2.70	2.75
5.55	5.75	Jan 10	25.00	1.70	1.80
4.10	4.25		27.50	2.60	2.70
2.90	3.00		30.00	3.75	3.95
6.75	7.20	Jan 11	25.00	2.30	2.60
n/a	n/a		27.50	n/a	n/a
4.40	4.60		30.00	4.50	4.75

Since options that expire in January could potentially exist for 2½ years, they are the ones that have the highest potential for being adjusted due to different corporate actions. Be especially careful when trading Jan options with quotes that seem "off." Check contract specifications for details on the underlying package.

Putting limits on a moving bear

When you're bearish on a stock you can either:

- ✔ Create a short stock position
- ✔ Create a long put position

If the stock goes down you can profit with either of these positions. The rewards are limited because a stock can only move down to zero. At the same time, the rewards are potentially high if the stock does become worthless.

Figure 11-2 presents this using risk graph overlays for the two positions.

Two main things for you to note from the risk graph are:

- ✔ The significant difference in losses
- ✔ The less than significant difference in gains

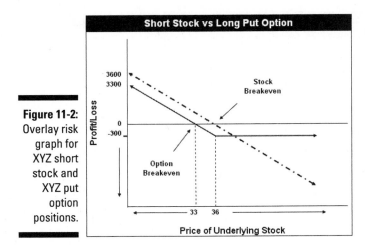

Figure 11-2:
Overlay risk
graph for
XYZ short
stock and
XYZ put
option
positions.

Relying on market timing

After trading for any period of time, you come to realize that it's pretty hard to identify the future direction for a stock, let alone how far it will go and by when. But selecting a proper time frame for an option is clearly an important part of trading these securities. That means you have to:

✔ Recognize the role probabilities play in trading stocks and options

✔ Be prepared to be "wrong" and limit your losses

✔ Pay the right amount of premium for moves that are realistic.

Basic option trading requires you to correctly predict the direction the underlying will move, the magnitude of the move and the maximum time it will take for the move to occur. All of these things are required for stock trading too — the difference is you can hold on to long stock position for months as it trade sideways. Managing a position this way doesn't mean you're necessarily trading successfully though.

There are times when a stock breaks out of a limited range, sideways channel, only to return back into the channel. If you've created a directional position based on the breakout, you must exit the position (stock or option) if the stock returns to the channel since the conditions that justified the trade no longer exist.

Predicting proper direction

In order for you to capitalize on either a stock or single option position, you need to correctly identify the direction of the underlying stock move.

Predicting the right direction is a challenge you face regardless of the security you select, so it seems reasonable to favor one that uses less of your capital for at least some of your trading. Only you know the answer to that.

Some general rules of thumb for increasing your probability of success include:

✔ Trading with the trend when using technical tools,

✔ Or (for proficient contrarians) trading against the trend when momentum is weakening and your indicators point to a pending turn,

✔ Trading undervalued stocks that are gaining some positive attention when using fundamental tools,

✔ In every trade, limit your losses with unbiased exit strategies.

Predicting the magnitude of the move

Time risk is the main disadvantage to trading options, but there is another risk that requires discussion. You can be correct about the direction and timing of a stock move and still have the magnitude be too small to make your option position profitable. This happens to all option traders.

How can you minimize these shortfalls? For the most part, it helps to have some tools — technical or fundamental — that provide estimated price projections.

Your overall trading profitability can be improved by focusing on higher probability trades (higher deltas indicating the move is more likely to occur) over lower probability "home run" trades. Allow gains to accumulate over time and you'll probably be fortunate to get a home run or two along the way.

Consider taking a portion of your profits off the table by exiting part of your total position when the move you anticipated is partially complete.

Option pricing models also help you identify higher probability trades by providing you with:

✔ Expected movement implied by the option price (implied volatility)

✔ An estimate of the probability the option will be ITM at expiration.

By using these option components in your trade analysis, you can determine if the option price is relatively expensive or inexpensive given the stock's history, past option pricing and market conditions. This is shown later in an example.

Predicting the right time

The forced time limits for an option provides newer traders with their first rules-based system when risk is properly managed. This means both:

- ✔ The trade represents a reasonable portion of the account
- ✔ The position is exited prior to the acceleration of time decay

A long option position has a clear, built-in exit rule. Ideally this isn't the only guideline you use to exit a position though.

There is no one size fits all criteria for selecting expiration periods since they can vary by strategy and your trading style. The most straightforward time horizon for option trading is associated with scheduled releases of news or reports that can prompt strong movement by a specific date. These include:

- ✔ Economic or industry reports such as unemployment figures or semiconductor orders
- ✔ Earnings releases

Some technical tools also provide estimated time projections, including price patterns or cycles. Identify your time horizons first, then check option chains.

Combining Options to Reduce Risk

In Chapter 4, a put option was combined with long stock to protect it by limiting the position risk. This was also accomplished when a call option was added to a short stock position. In both cases, the position cost increased.

The breakeven level for a stock is simply the entry price. Since option premiums represent a cost to you above and beyond your strike price contract rights, a breakeven value must be calculated using both the strike price and option price.

When creating positions that are focused on specific market outlooks, you can combine the following:

- ✔ Call and/or put options with stocks
- ✔ Different call options together
- ✔ Different put options together
- ✔ Calls and puts together

Adding long puts or calls to stock were the only combined positions discussed so far, but short options can also be used to reduce risk by:

✔ Further reducing the net cost of the position and/or

✔ Increasing the potential directions the underlying can trade while still realizing profits.

When a short option is properly combined with the underlying stock or a long option of the same type, it is said to be *covered*. That's because your risk (obligations) under the short contract can be satisfied using the stock or by exercising your rights under the long contract. Without such protection, the short contract is referred to as *naked*. That's kind of a good visual on your exposure.

Trading naked options allows you to receive a credit when you open a position — this credit is equal to the option premium. If all goes well the option expires out-of the-money (OTM) and you get to keep the credit. Different newsletters promote naked option strategies and this may seem like a great way to bring in monthly revenue, but seller beware.

Going naked a call option is the riskiest position you can create and I strongly advise against such a trade. Rather than creating a limited risk, unlimited reward consistent with good risk management, a naked call is an unlimited risk, limited reward position.

Unfortunately what often happens with these strategies is that months of smaller credits get wiped out with losses from just one or two trades that go against you. I'm not opposed to creating a trade for a credit, I just don't like doing it while completely exposing myself from a risk standpoint.

Risk can be limited by combining options for credits or debits using covered option positions. This section introduces spread trades which are limited risk, limited reward combination positions.

Spreading the risk with a debit trade

A vertical spread is a position that combines two options:

✔ One long and one short option of the same type (calls or puts)

✔ Having the same expiration month and

✔ Different strike prices.

It is referred to as "vertical" because that's how the strike prices line-up on when you look on an option chain. You can create a vertical spread for an initial debit or an initial credit. In each case the position has limited risk and limited reward.

Each option position in a vertical spread is referred to as a *leg*.

The type of vertical spread selected depends upon your market outlook. You vary risks and rewards by changing the strike prices used to establish the position. You can create two types of vertical spreads for a debit, one using calls and the other using puts. They are referred to by the outlook for the stock and include:

- **Bull call spread:** You create a bull call spread by purchasing a call option and simultaneously selling another call option that expires the same month. The short call has a higher strike price. Since the price of that higher strike call is less expensive, you pay a net debit for the trade. The short call ends up reducing the price of the long call, so this spread trade has less risk than buying a long call option alone.

- **Bear put spread:** You create a bear put spread by purchasing a put option and simultaneously selling another put option that expires the same month. The short put has a lower strike price. Since the price of that lower strike put is less expensive, you pay a net debit for the trade. The short put ends up reducing the price of the long put, so this spread trade has less risk than buying a long put option alone.

Going naked a put option is a very risky position, even if you're willing to buy the stock at the short put strike price. Short put assignment generally occurs when the stock is declining or bad news is released. Purchasing a stock in the market or though assignment at a time like this goes against reasonable risk management principles.

Assessing risk and reward for a call debit spread

Your maximum risk for the bull call spread is the initial debit you paid to create it, similar to a basic long call position. Since the position combines a short call to reduce the long call cost, it also reduces the risk for the position. Since you don't get something for nothing on Wall Street, reducing your risk this way comes at a price in the form of reduced rewards.

If ABC is trading at $37.65 and you are bullish on the stock, you can create a bull call spread by completing the following transaction:

- Buy 1 Jan 35 call @ $4.20 and
- Sell 1 Jan 40 call @ $1.50

The debit for the bull call spread position is $270 ([$4.20 − 1.50] × 100). This is also the maximum risk and occurs when ABC closes at $35 or less at expiration. At this price both calls will be worthless.

Unlike a basic long call, your maximum reward is limited for a bull call spread because the short obligation prevents you from realizing unlimited rewards. Your maximum reward is the gain you realize from the exercise-assignment transactions minus the initial debit paid for the position $230 [($40 – 35) × 100 – 270.00]. The maximum reward occurs when ABC trades at $40 or higher at expiration.

Your actual gain or loss may be somewhere between the max risk and max reward if ABC closes between 35 and 40. The bull call spread breakeven calculation is similar to the one for a long call. Using the strike price for the long call, you add the difference between the two option prices (the initial debit without the multiplier) to determine your breakeven level. In this example, the breakeven is $37.70 (35 + 2.70).

Figure 11-3 displays the risk graph for the ABC Jan 35-40 bull call spread using Optionetics Platinum, an options analysis software package.

Figure 11-3:
Risk graph for ABC Jan 35-40 bull call spread.

Since a vertical debit spread is a net long position, its value will suffer the same accelerated time decay within 30 days to expiration as a basic long option position. Incorporate a method to exit the spread prior to this time if the position is at risk of losing value this way.

The risk chart identifies the following important areas:

✔ Max risk of $270 displayed by the lower horizontal line

✔ Max reward of $230 displayed by the upper horizontal line

✔ A breakeven stock price of $37.70 displayed by a dark vertical line

✔ A range from losses to profits displayed by a diagonal line extending from the lower strike price to the higher strike price.

TIP

Risk, reward and breakeven calculations for vertical spreads are completed by assuming you're assigned on your short obligation and exercise your long rights.

Assessing risk and reward for a put debit spread

Your maximum risk for the bear put spread is the initial debit you paid to create it, similar to a basic long put position. Since the position combines a short put to reduce the long put cost, it also reduces the risk for the position.

If XYZ is trading at $50.85 and you are bearish on the stock, you can create a bear put spread by completing the following transactions:

- ✔ Buy 1 Jan 50 put @ $2.75 and
- ✔ Sell 1 Jan 45 put @ $1.30

The net debit is also the maximum risk. The risk, reward and breakeven calculations are *similar* to those for the bull call spread:

- ✔ Debit = Max Risk = (2.75 − 1.30) × 100 = $145.00
- ✔ Max Reward = [($50 − 45) × 100] − 145.00 = $355.00
- ✔ Breakeven = $50 − ($2.75 − 1.30) = 50 − 1.45 = $48.55

The maximum reward occurs when XYZ trades at $45 or lower at expiration.

Figure 11-4 displays the risk graph for the XYZ Jan 45-50 bear put spread using Optionetics Platinum, an options analysis software package.

Figure 11-4:
Risk graph
for XYZ Jan
45-50 bear
put spread.

The risk chart identifies the following important areas:

- Max risk of $145 displayed by the lower horizontal line
- Max reward of $355 displayed by the upper horizontal line
- A breakeven stock price of $48.55 displayed by a dark vertical line
- A range from losses to profits displayed by a diagonal line extending from the higher strike price to the lower strike price.

Consider entering a vertical debit spread when there is at least 60 days to expiration to give the position time to become profitable.

Never exit the long leg of vertical spread without also exiting the short side of the spread — otherwise you are significantly changing your risk profile. This applies even when it appears the short leg will expire worthless.

Summarizing your debit risks & rewards

In both vertical debit spreads your risks and rewards are limited. Each spread has less risk than its corresponding basic long option position because you reduce the initial debit by the price of the short option. The decreased risk comes at a cost in the form of significantly reduced rewards for you since the short option position also caps your profits.

Table 11-2 provides a summary of the risk, reward and breakevens for a bull call debit spread and bear put debit spread.

Table 11-2	Risk, Reward, and Breakeven for Vertical Debit Spreads	
	Bull Call Spread	*Bear Put Spread*
Risk	Initial debit	Initial debit
Reward	[(Higher strike − lower strike) × multiplier] − initial debit	[(Higher strike − lower strike) × multiplier] − initial debit
Breakeven	Long strike price + (long option price − short option price)	Long strike price − (long option price − short option price)

A trade risk graph provides specific risks, rewards and breakevens associated with a particular trade.

Spread Trade Floor Appeal

Traders on the exchange floors manage their risk by staying hedged in the market. This means when they make a market for your long call order and end up with a short call position, they will usually buy shares of stock or other long calls to cover this new short position.

When you enter an order for a vertical spread for a debit, the trader can execute your order without having to worrying about hedging the position. They basically just create a vertical spread for a credit. It's not that they're trying to trade against you — all they care about is staying hedged.

Vertical spread orders are appealing to floor traders because when they execute the trade, they don't have to do anything else. They're already hedged. That's why you can usually get a vertical spread order executed below the debit quoted in the market.

When you place an order for a new vertical debit spread, consider using a limit amount that is less than the quoted price for the combined position to reduce the impact of slippage. You probably won't be able to execute the trade at the mid-point of the spread, but you likely can get the order filled if you shave a little off the debit amount.

Spreading the risk with a credit trade

Debit spreads are not the only type of spread trade you can create using calls or puts. You can switch which strike price is purchased and which is sold in the debit spreads to create a credit spread instead. Once again, the spread requires that you buy one option and sell another of the same type expiring the same month. You can create two different vertical credit spreads:

- ✔ **Bear call spread:** You create a bear call spread by purchasing a call option and simultaneously selling another call option that expires the same month. The short call has a lower strike price. Since the price of a lower strike call is more expensive, you receive a credit for the trade. The long call ends up covering the short call, so this spread trade has significantly less risk than a naked short call option.

- ✔ **Bull put spread:** You create a bear put spread by purchasing a put option and simultaneously selling another put option that expires the same month. The short put has a higher strike price. Since the price of a higher strike put is more expensive, you receive a credit for the trade. The long put ends up covering the short put, so this spread trade has significantly less risk than a naked short put option.

Assessing risk and reward for a call credit spread

Your maximum risk for the bear call spread is limited to the difference between option strike prices minus the credit received when creating the trade. The position uses the long call to limit the short call risk which by itself is unlimited. Instead of placing an XYZ bear put spread for a debit, you can create an XYZ bear call spread for a credit.

You create the bear call spread by purchasing the higher strike less expensive call option and selling the lower strike more expensive call option:

- ✔ Buy 1 Jan 55 call @ $0.95 and
- ✔ Sell 1 Jan 50 call @ $3.20

For credit spreads, the net credit is also the maximum reward. The reward, risk, and breakeven calculations for a bear call spread follow:

- ✔ Credit = Max Reward = $(3.20 - 0.95) \times 100 = \$225.00$
- ✔ Max Risk = $[(\$55 - 50) \times 100] - 225.00 = \$275.00$
- ✔ Breakeven = $\$50 + (\$3.20 - 0.95) = 50 + 2.25 = \$52.25$

A bear call spread position reduces the risk by capping losses for the short call. Reducing your risk this way means your rewards are reduced. Your maximum reward is the initial credit for the spread. This occurs if XYZ closes below the short call strike price at expiration, resulting in both options expiring worthless.

Figure 11-5 displays the risk graph for the ABC Jan 50-55 bear call spread using Optionetics Platinum, an options analysis software package.

Figure 11-5:
Risk graph for XYZ Jan 50-55 bear call spread.

The risk chart identifies the following important areas:

- ✔ Max risk of $275 displayed by the lower horizontal line
- ✔ Max reward of $225 displayed by the upper horizontal line
- ✔ A breakeven stock price of $52.25 displayed by a dark vertical line
- ✔ A range from losses to profits displayed by a diagonal line extending from the lower strike price to the higher strike price.

If the underlying stock is near the short strike price on the last trading day before expiration, you run the risk of being assigned on the short option over expiration weekend, but may no longer have the ability to exercise your long contract rights. Close a vertical credit spread for a debit on the last trading day before expiration if the price of the underlying is near the short strike price.

Assessing risk and reward for a put credit spread

Your maximum risk for the bull put spread is limited to the difference between option strike prices minus the credit received when creating the trade. The position uses the long put to significantly reduce the short put risk which is high. Instead of placing an ABC bull call spread for a debit, you can create an ABC bull put spread for a credit.

You create a bull put spread by purchasing the lower strike less expensive put option and selling the higher strike more expensive put option:

- ✔ Buy 1 Jan 35 put @ $1.70 and
- ✔ Sell 1 Jan 40 put @ $4.10

For credit spreads, the net credit is also the maximum reward. The reward, risk, and breakeven calculations for a bull put spread follow:

- ✔ Credit = Max Reward = ($4.10 − 1.70) × 100 = $240.00
- ✔ Max Risk = [($40 − 35) × 100] − 240.00 = $260.00
- ✔ Breakeven = $40 − ($4.10 − 1.70) = 40 − 2.40 = $37.60

A bull put spread position reduces the risk by capping losses for the short put. Reducing your risk this way means your rewards are reduced. Your maximum reward is the initial credit for the spread. This occurs if ABC closes above the short put strike price at expiration, resulting in both options expiring worthless.

Figure 11-6 displays the risk graph for the ABC Jan 35-40 bull put spread using Optionetics Platinum, an options analysis software package.

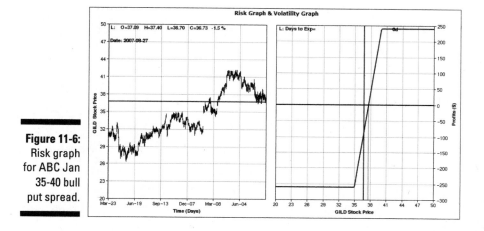

Figure 11-6:
Risk graph
for ABC Jan
35-40 bull
put spread.

The risk chart identifies the following important areas:

- ✔ Max risk of $260 displayed by the lower horizontal line

- ✔ Max reward of $240 displayed by the upper horizontal line

- ✔ A breakeven stock price of $37.60 displayed by a dark vertical line

- ✔ A range from losses to profits displayed by a diagonal line extending from the higher strike price to the lower strike price.

The cost of slippage is included in this risk graph.

Always monitor conditions for the stock after the close of trading on the last day of trading before expiration. You never want to allow a limited risk position to turn into a high or unlimited risk position because you failed to manage the trade though the end.

Summarizing your credit risks & rewards

The risk graph for a vertical credit spread is similar to that of the vertical debit spread with both risk and reward limited. It significantly improves the short call or short put risk graph by capping risks that are either unlimited or limited but high. This is accomplished by creating a position that covers the short option rather than leaving it naked.

Table 11-3 provides a summary of the risk, reward and breakevens for a bear call credit spread and bull put credit spread.

Table 11-3	Risk, Reward, and Breakeven for Vertical Credit Spreads	
	Bear Call Spread	**Bull Put Spread**
Risk	[(Higher strike – lower strike) × multiplier] – initial credit	[(Higher strike – lower strike) × multiplier] – initial credit
Reward	Lower initial credit	Lower initial credit
Breakeven	Short strike price + (short option price – long option price)	Short strike price – (short option price – put option price)

Although you can often execute a spread trade at a price more favorable than the current market price, always remember that if your risk parameters signal you should exit a position, just exit it. This can almost always be accomplished by placing a marketable limit order.

Chapter 12

Combining Options to Limit Your Position Risk

······································

In This Chapter

▶ Covering options with stock

▶ Reducing the cost of protection

▶ Expanding on vertical spreads

▶ Changing the spread time horizon

······································

*B*asic option positions reduce risk by reducing your position cost. However, the real power from these securities is unleashed when combining them with stock and other options. Starting with option positions covered with stock, I profile the risk and provide you with a strategy that discounts the cost of put protection for long stock. This strategy is known as a collar.

Covered option strategies with stock can be expanded to include just options when you vary different components of a vertical spread. By using the same strike price in the vertical spread while varying the expiration month for the two options, you create a calendar spread which adds time flexibility to the position. By allowing the strike prices to also change, you create a diagonal spread that provides even more flexibility for almost any short-term to long-term outlook.

Combining Options with Stocks

When you protect a short option position with stock or a long option of the same type, it is said to be covered. Calls can be sold when holding a long stock position to reduce the cost of the position and bring in some incremental income. Similarly, a short put can be sold against short stock to boost the returns. Both positions reduce risk slightly by reducing the stock's cost basis, but neither option protects it. Fortunately, you can add protection in the form of a collar strategy.

Creating "covered" positions

A covered position includes a short option with an obligation that you satisfy with stock or a long option of the same type for the same underlying. Rather than the unlimited or high risk associated with naked options, covered positions significantly reduce your risk. Approaching covered options from the stock side, you sell options against the underlying to bring in additional income and reduce the position risk by changing the cost basis.

Covered calls

When you own stock you can sell calls against it to bring in additional income. Because a credit is brought into your account when you sell the call, you also reduce the risk of the long stock position. A significant downside for you when bringing in this incremental income is that you're capping potential gains. If the market price of the stock moves up, rising above the strike price of the call, you'll be obligated to sell the stock at the lower strike price.

If for any reason you need to hold onto a stock position (i.e. capital gains or similar reasons), do not sell calls against it. Otherwise the covered call behaves just like a naked call — a position with unlimited risk.

Use long stock with a covered call to

- Reduce long stock risk incrementally by the short call credit
- As an income strategy for a portfolio position

When implementing a covered call strategy as a shorter term trade, your preference is to realize gains though assignment. For that reason, the short call strike price should be above the long stock purchase price. Always keep in mind that your risk with such a position is still pretty high — just because you have a bullish outlook for the stock doesn't mean it will necessarily go up in the short-term (or the long-term for that matter).

It's best to have a long option when the impact of time decay is at a minimum and it's best to have a short option when time decay accelerates — that is less than 30 to 45 days to expiration.

Covered puts

When you are short stock you can sell puts against the position to bring in additional income. Because a credit is brought into your account when you sell the put, you also reduce the cost basis of the short stock position resulting in slightly reduced risk for the position. The downside for you is that you're capping potential gains.

But why cap your gains this way? When I'm bearish on a stock, I prefer to capitalize on that with a long put or bear put spread.

The short put position is an obligation, not a right. You can't elect to have the stock put to you to offset the short stock position. The put doesn't serve as protection — you would need to buy a call to change the position risk from unlimited to limited.

If you're like me and like to reduce risk and maximize rewards, I'd focus more on vertical spreads than this particular strategy. For that reason, this strategy discussion is limited.

Covering the covered call position

You can use covered option position as short-term strategies or to increase income for longer term holdings. One main thing you need to keep in mind is that short options come with obligations not rights. The option leg is covered not the stock, which maintains high risk for the covered call.

Covered call strategy

A short call is a bearish position that is created for a credit. Since time decay works in your favor, you generally establish this position with 30-45 days or less until expiration. There are two reasons you create this position:

- You own the stock and you're long-term bullish on it, but moderately bearish in the short-term or
- As part of a trading strategy, you're short-term bullish on a stock and seek to boost returns by selling a call and being assigned on the stock.

Even though both of these are slightly different, the risk-reward profile for the combined position is the same. Your risk is high but limited due to the unprotected stock. This risk is slightly reduced by the call credit.

The covered call position is appropriate when you have a moderately bullish, short-term outlook for the stock. If you are extremely bullish in the short-term, a long call is a better strategy since it allows unlimited gains while the covered call position caps gains.

Your rewards are capped with a long stock-short call position because if the stock rises above the short call strike price by expiration, you will be assigned on the position and forced to sell your shares of stock.

Covered call risk profile

You purchase stock and sell a short call when you have a short-term bullish outlook for the underlying. The short call strike price should be above the stock purchase price so the stock gets called away for a profit. If you remain bullish at expiration, it's ideal for the stock to close just below the strike price so you can sell another call (assuming the original call expires worthless). You can continue to do this if your outlook is bullish and you own the stock.

Your risk associated with a long stock-short call position is similar to a basic long stock position – limited but high. Your maximum reward for the position is capped by the short option. After the stock rises above the short call strike price, you are at risk of assignment. If the strike price is higher than your stock purchase price, you profit when assigned. You calculate risk, reward, and breakeven for a long stock-short call position as follows:

> Max Risk = (Stock Purchase Price × # of shares) – Call Premium
>
> Max Reward = [(Call Strike Price – Stock Purchase Price) × 100] + Initial Credit
>
> Breakeven Level = Stock Purchase Price – Call Price

Your breakeven price for the position is the stock purchase price minus the option price when the position is sold. Below this level, losses accrue.

Never allow a short call that is part of a covered position become uncovered by selling the underlying stock. This turns a limit risk position into an unlimited one. If you wish to exit the long stock position, you must buy the call back first or exit both at the same time using a combination order.

Suppose ABC is trading at $37.72 and you're short-term bullish on it. With 30 days to go until expiration, the market for the near term 40 strike price call is $0.50. This represents a $50 credit when sold. Before entering a trade, you calculate your risk, reward, and breakeven for a position that includes 100 shares of ABC stock and one short call.

> Max Risk = ($37.72 × 100) – 50 = $3,722
>
> Max Reward = [($40 – 37.72) × 100] + 50 = $228 + 50 = $278
>
> Breakeven = $37.72 + 0.50 = $37.22

Figure 12-1 displays the risk graph for the ABC covered call strategy. Your breakeven appears as a vertical line drawn where profits = 0 (37.22).

Figure 12-1:
Risk graph
for long ABC
stock with a
short call.

The risk graph includes three curved lines displaying the expected value of the position given ABC's price and the implied volatility of its options. The price of the short option decreases as expiration near.

A short call that is covered by long stock does not protect the long stock. The position risk remains similar to long stock alone.

Reducing protected stock costs

Covering a short call obligation and protecting a long stock position are not the same thing. Although the covered call strategy is considered a relatively conservative approach to investing, it actually leaves you exposed to risk that is very similar to long stock. Another way you can manage stock risk for less money than a protective put strategy (see Chapter 10) is by creating a collar on the stock. You create a collar using the following:

- ✔ Long stock
- ✔ Protective put on the underlying stock
- ✔ Short call on the underlying stock

By selling a call in combination with a protected stock position you reduce the cost of that protection. Your only obligation is from the short call because the put represents a right. The short call remains covered by the stock.

A short option represents an obligation that is only considered covered if there are no other obligations or requirements for the associated stock or long option.

Defining a collar

You create a collar by purchasing a put and selling a call for a new or existing stock position. It is a limited risk, limited reward position that:

- ✔ Significantly reduces long stock and covered call risk from limited, but high to simply limited
- ✔ Significantly reduces long stock rewards from unlimited to limited

A covered call strategy is often considered a short term trade or income generator while a collared position is considered a protected position. The main goal of the short call is to reduce the cost of protection. This slightly reduces the risk of a protected put position.

Once you sell a call short you are obligated to sell the underlying stock when assigned. Do not create a collar around a position unless you're willing and able to part with the underlying stock.

Collaring long stock

A collar is a hedged position that has limited risk and limited reward. Your risk is limited to the downside by the put strike price and your reward is limited to the upside by the call strike price. If the stock goes below the strike price you don't necessarily need to exercise the put. You can decide to sell the put for a profit instead.

The long put and short call strike prices create a cap on long stock risks and rewards, respectively. The two option positions in combination provide a collar around the stock price.

As a general example, you can use a collar when you have a definite short-term bearish view on a stock position that you prefer to hold in anticipation of longer term gains. In this instance, you would want to have both the put and call as close to at-the-money (ATM) as possible to minimize both the downside risk and the cost of the protection.

The term _peg_ is used to describe the cap a short call creates on long stock appreciation. You may see this applied to the short call position when reviewing account balances.

Profiling collar risks

The risk associated with a collar strategy is significantly less than long stock. The long put caps the risk, while increasing the position's cost. This cost is slightly off-set by the credit received when selling the call.

Suppose you own 100 shares of ABC at $37.86 and you're bearish on it over the next 1½ months. You want to protect your position, but don't want to spend a lot of money to do it. You decide to create a collar around ABC using next month options which expire in 45 days.

Before buying a 37.50 strike put option for $1.20 and selling the 40 strike call option at $0.70 you complete the following key calculations:

Net Debit = $(1.20 - 0.70) \times 100$ = $50

Max Risk = [(Stock Purchase Price – Put Strike Price) $\times$ 100)] + Net Debit = [($37.86 – 37.50) $\times$ 100] + 50 = $86

Max Reward = [(Call Strike Price – Stock Purchase Price) $\times$ 100] – Net Debit = [($40 – 37.86) $\times$ 100] – 50 = $164

Breakeven = Stock Purchase Price + Net Debit = $37.86 + 0.50 = $38.36

Your risk for the position is the difference between your stock purchase and the put strike price, plus the net cost of the options. In terms of the maximum reward, after the stock rises above the short call strike price, you are at risk of assignment and will be obligated to sell your shares at the strike. If the strike price is higher than the stock purchase price plus option premiums, you profit when assigned.

Figure 12-2 displays your risk graph for the collar position.

Figure 12-2: Risk graph for a long ABC stock with a collar.

Varying Vertical Spreads

A vertical spread is a position that combines a long option and a short option for the same underlying that meets all of the following:

- ✔ Are the same type (call or put)
- ✔ Expire in the same month
- ✔ Have different strike prices

You can create a vertical spread for a net credit or a net debit depending on your outlook for the stock and the current level of volatility implied in the options. By changing the strike prices, you can change the risk profile for a given vertical spread.

A calendar or diagonal spread is long the closer month option and short the further month option is equivalent to holding a naked position. These are not strategies consistent with good risk management.

It's also possible to create a spread that varies the time until expiration for the two options rather than the strike price. This position is known as a *calendar spread* and is similar to a vertical spread using the same strike price, but different expiration months.

You can also vary both the expiration month and strike prices for the two options. This is a *diagonal spread* referring to the diagonal line that can be drawn between strike prices on an option chain.

Calendar spreads and diagonal spreads that use a long option for the later month leg of the spread are limited risk positions.

- ✔ Call calendar and diagonal spreads have unlimited reward potential after expiration of the short option.
- ✔ Put calendar and diagonal spreads have limited, but high reward potential after expiration of the short option.

Changing your vertical spread risk profile

You can change the risk profile for a given vertical spread by changing the strike prices used in it, while maintaining your outlook for the stock. That's one reason you need to explore different vertical spreads. Although a few vertical spreads might satisfy your outlook, there may be one that is best suited to your risk. Calculating the reward-risk ratio for different spreads is one way to obtain an apples-apples comparison for the different alternatives.

You can create vertical spreads for a debit or a credit. To help keep the outlook and credit/debit result clear, consider the outlook for the more expensive option. A short call is bearish and brings a credit into your account. The short call option in a bear call spread is more expensive so this is a credit spread.

In addition to identifying the vertical spread with the best reward-risk ratio, you may also uncover a volatility skew that makes one particular position stand out. A *volatility skew* is a condition that arises in the option markets where options for the same underlying have implied volatilities (IVs) that are significantly different from the others. This can happen when demand factors impact option prices.

There are two types of volatility skews:

- ✔ **Price skew:** Options expiring in the same month have IVs that deviate from normal conditions (i.e. ITM options higher IV than OTM options).

- ✔ **Time skew:** Options expiring in different months have IVs that deviate from normal conditions (i.e. options expiring sooner have IV that is higher than options expiring later).

You capitalize on volatility skews by selling the option with atypically high IV and/or buying the option with the atypically low IV as part of the strategy.

When uncovering a volatility skew, be sure to check the news for the company to determine if there is a specific reason for the condition.

Spreading time with calendars

You create a calendar spread by combining a long option and a short option for the same underlying that meet the following:

- ✔ Are the same type (call or put)
- ✔ Expire in different months
- ✔ Have the same strike price

The longer term option costs more than a shorter term option with the same strike price, so you create the position for a net debit to your account.

You may decide to use a calendar spread in place of a vertical spread if your

- ✔ Short-term outlook is neutral to bearish while your long-term outlook is bullish (call calendar spread)
- ✔ Short-term outlook is neutral to bullish while your long-term outlook is bearish (put calendar spread)

In both cases the short-term, short option reduces the cost of the later month long option. The strategy isn't appropriate if you're strongly bearish or bullish because of either of the following:

- ✔ The short-term option will be assigned
- ✔ The long-term option will lose too much value

Your risk is limited when using the long option as the longer term leg of the spread for both call and put calendar spreads.

When a debit spread position includes two options that expire in different months the reward and breakeven levels are estimates based on the price of the underlying and volatility at the earlier expiration for the short option.

Assessing calendar risk and reward

When creating a call calendar spread you buy a longer term call and sell a shorter term call, both at the same strike price. The longer term call is more expensive so the position is generally created for a net debit. This initial debit is your maximum possible risk. Managing this trade is a little different than a vertical spread because you need to consider two time horizons.

Although I specifically describe a call calendar spread here, a similar breakdown occurs for a put calendar spread position. There are three scenarios to consider at expiration for the short option:

- ✔ **Scenario 1:** The stock moved significantly higher than the calendar strike price and the short call was assigned. In that instance you need to determine which approach is best:

  - Exercising your long call option to satisfy the short call assignment

  - Buying the shares in the market and selling your long call if time values remains (see Chapter 9)

  - Buying the shares in the market and creating a bull call spread by holding the long call and selling a higher strike call option for the same month

- ✔ **Scenario 2:** The stock moved significantly below the calendar strike price and the short call expired worthless. In that instance you need to determine which approach is best:

  - Selling your long call option if it still has value

  - Creating another spread with the long call if bullish

Consider your outlook for the stock to determine if you want to maintain the long call position. If bearish exit the position. This highlights the importance of identifying a downside exit price for the stock prior to creating a calendar spread. Your decision-making is much easier by knowing this value in advance. In fact, by expiration you may not have a decision at all if you already exited both legs of the position as part of your trade risk management.

A *near month option* is one that is the closest to its expiration date. A *next month option* is one that expires in the month that follows the near month option.

✔ **Scenario 3:** The stock is near the calendar strike price and the short call expired worthless. In that instance you need to determine which approach is best:

- Selling your long call

- Creating another calendar spread using the existing long call and selling another closer term option at the same strike price

- Creating a bull call spread using the existing long call and selling a higher strike call option for the same month

After the short term has expired you may be left with an unlimited reward (long call) or limited but high reward (long put) position.

Profiling calendar spread risk

It's difficult to calculate potential rewards and breakeven levels for calendar spreads with a later month, long option because of the different expiration months for the two legs. Of course this doesn't mean you shouldn't try to understand them. Fortunately, the strategies are reasonable to include in your arsenal because you can identify a limited, maximum risk for the position.

Options analysis applications can estimate rewards and breakeven levels for calendar spreads using probabilities based on historical and implied volatilities. This data can be extended to risk graphs which are also available.

Figure 12-3 provides a risk graph, accompanied by a price chart for a call calendar spread.

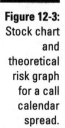

Figure 12-3:
Stock chart
and
theoretical
risk graph
for a call
calendar
spread.

Profits are now displayed on the x-axis and price for the underlying on the y-axis. This coincides with price levels for the stock chart.

You must always understand the risks and margin requirements for positions you create. Paper trading helps you better appreciate risk. Contact your broker to be sure you truly understand option margin requirements.

Defining diagonal spreads

Diagonal spreads are vertical spreads with different expiration months. You can vary calendar spread risks and rewards by varying the strike prices used for the options. You create a diagonal spread by combining a long option and a short option for the same underlying that meet the following:

- ✔ Are the same type (call or put)
- ✔ Expire in different months
- ✔ Have different strike prices

The longer term option may or may not cost more than a shorter term option — it just depends on the strike prices and expiration months selected for the two. This means that both debit and credit spreads are possible when using a diagonal spread strategy.

Diagonal spreads can morph into different strategies after the short option is exited or expires.

Because so many diagonal spread combinations are possible, it's more difficult to categorize short-term versus long-term views for the underlying stock. That's not really bad news, it's more of a comment on your flexibility when using these spreads.

You may decide to use a diagonal spread in place of a calendar spread if your

- ✔ Short-term outlook is slightly more bullish than neutral and your long-term outlook is bullish (call diagonal spread for a debit)
- ✔ Short-term outlook is slightly more bearish and your long-term outlook is bullish (call diagonal spread for a credit)
- ✔ Short-term outlook is slightly more bearish than neutral and your long-term outlook is bearish (put diagonal spread for a debit)
- ✔ Short-term outlook is slightly more bullish and your long-term outlook is bearish (put diagonal spread for a credit)

These diagonal spread combinations are provided as a calendar spread comparison in case you have a dilemma trying to find one that fits your outlook and objectives. The same may hold when considering vertical spreads — a diagonal spread may be more appealing if you feel the long option could benefit from more time or if a volatility time skew exists.

If you exit or allow to expire a long option position that covers a short option, you have a naked option position. Risk ranges from limited but high to unlimited.

Your risk is limited when using the long option for the later month leg of the spread for both call and put diagonal spreads. These spreads present the same type of timing problems as calendar spreads when calculating the reward and breakeven values. They should be considered estimates rather than absolutes when using options analysis applications.

If considering a diagonal spread that uses the short option for the later month expiration, think of it as holding a naked position.

Assessing risk and reward for diagonal spreads

Suppose you're moderately bullish on a stock in the short-term and believe that when the market strengthens in a couple of months, it will give a nice boost to the stock. It is currently trading at trading at $46.64. You note there is currently a modest time skew between next month options and those that expire three months later.

You wish to purchase a call that is near the money and want to finance the trade with a short call that expires sooner. To reduce the chance of assignment, you decide to use a diagonal spread in place of a calendar spread.

The next month $50 strike price call expires in 35 days and has a bid at $1.80 (IV of 34.6). The 47.50 strike price call expiring three months later has an offer price of $3.10 (IV of 32.4). The risk for the position is the initial debit which is $130.00. The reward and breakeven are variable.

Figure 12-4 displays the risk graph for the call diagonal spread. If the stock is below $50 at the closer term expiration and the short call expires worthless, you have a few alternatives available for the remaining long call.

Figure 12-4: Stock chart and theoretical risk graph for a call diagonal spread.

Chapter 13

Benefiting from Exchange-Traded Funds

*E*xchange-traded funds (ETF) are relatively new investment products well received by Wall Street so the ETF universe should continue to grow. Much more importantly, they are a great tool for retail traders enabling you to trade a variety of markets and sectors individually or with options. No wonder I'm a fan.

ETFs enable you to reduce risk by offering un-leveraged access to certain asset classes and implementing strategies only previously available to larger investors. ETFs can also reduce volatility. As an option trader I don't feel the need to completely avoid volatility — quite the contrary. It has its place on the trading side. But that place may be best explored after you've taken care of you longer term financial goals.

Introducing the Exchange-Traded Fund

An exchange-traded fund (ETF) is a security that is made up of different component stocks, bonds, and/or commodities and is typically designed to track a specific index or segment of the market. If you're not very familiar with these instruments, one of the best ways to understand them is by comparing them to market indexes. There are many similarities between the two, but one important difference makes ETFs very powerful: you can own an ETF. That means you expand the option strategies available to you.

Because ETFs track a group of securities, ETF volatility is less than that of its component stocks, bonds, or commodities. That's because a strong decline in one security in the group is offset by less severe declines or gains in the other components. Option traders don't want to shy away from volatility, but can benefit from recognizing when using a less volatile instrument is helpful. And this concept is a must to understand if trading options derived from a security that is less volatile.

ETFs are similar to mutual funds, but trade like a stock. This means you don't have to wait until the end of the day to exit a position.

Comparing ETFs to Indexes

ETFs are similar to indexes in that they both are based on a group of specific, related securities. An index is a measurement of the market value for these component stocks, bonds, and/or commodities, while an ETF is a security that allows you to own that measurement. Most ETFs actually track a specific index. See Chapter 9 for an index review.

One of the best characteristics ETFs and indexes share is they both have options available for trading. Since you can own an ETF you can create combination positions to include index-like products via the ETF. You'll find this is a really nice strategy addition given the size of the ETF universe. Navigating through all the available products should be easier with some of the resources identified at the end of this section.

Check with your accountant to fully understand the tax implications of investing and trading ETFs.

Connecting the common ground

Clearly a measure (index) and a security (ETF) are different beasts, but for now consider these similarities (ETFs share the following characteristics with indexes):

- ✔ Available for a variety of asset classes, sectors, and regions
- ✔ Both impacted by the index construction weighting method
- ✔ Offered by a variety of financial service firms

If you're looking for a segment of the market to invest or trade, there's a good chance there's an ETF that will fit the bill for you. There's been explosive growth in these instruments so don't hesitate seeking an ETF for a market you wish to trade or a risk you wish to hedge.

Weight management for ETFs

ETF managers use weightings similar to the index weighting method to achieve similar returns.

The weighting method used for index construction determines the impact a component security has on the index value. Although an ETF won't always track an index exactly, the weighting method affects ETF value changes given component changes. Here's what you want to remember about construction methods for stock indexes:

- ✔ A market-capitalization weighted index is impacted more by higher capitalization stocks.

- ✔ A price weighted index is impacted more by higher priced stocks.

- ✔ An equal-weighted index is impacted equally by all component stocks.

Checking out the differences

Before moving on to ways you can access ETFs, here are some differences between ETFs and indexes:

- ✔ You can own an ETF but not an index.

- ✔ The actual components used to create an ETF may be different than the component securities and can include futures and swap arrangements.

- ✔ ETFs can be leveraged or have an inverse relationship with the index it tracks.

ETFs not comprised of the exact basket of component securities can have moderate daily fluctuations known as premium or discount trading. Some also possess an additional degree of risk of catastrophic losses if the fund company used more exotic trading instruments (such as swaps) if not hedged properly.

Stock risk is high, but limited to the total amount invested when purchased in a cash account.

ETFs and risk

Your risk with an ETF is the same as stock ownership; limited, but high depending on the price of the ETF and whether it was purchased with cash or on margin. Some of the managed products have yet to be tested under extreme market conditions.

Certain ETFs have gained popularity because of their uniqueness in the market. There is a family of ETFs that offers leveraged, inverse, or both attributes in the ETF. For instance, QID is the Proshares Ultrashort QQQQ which tracks the inverse value of the Nasdaq 100 Index by two. Owning the QID is like being short 200 shares of QQQQ. This means you have a second means of creating a limited risk bearish position for some indexes. Of course put options tops this list of alternatives.

Many ETFs are passively managed and based upon a specific index such as the S&P 500 Index. Some newer ETFs are actively managed by portfolio managers who select specific securities for investment. Always check the ETF prospectus or tear sheet to determine which index, if any, the ETF tracks.

Pinpointing ETF resources

ETFs trade on major U.S. stock exchanges. Buying and selling these securities is the same as buying and selling stocks — you enter an order via your broker using the same order entry process. ETF popularity has also given rise to the availability of research and scanning tools for these securities on broker web sites.

Avoiding "analysis to paralysis" can be tough given the broad range of ETFs available. By identifying your objectives first, you have a better chance of staying on track so you can move forward implementing ETF strategies. When accessing a particular web site or other product materials, consider the objective of the site sponsor to be sure all of your needs are being met. For instance, the American Stock Exchange (AMEX) benefits when you trade ETFs listed on their exchange since that's how they make their money.

Table 13-1 provides a brief list of ETF web resources to consider accessing.

Table 13-1		ETF resources
Sponsor	*Site*	*Access*
NASDAQ	www.nasdaq.com Search site for "ETF heatmap"	Performance ranking for 100 ETFs
Nuveen	www.etfconnect.com	ETF listing with sorting and ranking features
AMEX	www.amex.com	ETF listings
Alps Dist	www.sectorspdr.com	Listing of family specific sector ETFs
Barclays	www.ishares.com	Listing of widely held Barclays ETF products

Risk can be reduced with ETF option strategies since the initial investment is significantly reduced.

Distinguishing ETF and index options

Index options and ETF options both provide you with a way to use option strategies on a group of related securities. The two products differ in three important respects:

- ✔ Because ETF options have an underlying security you can own, they lend themselves to combination strategies.
- ✔ Index options are cash-settled while ETF options are settled using the underlying instrument.
- ✔ Index options are European style or American style while ETF options are only American style.

If you want to avoid assignment on all but the exercise day, then an index option may be your only alternative.

Leverage is a double-edged sword. It can magnify your losses just as it magnifies gains.

Naturally there are similarities as well. Whether using index option or ETF option strategies, be sure to consider the following:

- ✔ **Contract liquidity:** Not all options are actively traded. Be sure spreads don't significantly impact your slippage costs.
- ✔ **Impact of dividends:** Certain groups of stocks provide higher dividend payouts. Be sure to incorporate dividends in option pricing calculators.
- ✔ **Volatility:** Because both represent baskets of securities they tend to be less volatile then their components.

Checking out strategies and new instruments by paper trading is a good way to get an inexpensive lesson for unexpected risk for either of these securities.

Index and ETF values are both affected by dividends and as a result, so are the options for them. As soon as dividend announcements are made these values are priced into calls and puts currently available. Option calculators allow you to incorporate dividend payments that occur during the life of the option.

Identifying ETF option advantages

Because this book focuses on option trading, the number-one advantage of ETF options over index options is the opportunity to access combination strategies. ETF options are more flexible because you can own the underlying security.

ETF option characteristics also make them more straightforward. You won't be worrying about different exercise, expiration or last trading days for ETF options because they are all American style, just as with stocks. If you have

already traded stock options, ETF options are a pretty natural next step
for you.

ETFs have expense ratios just like mutual funds. Because so many ETFs are
passively managed they are generally lower than mutual funds fees, but compare ETFs to be sure you're accessing one with reasonable ones.

By using ETFs in your investing, you quickly and inexpensively access a group
of securities which can reduce the fluctuations (volatility) in your portfolio.
This topic is covered more in the next section, but basically you're able to
accomplish a big investing goal: diversification. ETF options provide this at a
significantly reduced cost, reducing your risk.

As with stocks, not all ETFs have options available for trading. For those that
do, not all will have LEAPS available. These are long-term option contracts
that have expirations ranging from more than nine months to 2½ years.

Two additional risks ETF options and ETF LEAPS introduce for you the
following:

- ✔ Time risks associated with options in general because these securities
  can expire worthless
- ✔ Potential leveraged losses on the downside

Weighing out my choices, I'm personally okay with increasing the potential
percentage loss when I'm significantly reducing my initial investment. But
remember, this is a personal choice and you must weigh your own risk tolerances and preferences against using such approaches.

Commissions are charged on ETF purchases and sales, which can raise the
cost of using these products for investing or trading. Many mutual funds can
be bought and sold without a commission if held a minimum period of time.

Accessing combination strategies

When combining ETFs with ETF options, you have access to an index-based
security that you can protect, reduce its cost, or both. Using ETFs, you can
incorporate these strategies to manage risk:

- ✔ **Protective put position:** Long ETF combined with a long put. Limits the
  ETF downside risk to the put strike price and slightly increases the cost
  of the ETF. A high, but limited risk is turned into a limited risk position.
  Potential rewards remain unlimited above the price of the ETF plus ETF
  option.
- ✔ **Covered call position:** Long ETF combined with a short call. Reduces the
  cost of the position, moderately reducing risk. It is an income-generating
  strategy for a short-term bearish outlook on a long-term holding.
  Potential rewards are capped by the call strike price, so a previously
  unlimited reward position becomes limited.

> ✔ **Collared position:** Long ETF combined with a long put and a short call. Limits the ETF's downside risk to the put strike price and increases the cost of the ETF. This net increase to cost is less than a protective put position because the credit brought in by the call slightly off-sets the put cost. As a result, the high, but limited risk is turned into a limited risk position. Potential rewards are capped by the call strike price, so a previously unlimited reward position becomes limited.

Not all ETFs have options available for trading. When researching ETFs for investing or trading, be sure to check whether options trade for the underlying and how liquid the fund and option contracts are.

Reducing Portfolio Volatility with ETFs

Volatility is a measure of security movement and varies by asset. An ETF is less volatile than one of its component stocks. However, if you decide to use longer term ETF option strategies for investing, you still have to be sure to purchase long options when the volatility conditions are right. If you have access to options analysis software, check relative historical volatility (HV) and implied volatility (IV) levels for the options. If you don't have access to IV charts you can get a quick view of relative volatility conditions for an ETF using Bollinger bands on a price chart.

In addition to the important role implied volatility has in option pricing, relative levels for each will help an individual select a strategy appropriate for market conditions.

Revisiting volatility

An exchange-traded fund's (ETFs) *historical volatility* (HV) calculation is just like the one for stock — it uses past price changes over a certain period of time to quantify the range an ETF travels. It allows you to complete an apples-to-apples comparison to:

> ✔ Different HV time horizons for the ETF
>
> ✔ The implied volatility of the ETF
>
> ✔ The HV of another security

Implied volatility (IV) is the option volatility implied by current market prices. It includes different market participants' expectations for the ETF, along with demand factors for that particular option. IV is a "plug" figure in option pricing models meaning it's the value needed to correctly price an option after all of the known values such as strike price, ETF price, and so on are considered. *Vega* is the option Greek that measures the expected change in option value for every 1% change in implied volatility.

Getting just a current reading of the IV for an ETF is usually not enough to gain a sense of relative levels unless you are so familiar with the ETF's price movement that you know when the reading is in-line with typical values. By using a chart to compare current IV to previous levels, you gain a much better sense of whether the values represent high, low, or average readings.

Trends and volatility are two primary factors impacting market conditions. There are three possible trends for the markets to exhibit: upward, downward, or sideways. In terms of volatility, the markets can be quiet traveling over a moderate range over a given period or more explosive with wider ranges reached over the same period.

Figure 13-1 displays an IV chart for a broad-based stock market index ETF. Different lines are used to identify IV for different expiration periods.

Figure 13-1:
Two-year implied volatility chart for SPY.

While checking relative IV levels, you should also compare current IV levels to HV. This provides you with a comparison of expectations versus past movement and will alert you to something unusual that may be happening. "Unusual" may be a trading opportunity or it may be a trading pothole you want to navigate around. Figure 13-2 displays an HV chart for the same broad-based stock market index ETF used in Figure 13-1.

Volatility and risk

Volatility is a measure of risk and reward because the moves a security makes has a direct impact on your returns. The bigger the price swings in an ETF, the bigger the potential risk since declines can occur rapidly. You may decide to accept this high potential risk because price swings go both ways — gains can accumulate quickly too.

When buying options you pay more for those based on an underlying security that is more volatile since its past movement (measured by historical volatility) is a major component in the option's implied volatility (IV). It's really important to understand that IV is part of the time value portion of an option — the portion that decays each day you get close to expiration.

Figure 13-2:
Two-year
historical
volatility
chart for
SPY.

The fact that this risk measure increases an option's cost makes it that much more critical for you to understand both volatility measures (HV and IV). It's not just about increased risk and reward, it's about paying for this risk. Do what you can to minimize the cost by purchasing volatility when IV levels are relatively low and selling it when value decay accelerates near expiration.

Historical volatility (HV) also referred to as statistical volatility (SV) does not predict the future volatility of an asset. It uses past data to quantify movement of the asset and allow for an apples-to-apples comparison to other assets.

Security risk

Risk varies by security type and is inherent in the stock, bond, and commodities market. While diversification alleviates some market risk, it doesn't create a risk-free investment. Investors accept market risk to address another financial risk — the risk that savings will not outpace inflation.

You must always understand the risks associated with the securities you choose for investments and trading. If you don't thoroughly understand these risks, you should continue to use securities you do understand.

Generally higher risk for an individual stock translates to higher volatility which means rewards can be greater with an investment in an individual stock. Table 13-2 summarizes the relative risk/volatility levels for stocks, sectors and the market as a whole.

Table 13-2		Relative Risk Levels
	Proxy or Security	*Volatility*
Market	Broad-based index or ETF	Low relative to sectors and stocks
Sector	Sector index or ETF	Generally high than market but less than individual stock
Stock	Individual Stock	Generally high relative to markets or sectors

Investing with ETFs

Although most of the discussions in the book address trading topics, you have to admit it's hard to focus on trading if things in your investment portfolio aren't in good order. Exchange-traded funds (ETFs) provide you with inexpensive access to a diversified group of stocks via broad-based index ETFs or a combination of sector ETFs, similar to mutual funds. What ETFs have that mutual funds don't offer is protection via option strategies.

ETF investing opportunities available to option traders include:

✔ Investment in diversified market portfolio via broad-based sector ETFs

✔ Development of a diversified market portfolio via sector ETFs

✔ Protective put positions using ETFs

✔ Collared positions using ETFs

✔ ETF LEAPS portfolios

Since mutual funds similarly provide an inexpensive way to diversify, the best thing ETFs bring to your investment plan is the opportunity to protect the portfolio with options.

Portfolio management includes the allocation of assets across and within asset classes. This means you seek to diversify holdings by investing in different types of assets (i.e. stocks, bonds, and commodities) while diversifying within those assets as well.

This section provides one approach to investing using a protective put position for the S&P 500 Index ETF (SPY). Unfortunately it has to be said that this is just for illustrative purposes — it's not a recommendation since everyone's situation is different.

Traders managing their investments should complete an investment analysis and trading analysis at separate times since the holding period time horizons are different for each. It's difficult to exit a short-term position on market weakness and not think about similarly exiting your longer term holdings.

Selecting ETFs for investment (for illustrative purposes only)

Although an ETF may track a major index, it doesn't mean that particular ETF is your best choice. Things to look for when selecting an ETF include:

✔ **How well it tracks the index or benchmark:** The most thorough way to determine how well a passive ETF tracks its benchmark index is to perform a correlation analysis for the returns of the benchmark and the

ETF. This requires access to daily closing values for an extended period of time, minimally a year.

There are Web sites that allow you to obtain correlation results for either a limited period of time or using a limited number of ETFs. Smart Money has a Correlation Tracker in the subscription portion of its Web site that is licensed to a variety of ETF providers (no fee). One of the best ways to find current correlation tools information is by completing a Web search on "ETF correlation".

✓ **The liquidity of the ETF:** If you find an ETF that uniquely meets your needs and you're planning on holding it for a longer time, liquidity is less of an issue. If you plan on being more active with the ETF consider those with volume of one million daily shares as a quick rule of thumb.

✓ **Whether options are available and option liquidity:** For both ETFs and options, the Bid-Ask spread can be used as a relative measure of share or contract liquidity. Large spreads indicate less liquid, while small spreads indicate more widely traded issues. Use option chain data to check spreads for the highest open interest contracts to get the best feel of whether the option contracts will meet your needs.

✓ **The expense ratio for the ETF:** Expense ratio data and the instruments used by the fund to track an index should be available via the research portion of your broker's Web site, or using prospectus and tear sheet data from the ETF provider or other ETF resources.

✓ **What instruments the fund uses to obtain its results:** Some funds may use more exotic derivatives to track its target index. Read the prospectus to determine if these securities add any additional risk to the ETF.

The asset allocations you hold depend on your individual needs, constraints, and risk tolerance, as well as your outlook on different groups. There is no one size fits all for investing.

Assessing market conditions (illustrative)

Suppose one of your main investment goals is to obtain results that are similar to the S&P 500 Index (SPX). The actual annual returns for the past 30 years for this index suits your risk tolerance and time horizon. Using this as your portfolio benchmark, you want to select an ETF that serves as a good proxy for the index — SPY fits the bill.

It's early fall 2007 — you just added $10,000 to an investment account and need to decide how to put the money to work. You are primarily focused on whether you should allocate this money to a broad-based market index now or wait for your next portfolio assessment scheduled in a few weeks.

You plan on evaluating the following to help with your decision-making:

- Weekly chart for SPY with volume, a volume indicator, and two moving averages
- Weekly chart for SPY with a momentum indicator and Bollinger bands
- Arm's Index readings for the New York Composite Index (NYA) with an NYA overlay
- Weekly VIX chart with SPX overlay and relative strength comparison

Even though you tend to avoid using market timing techniques for your investment dollars, you're still leery about creating new positions in the fall. You can't help but think about the quick, strong declines (a.k.a. crashes) that have occurred in the past. Unfortunately, you know nice rallies have developed during this time too.

No one knows what the market will do in the next day, week, month, or year.

Figures 13-3 and 13-4 display the weekly charts referenced for SPY.

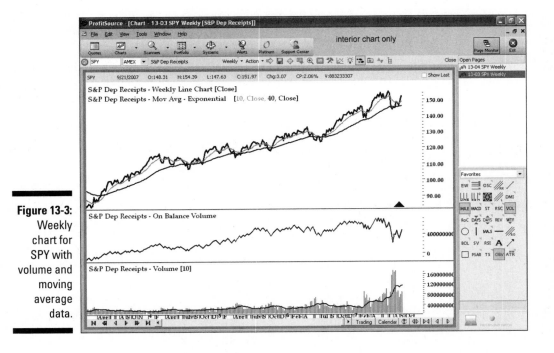

Figure 13-3:
Weekly
chart for
SPY with
volume and
moving
average
data.

Figure 13-4:
Weekly chart for SPY with momentum and Bollinger bands.

SPY is well correlated to the SPX and serves as a reasonable proxy to complete market analysis. Rather than analyzing SPX for your market assessment and SPY for position analysis, you decide to use SPY in the market analysis as well. Using the charts you note that:

- **SPY is in a long-term uptrend:** The 10-week exponential moving average (EMA) is trending upward and is higher than a slightly upward trending 40-week EMA.

  Check longer term trends first since they tend to be stronger.

- **ETF volume still needs to confirm the move:** Volume is a little bit of a concern because last month's strong decline was accompanied by strong volume, while the more recent recovery occurred on lighter volume. In addition, the current on balance volume (OBV) reading has not yet confirmed the recovery. It's possible it can diverge from here.

- **Momentum is not confirming the move:** Typically, sustainable moves for SPY are accompanied by movement of the 13-week ROC above its 21-period simple moving average (SMA). ROC remains below the SMA, but is not signaling a divergence since it is moving upward.

- **Bollinger bands showing decreased volatility:** Price recently moved above the 20-week SMA as the bands were contracting.

Technical tools can confirm a price move or may diverge from price actions providing a warning about the current trend.

These chart conditions do not provide an overwhelmingly bullish picture, but you can't ignore the long-term trend for the ETF . . . especially since many indicators lag price. You decide to evaluate put options to protect your existing SPY position given the current volatility environment. You continue your market analysis by evaluating the daily Arm's Index (TRIN) chart.

The Arm's Index is a breadth indicator that uses advancing and declining stock data for the New York Composite Index (NYA). For more detail on applying this tool, See Chapter 5. The indicator is currently in neutral territory and is strengthening after the recent decline in NYA. This index has a strong positive correlation with SPX and SPY. Recent spikes down on the chart may have signaled a bottom was formed in August.

Many ETFs are actually unit investment trusts which are similar to mutual fund investment companies.

Figure 13-5 displays the weekly charts for the VIX with an SPX overlay and a relative strength comparison line.

Figure 13-5:
Weekly chart for VIX with SPX overlay and relative strength line.

The VIX and SPX have a strong negative correlation with spikes down in the VIX coinciding with upward moves in the SPX. The VIX is currently heading downward indicating a bottom may have formed last month in the SPX.

The VIX is a measure of implied volatility for SPX options and is also referred to as the "Fear Index."

Establishing a position

Rather than waiting to invest the money because of fear about what may happen, you decide you need to invest the money based on what your technical and sentiment tools are telling you. You are still committed to hedging your risk with the purchase of protective puts.

SPY is trading at $151.97. You purchased 100 shares of SPY in early January at $141.67 which are now valued at $15,197. You consider purchasing an additional 50 shares of SPY for approximately $7,600 providing you can purchase sufficient puts to reasonably hedge all 150 shares.

Since you are buying the options, you consider both November and December expiration months to provide the desired protection while still allowing time to sell the contracts before your 30 days to expiration rule. In either case, you can re-evaluate SPY conditions when you sell the puts and roll the contracts out to a later month. You choose not to look beyond December in the event SPY makes a big move upward by mid-November.

After a quick look at the puts for the two months, you note the December options are trading for about $1.00 per contract more than the November contracts. You decide to focus on December options to take you through most of the Fall before reaching that 30-day mark. Table 13-3 provides a partial option chain for December SPY puts.

Table 13-3	Partial Option Chain for December SPY Puts				
Strike Price	**Bid x Ask**	**Delta**	**Gamma***	**IV**	**OI**
150.00	4.20 × 4.30	−39.00	2.62	19.33	88,278
152.00	4.80 × 5.10	−44.32	2.75	18.94	10,409
153.00	5.20 × 5.50	−47.08	2.82	18.60	17,689
154.00	5.60 × 5.90	−49.96	2.89	18.12	10.275

* The rate of change for gamma is greatest when you move away from the ATM strike price of 152.00.

Check option delta values when wanting to hedge a position.

The tightest Bid-Ask spread is for the 150.00 strike price puts, reflecting the high open interest and strong market for this put. This should reduce costs on both entry and exit. Although the 154.00 strike price put has a delta near -50 offering a near perfect hedge, you're considering purchasing four 150.00 strike price puts to reduce slippage costs and gain additional delta protection for slightly less money.

Calculating delta you obtain:

SPY	150 shares $\times$ +1 = +150 Delta
154.00 Call	$3 \times -49.96 = -149.9$
150.00 Call	$4 \times -39.00 = -156.0$

Stock delta is +1 per share.

The 150.00 strike price put deltas exceed the SPY position, resulting in a slight directional bias to the downside. Calculating premiums you obtain:

154.00 Call	$3 \times \$5.90 \times 100 = \$1,770$
150.00 Call	$4 \times \$4.30 \times 100 = \$1,720$

Since the position is an investment and has protection beyond the number of shares held, you do not identify an exit for a loss price level. At the 30 days to expiration mark, a new hedge will be implemented.

Tilting Your Portfolio with Sector ETFs

A portfolio tilt is an investing approach that attempts to beat a market benchmark by allocating a portion of the funds to an asset that is highly correlated with that benchmark and adding smaller allocations in sectors that are outperforming the benchmark. Alternatively, underperforming sectors can be underweighted.

Both sector index options and exchange-traded fund (ETF) options can be used to implement the tilt portion of the portfolio. Using the protected SPY position created in the last section as a base portfolio, sector ETFs are added to tilt the portfolio. Assume there is $5,000 available for ETF sector allocations.

Adding sector ETFs to a portfolio

The goal of a portfolio tilt is to add a moderate investment in outperforming sectors and/or create a bearish position on underperforming sectors. You can accomplish this using the sector ETFs from a specific family of ETFs and comparing the relative strength for each. This next section outlines one basic approach to selecting outperforming sector ETFs during bullish periods.

Using SPY as the proxy ETF for the benchmark index — the S&P 500 — the sector ETFs in the same family are used for the tilt. The method used to create the tilt is a long only approach with a very basic moving average market timing tool to identify bullish periods. Long positions are the only ones considered to minimize risk and the approach remains out of the market during bearish periods since all of SPDR Sector ETFs have a strong positive correlation with SPY.

Past performance does not guarantee future returns.

Selecting strong sectors

Relative strength comparison lines are constructed by dividing the price of one security (A) by the price of another (B). A rising line indicates A is outperforming B, while a declining line indicates that A is underperforming B. This line does not provide you with information about the trend of A or B — both may be rising or declining. A relative strength line provides good, unbiased information on a chart to compare two securities.

Using a technology index and utility index and comparing each to a benchmark index, you'll obtain unrelated ratio values because the two sector indexes are trading at unrelated levels. To compare the performance of technology to utilities, you need to either of the following:

- ✔ Plot a relative strength comparison for these two indexes
- ✔ Calculate the change in value for the sector versus the benchmark

By using changes in the relative ratios instead of the absolute ratio you have a value that can be compared. This allows you to rank a group of indexes. Another alternative is to simply calculate the change in values for each index over a given period. Again, you can't use index values to rank the sectors but you can rank the week over week percentage change in value (rate of change).

Put options provide a limit risk alternative to shorting stock.

Identifying an approach

Using SPY and the nine major Select Sector SPDR ETFs, an investment in an outperforming ETF will be made to tilt an ETF portfolio. The nine ETFs are included in Table 13-4.

Table 13-4	Select Sector SPDR ETF List
Sector	*Symbol*
Materials	XLB
Energy	XLE
Financials	XLF
Industrials	XLI
Technology	XLK
Consumer Staples	XLP
Utilities	XLU
Healthcare	XLV
Consumer Discretionary	XLY

Outperforming sectors are identified during bullish periods as follows:

1. **On a weekly basis rank the ETFs using three-month returns. The top ranked ETF is the one with the best returns over a three-month period**

2. **Invest in the top ranked ETF.**

3. **Maintain investment in ETF until it drops below the third rank (ranks 4 – 9) for two consecutive weeks.**

4. **Identify new ETF for investment by repeating steps 1 through 3.**

By requiring a two-week drop in rankings, there are fewer changes to the tilt, keeping costs to a minimum.

Many technical tools can be used to provide you with unbiased rules to follow.

Tracking bullish and bearish periods

Different sectors outperform the market at different times, but when a strong bear market enters the picture you'll find few sectors come out unscathed, at least in the short-term. To minimize the risk on this basic tilt model, no sector investment is made during bearish periods.

Two other ETF-like securities are currently available for trading. They include the widely held Merrill Lynch HOLDRS and the lesser traded Exchange-traded Note (ETN) from iShares.

Once you feel comfortable the mechanics and risks associated with a tilt approach, consider using a long ETF plus long put combination for top ranked ETFs during bearish periods or long puts on bottom ranked ETFs.

Using daily chart for SPY with 50-day and 200-day simple moving averages (SMAs) plotted, bullish periods are identified as those periods when the 50-day SMA is above the 200-day SMA. Bearish periods are identified as those periods when the 50-day SMA is below the 200-day SMA. So as the 50-day SMA crosses below the 200-day SMA, a bearish period is identified. In terms of the portfolio tilt, this means the sector ETF position is exited.

The advantage of using SMAs to identify bullish and bearish periods is that it represents an unbiased measure that signal the change. The disadvantage to this method is that there is a reasonably long lag in signals since SMAs use historical prices. It's a trade-off and its validity is one you have to decide for yourself.

Using the signal to identify bullish and bearish periods, it's assumed that $5,000 is the initial investment in the outperforming ETF as a new bullish period is signaled. The only re-balancing that occurs with the tilt is after the next bearish-bullish cycle takes place.

Measuring results

Using data from 1/3/2000 to 9/21/2007, there were two bullish periods in which the tilt was in place:

- ✔ 1/3/2000 to 11/3/2000
- ✔ 8/8/2003 to 9/21/2007

Table 13-5 provides some additional statistics for the approach. The SPY columns provide buy and hold comparison returns for the two bullish periods

Table 13-5	Select Sector SPDR Portfolio Tilt Results			
	Period 1	*Period 2*	*SPY 1*	*SPY 2*
Beginning Value	$5,000	$5,000	$5,000	$5,000
End Value	$5,135	$14,080	$4,855	$7,599
# of Trades	4	16	1	1
# Gains	3	11	--	--

(continued)

Table 13-5 (continued)

	Period 1	Period 2	SPY 1	SPY 2
# Losses	1	5	--	--
Largest Gain	5.28%	41.65%	--	--
Largest Loss	(4.62%)	(4.39%)	--	--
Consecutive Gains	3	6	--	--
Consecutive Losses	1	2	--	--

The last position entered produced large, atypical gains. Adding mean, median, and standard deviation calculations to those identified in Table 13-4 will help you assess the consistency of results. It's deemed that after removing this last trade the results are still acceptable. The new largest gain is now 27.09% and the end of period value $9,940.

Always complete your own assessment for any system approach you consider implementing to determine suitability.

Selecting the right approach

Investing in the markets requires a reasonable plan that suits your risk tolerances and preferences. From a financial standpoint you may be able to afford a market decline of 10%, but that doesn't mean it suits you. Some less than scientific ways to identify whether you're risking more than maybe you should is by gauging how you sleep at night or your irritability levels during market declines. These measures do matter.

Selecting an approach that works for you takes an investment in time. Don't expect to map out your perfect plan the first go around. By identifying a reasonable approach that manages risk and then testing it, paper trading it, and/or initiating small positions to start, you'll develop a plan that's suitable for you.

Using a sector approach with a portion of your investments has advantages and disadvantages. Considering both is an important part of building your own plan.

Advantages of sector investing with ETFs

The main advantage to sector trading is that it allows you to benefit from gains in outperforming sectors and ideally eek out slightly better returns than a simple buy and hold approach using a passive fund. Other advantages to sector investing includes:

✔ Produces less volatile result than individual stock positions

✔ Reduces trading stress by minimizing portfolio decision-making

✔ There are a variety of ETF choices making it a flexible approach

Disadvantages of sector investing with ETFs

The main disadvantage to sector trading is that strong declines in the markets are often widespread — usually all sectors will drop together. This means that you cannot bank on profits week after week, month after month. Sector investing may only moderately outperform a declining market. Other disadvantages include:

✔ Costs of trading including slippage, taxes, and commissions

✔ Represents risk that is not hedged

✔ Cost of protection for the core holding may offset or exceed gains from sector approach

✔ Approaches generally based on past data which cannot be guaranteed in the future

✔ Requires identifying suitable sector proxies for a group of ETFs

✔ Is not a substitute for effective risk management

Part IV:
Advanced Strategies for Option Traders

In this part . . .

Option strategies go beyond stock trading alternatives. When trading options you can benefit from large moves in a stock, regardless of the direction of the move when using the right strategy. There are also ways you can create a perfectly hedged position that has minimal risk from moves in the underlying. Through position adjustments you can maintain a completely neutral market view, but still profit. The key to these strategies is changing volatility — a topic addressed throughout this part.

Chapter 14

Profiting Without a Market Outlook

I keep mentioning that on any given day the market can move three ways — it's really to reinforce the fact that no one knows what the market will do in the next month, week or even day. If knowing exactly what's next is a trading goal, you really have to find a way to shift your thinking. Managing your risk is the first and foremost rule of trading.

The strategies I've covered so far only scratch the surface of option benefits. It's a pretty deep scratch since a lot of them significantly decrease risk, but they're still on the surface. This chapter introduces a trading approach unique to options — profiting without a directional outlook for the underlying stock. By incorporating delta and gamma analysis into your approach, you can apply strategies that make money if the market goes up or down. Part of this analysis includes adjusting trades so you can take some profits off the table while gearing up for the next move follows. Whichever way that move is.

Limiting Directional Risk

How would you like to anticipate a big move, be wrong about the expected direction of the move and still profit? Rather than direction, the next two strategies rely on increasing volatility. Anticipating this environment is more straightforward than anticipating direction because volatility changes often occur when scheduled reports and other news items are released.

It's generally easier to anticipate a change in volatility for a stock than a change in price.

Two basic strategies that allow you to profit under such conditions include:

- ✔ A straddle
- ✔ A strangle

Both of these position combine a long call and a long put. The strategy works best when the stock moves enough to have the call or put realize gains that cover the cost of both options with some profits to spare.

Capitalizing on a big move

A straddle is a combination position you create by purchasing both a call and put for the same underlying stock. You use the strategy when you expect a big move to occur in the stock, but you're not sure of the direction. You construct a straddle using:

- ✔ A long call and long put
- ✔ The same expiration month
- ✔ The same strike price

The reason the basic form of this strategy requires a large directional move is because all of the profits are expected to result from one leg of the position while the other leg expires close to worthless. The reality is that there are a few different ways the straddle position can realize profits.

Straddling opportunities

In terms of finding straddle opportunities, there are a few different times you can anticipate big moves:

- ✔ When observing sideways trending consolidation patterns on a price chart, you'll find it's not uncommon for price to break away from the pattern and make a big move.
- ✔ Prior to scheduled events such as earnings reports and company announcements get released.
- ✔ Prior to scheduled events such as economic reports. The biggest swings generally occur when the news is counter to the market's expectations.

The advantage of a straddle is that it doesn't matter which way the price moves, as long as it moves. Using straddles helps you trade with the odds because rather than betting on one direction, there are two possible directions for the stock to move.

For a straddle to be profitable, the stock doesn't actually have to move above or below the position breakevens. There are times when a smaller move is profitable since the OTM option will probably not decrease as quickly as the ITM option increases. The IV for both options usually increases as well.

Straddling the markets

The position can be profitable given three different scenarios for the underlying stock:

- When the move results in an increase in the value of the call or the put by an amount that exceeds the cost of both options
- When a smaller move increases the in-the-money (ITM) option faster than the out-of-the-money (OTM) option decreases
- When the move allows you to sell one option for a profit, then changes direction allowing you to sell the other option for a modest gain or loss

You want to purchase a straddle when implied volatility (IV) is relatively low and expected to increase. Since there are two long options in the position, you also need to provide enough time for the stock to react without giving up too much value to time decay.

Since a straddle is comprised of two long options, your maximum risk is the net debit you paid to enter the position. The stock can move up or down for you to gain — it just has do so with some magnitude. Since there are two directions the stock can move and still realize profits, there are two breakeven points associated with the position.

For you to profit from a downward move, the stock must go lower than the strike price minus the net option cost. Below this level your gains are limited, but high. For you to profit from an upward move, the stock must go higher than the strike price plus the net option cost. Above this level, your gains are unlimited.

Figure 14-1 displays a generic view of the straddle risk graph which is drawn by overlaying a long call risk graph (thicker line with dotted line) on a long put risk graph (thinner line with dashed line).

Figure 14-1:
Straddle risk chart (long call + long put).

It's ideal to purchase a long straddle when implied volatility (IV) is relatively low and to sell it when IV is relatively high.

Benefiting from a big move

Remember Wall Street worrying equals market volatility.

To show you what I mean, I set up an example trade here. Monitoring an investment bank stock you like to trade options on (symbol GS), you notice that it's pretty quiet a few days ahead of a holiday weekend. The stock recently took a slide recently after some hedge fund headlines, but typically it performs well. The company's earnings announcement is due two days after the Fed meeting. After noting low relative implied volatility (IV) levels, you decide to take a look at a straddle anticipating increased volatility as the news comes out in the very near future.

Figure 14-2 displays a daily bar chart of GS with volume, Bollinger bands and two horizontal lines. The lines denote an upper area of resistance and a lower extreme level reached a couple of weeks earlier.

The dotted lines represent potential moves for the stock.

Figure 14-2:
Daily bar chart for GS with volume and Bollinger bands.

Time decay accelerates in the last 30 to 45 days for a long option. This means a straddle is impacted twice as much since the position includes two long options. When purchasing a straddle, be sure to leave enough time for the event to occur and still be outside of the window for accelerated time decay.

Figure 14-3 displays the six-month implied volatility chart for ATM options.

Figure 14-3:
Six-month
IV chart for
ATM GS
options.

The two news events you expect to cause volatility will both pass about 30 days prior to October expiration. Since the stock closed at $178 you check the Oct 180 strike price calls and puts obtaining the following:

Oct 180 Call Bid: $9.20 by Ask: $9.50

Oct 180 Put Bid: $10.50 by Ask: $10.80

The quotes reflect IV levels of approximately 37%. You enter a trade by placing a limit order to buy the straddle at a discount as follows:

Buy to Open 2 GS Oct 180 calls and simultaneously

Buy to Open 2 GS Oct 180 puts, for a net debit of $20.10.

Volatility in the market and individual stocks tends to be cyclical.

Your risk for the position is the initial debit (sum of the two long options times the multiplier and the number of contracts).

[(Price of Put + Price of Call) × multiplier × # of contracts] = Max Risk

[($9.40 + 10.70) × 100 × 2] = $20.10 × 100 × 2 = $4,020

Your potential reward for the position is limited, but high to the downside (long puts) and unlimited to the upside (long calls).

There are two breakeven levels for this position, one to the downside and one to the upside. The downside breakeven is equal to the straddle strike price minus the sum of the call and put option prices. The upside breakeven is equal to the straddle strike price plus the sum of the call and put option prices.

Downside Breakeven: Strike Price – (Price of Put + Price of Call)

$180 – ($9.40 + 10.70) = $180 – 20.10 = $159.90

Upside Breakeven: Strike Price + (Price of Put + Price of Call)

$180 + ($9.40 + 10.70) = $180 + 20.10 = $200.10

The Fed meeting (Tuesday) and earnings report (Thursday) occur the week of September option expiration. You plan on exiting half the in-the-money (ITM) leg if price makes a move that is 80% to the target region. On the day earnings are released, you plan on closing out the remaining options. This is one full month before expiration.

If you purchase an even number of contracts for straddle positions, you have an opportunity to do some profit-taking while allowing greater gains for the portion of the trade left in place.

Reviewing the straddle risk profile

Your risk with a long straddle is limited to the initial debit paid since the position combines a long call and a long put. A strong move up or down in the underlying will result profits.

Figure 14-4 displays the straddle risk graph with an adjoining price chart.

Figure 14-4:
Risk graph
for GS
straddle
with price
chart.

This risk graph includes three curved lines which estimate the position value given various days to expiration. The curved line closest to the straight lines (expiration) use 18 days to expiration — note how large the gap is between this curve and the value at expiration. This is the time decay factor.

Using the target areas identified in the daily bar chart for GS, you plan on exiting half of the ITM leg will be exited if the stock moves up to 198.50 (80%) or down to 161.50 (80%). On the day of the Fed meeting, the stock closed at 200.50 and one call was exited at a price of $22.80 (IV = 40%). Two days later when earnings are released the remaining call and two puts were sold for $30.10 and $0.70, respectively. The net gain for the position follows:

$$[(\$22.80 + 30.10 + 0.70 + 0.70) \times 100] - 4{,}020 = \$5{,}430 - 4{,}020 = \$1{,}410$$

Reducing straddle risk & reward

A strangle is very similar to a straddle, but reduces the risk and generally the reward for the position. You accomplish this by purchasing a call and a put with different strike prices that are out-of-the-money (OTM) and expire the same month.

Since OTM options are less expensive, the initial debit is smaller and you have less money at risk. Reducing your risk usually means giving up something and that something is usually gains. The move generally needs to be larger for a strangle since both options begin OTM.

A strangle requires a bigger move than a straddle since there is a spread between the strike prices.

Defining a strangle

A strangle is created by purchasing a call and a put:

- ✔ For the same underlying stock
- ✔ Using the same expiration month and
- ✔ Different strike prices that are both usually OTM

The ideal scenario is for a move in the underlying to be sufficient to sell one leg of the strangle while covering the costs (and then some) for both legs. When this happens, it's not uncommon for the remaining OTM option to expire worthless or with little value. It just depends on conditions.

A strangle is a straddle that reduces potential risk by reducing the cost of the position.

Using the straddle set-up, you decide you want to risk less on the position by placing a strangle instead of a straddle. You still believe the move can be large enough to yield profits. With the stock closing at $178 you check the Oct 185 strike price call and the 170 strike price put obtaining the following:

Oct 185 Call Bid: $6.90 by Ask: $7.20 (IV = 36)

Oct 170 Put Bid: $6.50 by Ask: $6.70 (IV = 40)

You enter the trade by placing a limit order to buy the strangle at a discount as follows:

Buy to Open 2 GS Oct 185 calls and simultaneously

Buy to Open 2 GS Oct 170 puts, for a net debit of $13.90.

The short strangle is an extremely risky position since it combines a limited but high risk if the stock moves down (short put) and an unlimited risk if the stock moves up (short call).

Your risk for the position is the initial debit (sum of the two long options times the multiplier and the number of contracts).

[(Price of Put + Price of Call) × multiplier × # of contracts] = Max Risk

[($7.20 + 6.70) × 100 × 2] = $13.90 × 100 × 2 = $2,780

Your potential reward for the position is limited but high to the downside (long puts) and unlimited to the upside (long calls).

There are two breakeven levels for this position. The downside breakeven is equal to the put strike price minus the sum of the call and put option prices. The upside breakeven is equal to the call strike price plus the sum of the call and put option prices.

Downside Breakeven: Put Strike Price – (Price of Put + Price of Call)

$170 – ($7.20 + 6.70) = $170 – 13.90 = $156.10

Upside Breakeven: Call Strike Price + (Price of Put + Price of Call)

$185 + ($7.20 + 6.70) = $185 + 13.90 = $198.90

The exit for the GS strangle is similar to that of the strangle, which includes an exit of all option positions by the close on earnings day.

The term leg is used to describe the different securities in a combined position.

Reviewing the strangle risk profile

By separating the strike prices and using two OTM options, there is a range of prices in which both options expire worthless, resulting in the maximum loss. Rather than a v-shaped bottom, the strangle risk graph has a flat loss region which moves upward towards profits similar to a straddle.

Figure 14-5 displays the risk graph for the GS 185c-170p strangle with an adjoining price chart.

Figure 14-5:
Risk graph
for GS
strangle
with price
chart.

Exiting the position on the same day as the straddle yields the following:

$$[(\$18.80 + 25.5 + 0.30 + 0.30) \times 100] - 2{,}780 = \$4{,}490 - 2{,}780 = \$1{,}710$$

Always have an exit strategy before you exit a position. Including specific price levels where you exit for a loss and exit for a profit is a great risk management tool to use whenever possible.

Neutral View versus Neutral Position

The term *neutral* can have two meanings in the market and it's important to clarify them here. You may hear of an analyst having a neutral view on a stock, suggesting it is neither a buy nor sell and that it will likely move with the market. The other use refers to a neutral strategy which is one that can benefit from a move upward or downward — there is no directional bias.

Options help you implement neutral strategies. Straddles and strangles are examples of such strategies, but there's more to these positions than meets the eye. Optimizing a neutral trade means looking once again at delta.

Hedging a position means you invest in securities that go up in value when the original security goes down.

Defining a neutral approach

A neutral approach is a combination of stock and options or just options that limit directional bias. As a result, trading with a neutral approach allows you to realize gains whether the market goes up or down. When market moves are accompanied by increased volatility, neutral strategies can really benefit.

You successfully implement long delta neutral strategies by focusing on delta and gamma during low implied volatility (IV) periods. Using these measures allows market conditions to dictate the positions you establish rather than trying to force a particular strategy or view on the market.

It's important to note delta neutral trading isn't the "holy grail" for option approaches. You still need to consider the position's risk profile to see if the trade has a reasonable reward:risk ratio and is one that fits your risk. Stocks that are trading sideways can continue to do so for extended periods so there are no guarantees that the position will yield profits.

Delta neutral trading does not guarantee profits — you still must evaluate potential risks and rewards for a position and identify reasonable positions sizes and exits to minimize losses.

Identifying neutral positions

Neutral approaches were introduced with hedged positions in Chapter 10. Using puts for the underlying stock, you protect a position since a move down in the stock price results in a move up in the put's price. When this movement is one to one — the put goes up $1 for every $1 decline in the stock — the stock is *perfectly hedged*. This occurs when the put is deep ITM and has a delta of -1.0. The combined position behaves neutrally to price changes.

The relationship between stock and put movement can vary depending on the put(s) used for the strategy. When the movement between the two is less than one to one the position is referred to as a *partial hedge*. This occurs when the cumulative delta for the put position is less than -1.0 in absolute terms.

A problem you encounter when using options to hedge a stock, is that delta changes as the price of the underlying changes. So what may initially be a perfect hedge can turn into a partial hedge. The expected change in delta is measured using gamma and varies depending on the moneyness of the option.

The stock-put position is not the only one available to you for hedging purposes. By combining other stock and options or just options, you can achieve perfectly and partially hedged positions that are neutral.

Delta neutral trading is more geared towards longer time frames (on the higher end of 30 to 90 days). This gives the position time to yield profits.

Calculating delta for combination positions

Stock has a +1 delta per share while option deltas vary. You calculate the position delta by adding the deltas for all of the individual legs.

Suppose you held a protective put position with two puts and 100 shares of long stock. If each put has a delta of –45 (net –90), you calculate the delta for the combined position as follows:

(Shares of Stock × Stock Delta) + (Contracts × Option Delta)

Together, the puts move up $0.90 for every $1 decline in the stock. This is a partial hedge with a minor loss in the position when the stock goes down. Your position gains modestly when the stock goes up. As a result, it is has a slight directional bias to the upside.

Delta values can be used to identify the directional bias for a position. Combined delta values that are less than 0 have a downward directional bias while those with deltas greater than 0 have an upward bias. The bias indicates the direction for the underlying to move for the position to realize gains.

Trading with Delta

Delta is the Greek value that tells you the expected change in an option for every dollar change in the underlying stock. You can access delta values using an options calculator based on one of a variety of different option pricing models. This is important from the standpoint of understanding that each pricing model has assumptions you need to keep in mind.

You can gain an intuitive sense about delta values by considering an at-the-money (ATM) call option. Suppose ABC is trading at $50. It's expected that a 50 strike price call option will have a delta of 50, so if ABC goes to $51 the call option will increase by $0.50. Why 50? One model assumption is that a stock has a 50% chance of going up and a 50% chance of going down. So the call option has a 50% chancing of being ITM.

A problem arises once the stock actually moves up and the option price changes. Using an options calculator again you'll find delta has gone up. Trading neutrally with this moving target presents a challenge. Fortunately, the change in delta is not some random amount. By looking at an option's gamma you'll have some idea of the expected move in delta.

Gamma is like the delta for delta. It represents the expected change in delta for each $1 change in the price of the underlying stock.

Monitoring two key Greeks

Trading neutral strategies means monitoring the position delta and gamma, along with the stock and option price movement. And in case I haven't mentioned it in awhile — managing your risk. Delta and gamma values are accessible via an options calculator. Their impact on option prices is also covered in Chapter 3. Options analysis software may also provide you with a graphical view of both of these values.

Understanding changes in delta

Delta is primarily effected by the option strike price relative to the price of the underlying, but there are other factors as well. Both volatility and the time remaining until expiration impact delta values.

- ✔ As volatility increases, all option deltas move towards 0.50 (+0.50 for calls and –0.50 for puts).
- ✔ As time to expiration decreases, all options deltas move towards 0

These are trends often describing general shifts for delta. A 10% increase in volatility does not cause a call option with a +0.80 delta to jump to a +0.50.

Assessing gamma changes on delta

Understanding changes in delta also means understanding the option greek gamma. Gamma is greatest for ATM options, then decreases once the option becomes more ITM or OTM. As a result, you'll find the biggest moves in delta occur for your ATM options.

Gamma is greatest for ATM options so delta changes the most when holding an ATM option.

Like delta, gamma is a moving target, but on a smaller scale. Some general characteristics you should note about gamma is the following:

- ✔ Gamma is always positive
- ✔ Gamma is highest for ATM options
- ✔ Gamma increases as you approach expiration

Since gamma is always positive, when the price of a stock goes up $1 a call delta increases by gamma. The put delta also increases, but this translates to a reduction in the magnitude of the put's delta since a put delta is negative.

Creating a delta neutral straddle

Creating a straddle allows you to realize gains whether a stock moves strongly up or down. Sometimes it's not even necessary for the move to be that big — the stock just has to keep moving. You establish a straddle position by purchasing a long call and a long put, with the same expiration month and strike price. That strike is either at or near the money, so paying attention to gamma and delta when initiating a neutral position is important.

The changing nature of both option pricing factors also make it necessary to monitor delta and gamma throughout the position's life. A once neutral position can become directionally biased within one day's trading. In terms of a straddle that's not terrible news since 1/2 the position will then be profitable. Returning to delta neutrality may mean adding to the position or taking profits off the table.

When purchasing at or near the money straddles, you are predominantly purchasing time value. You must manage your risk by minimizing the effect of accelerating time decay on such a position by closing it at least 30 days prior to expiration.

Checking delta status

Gong back to the GS straddle example earlier in this chapter, the initial position delta is obtained using the options calculator from Optionetics Platinum:

GS Oct 180 call trading at $9.40: (Call delta = +51.191)

GS Oct 180 put trading at $10.70: (Put delta = –48.688)

Position Delta: $[(2 \times +51.191) + (2 \times -48.688)] = +102.382 - 97.376 = +5.006$

The position was similar to one that was long five shares of stock.

What about a few days into the position — is there directional bias? It actually didn't take long at all for bias to be introduced. The next trading day GS dropped seven points, decreasing the magnitude of the call deltas and increasing the magnitude of the put deltas. Within a week, the bias was positive once again.

An increase in the volatility of the underlying causes all option deltas to move *towards* 50. This increased volatility increases uncertainty as well as the potential for a deeper ITM option to expire OTM. Delta decreases towards 50. However, this increased uncertainty also increases the chance an OTM option will expire ITM, increasing delta towards 50.

Table 14-1 displays stock and option prices, delta and gamma values, and the position delta on different days over the 24 calendar day life of the straddle. The table assumes all options were held for the 24 days.

Table 14-1	**Position Delta**				
	T	*T+1*	*T+8*	*T+16*	*T+24*
GS Price	177.95	170.95	178.98	188.47	207.55
Call Price	9.40	6.80	11.10	14.9	30.10
Delta	+51.191	+40.762	+52.976	+67.179	+86.906
Gamma	1.613	1.539	1.425	1.459	0.741
Put Price	10.70	15.20	11.10	5.4	0.70
Delta	−48.688	−58.667	−47.061	−32.363	−7.106
Gamma	1.569	1.485	1.439	1.509	0.637
Position Delta	+5.006	−35.810	+11.830	+69.632	+159.600

Maintaining a delta neutral position

The method of using primary support and resistance areas is reasonable for identifying price targets, but there are no guarantees price will reach either. That could be a problem with a straddle. Applying this technical analysis tool primarily for risk (and profit-taking) is good for identifying extreme points.

Stock deltas are considered fixed — 1 long share of stock always represents +1 stock. Option deltas on the other hand are variable covering a range of values determined primarily by the option's moneyness.

With the benefit of hindsight, wouldn't it have been nice to return the straddle towards delta neutrality by going long another call on T+1 (position delta from −35.810 to 4.952)? What if two calls were exited on T+16 when the position only had about one week remaining (position delta from +136.81 to 2.453)?

So to what extent do you need hindsight to act on T+1 and T+16? When preparing this, I just picked random trading days along the way and looked at the easiest way to return the position to delta neutrality. Timing issues certainly come into play when thinking about adding to or reducing a position, but hopefully this quick example provides incentive to incorporate delta neutral trading into your overall approach to the markets.

Reviewing changes to the risk profile

Are you wondering how adding a call to the position impacted the risk profile of the trade? First, the dollars at risk is the total debit for the position, which now includes an additional call. Assuming the call was purchased at $7.00, the net position risk was $4,720. The directional bias with this addition was reduced most of the days tracked.

When adding to or reducing a position, it helps to review the current risk graph to most easily see the impact the change has on the strategy.

The original call was exited on T+22 at the more favorable price of $22.80. As a result, both approaches to the trade yielded a gain of $1,410, but the delta neutral approach relies less on potentially subjective price targets and had less directional risk.

Figure 14-6 provides an updated risk graph for the adjusted straddle position on the T+1 date. In this case, the risk area decreased slightly because the straddle acted as it was supposed to — increased volatility resulted in the put value increasing at a faster rate than the call decreased. When the third call was purchased there were already profits in the position, reducing the impact of the additional debit.

The stock prices that occur between strangle strike prices identifies the range for maximum risk. At these prices, both options expire worthless.

The "risk area" refers to the distance between the two trade breakevens. In the straight straddle the breakevens were 159.90 and 200.10 (40.20) while the adjusted straddle breakevens were 156.40 and 195.73 (39.33).

Figure 14-6:
Risk graph for adjusted GS straddle.

Understanding Trade Adjustments

Adjusting a trade is something you do to maintain delta neutrality — not something to avoid taking losses when a position has gone against you. In the GS straddle example I added to a leg that had declined in value, but the position as a whole increased in value. The straddle was basically working as it should with the ITM leg increasing at a faster rate than the OTM leg was decreasing. An increase in volatility also helped.

"Adjusting" is not synonymous to "avoiding". If a position has gone against you and is not acting properly, you should exit it and take your losses.

The purpose of adjusting trade is to keep the positional bias to a minimum. You accomplish this by maintaining delta neutrality, but not at all costs. At some point you may need to simply exit the position. Factors that impact your decisions include:

- Time to expiration and whether the adjustment buys or sells time value
- Relative implied volatility (IV) levels
- Trading costs

A quick comment on the last item — straddle positions can be hedged with stock which may be a more cost effective approach at for some adjustments.

Deciding when to adjust a trade

Focusing on a straddle position, trade adjustments should be made once the position becomes overly reliant on the stock moving in one direction. That's when one leg really begins losing value. If you've purchased the straddle in a high IV environment and IV declines, then the ITM leg is not gaining at a faster rate than the OTM leg and it's probably time to cut your losses.

Different aspects of trading are referred to as "art not science". While you can specifically identify some trading rules and mechanical steps, others parts of trading require experienced assessment of conditions and a best guess of how to proceed.

So far my answer about "when" has been kind of fuzzy. Unfortunately it's the nature of the beast and looking back at a position you may find a more optimal adjustment time or method. The following should help you more successfully implement delta neutral strategies:

✔ Experience with the specific strategy, in this case straddles

✔ Understanding the cyclic nature of IV for a specific stock

✔ Analyzing how a stock behaves after different events

Some traders make adjustments every trading day to start out as close to delta neutral as possible. Others may use specific delta values above or below zero to trigger adjustments. It just depends on style.

It's reasonable to consider a set time schedule for adjustments or to base adjustments around different event dates. Just be sure you understand the implications of the position delta you hold and how it may deviate from a delta neutral approach.

Making money in the markets can be done in a variety of ways. It's bets to find approaches that suit your temperament, time, and style.

Deciding how to adjust a trade

Straddles can be adjusted in the following ways:

✔ Purchasing more calls (+delta) or puts (–delta)

✔ Selling calls (–delta) or puts (+delta)

✔ Buying stock (+delta)

✔ Selling stock (–delta)

Deciding which approach is best depends on your cost of trading (commission and slippage) and how many contracts you use to create positions. Even though you hold rights with the two option types, you may decide shorting stock is not a way you want to reduce delta. This means the fourth alternative is only possible if you hold a position that is long stock.

Another factor for you to consider is how much time remains to expiration. You may be at a point when it's best for you to do some profit-taking by closing out one or more positions if the 30-day to expiration mark is coming.

If there is plenty of time to expiration and IV is relatively low, you can purchase more of the original strike price options or improve delta neutrality by selecting options with strike prices that best adjust the position to a net delta of zero.

Chapter 15

Keying In on Volatility for Trading Opportunities

In This Chapter
▶ Monitoring option volatility for prospects
▶ Trading implied volatility price skews
▶ Identifying the best strategies for current conditions

Although stock prices exhibit some cyclical properties, the cyclic nature of volatility is much more reliable for certain stocks. Even the market as a whole can display such tendencies as seen by the VIX (see Chapter 5). Using relative volatility levels for strategy selection can help put the odds in your favor by capitalizing when volatility changes.

Ratio spreads and backspreads are strategies that also benefit from volatility changes. Incorporating delta neutral concepts can then help improve strategy success. As your experience builds, you'll develop more skill implementing approaches that are well-suited to existing market conditions.

Analyzing Implied Volatility Levels

Implied volatility (IV) is impacted by some of the following factors:

- ↙ Past price movement (historical volatility)
- ↙ Time until expiration
- ↙ Expected future movement given scheduled events before expiration
- ↙ Demand factors for the specific option

IV determines the time value for an option. The greater the value of the listed factors, the greater the option's extrinsic value. Because they all vary, it's really important to buy and sell options under proper IV conditions.

It's all relative

There are two types of volatility for you to consider when analyzing an options trade:

- ✔ Historical volatility for the underlying security
- ✔ Implied volatility for the option

Because you're paying for implied volatility (IV), focusing on this measure is pretty critical. But that doesn't mean you can ignore historical volatility (HV) — far from it. HV allows you to take the first step in determining whether IV is reasonable. So when gauging an option's IV level, you need to look at both types of volatility.

An option's intrinsic value is its "moneyness" factor. For a call option, intrinsic value is the stock price above the call strike price and for a put option, it is the stock price below the put strike price. Intrinsic value is set to zero for any options that are out of the money.

Evaluating past movement

Historical volatility (HV) provides you with information about past stock movement.HV can be calculated using any number of trading days, but the measure itself gives you information about annual movement. The data is extrapolated which means what happens during the shorter term is extended to a one-year period using statistical techniques.

HV periods include 6-day, 10-day, 20-day, and 100-day. The movement that occurs during these periods varies depending on what's happening in the markets and for the security. An annualized measure that is created using 10 trading days can suggest much more volatility than one using 100 trading days. But, that really depends on events taking place over the last 10 and 100 trading days. If it's summertime and Wall Street was vacationing in the Hamptons, the ten-day measure may understate volatility.

The best way for you to get a good feel for past volatility in a stock is by viewing HV charts. This quickly provides you with a visual on HV conditions.

Extrinsic value is the time value component of an option price. It's what is leftover after intrinsic value is determined.

Figure 15-1 displays a 12 month HV chart for Akamai Technologies Inc (AKAM), a computer services company. The chart includes 6-day, 10-day, 20-day, and 100-day HV measures and is courtesy of Optionetics Platinum.

One year typically consists of 252 trading days.

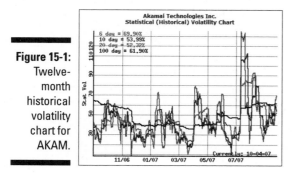

Figure 15-1:
Twelve-month historical volatility chart for AKAM.

You can see that the six-day measure (69.90%) reflects increased volatility during the last few days. The 10-day (53.99%) and 20-day (52.32%) measures include this recent volatility, along with quieter trading days which bring down their respective values.

It appears these "quieter" periods may be less typical for the stock, given a 100-day HV at 61.90%. This 100-day measure is telling you that if the stock moves similar to the last 100 trading days in the next 252 trading days, its volatility for that period will be 61.90%.

Note the different spikes in volatility which has recently reached one-year highs. Expect options for this stock to have implied volatility levels that incorporate these HV spikes in its value.

What may be typical historical volatility (HV) levels for one security may be high for another. Viewing a stock's HV chart gives you the quickest feel for recent volatility for a stock and more importantly, how this movement relates to what's happened in the past.

Viewing implied volatility

Implied volatility (IV) levels change over time, similar to historical volatility (HV) levels. When using an options calculator to determine the current IV for a particular option, you'll want to take the next step of viewing an IV chart that displays at-the-money (ATM) IV values to determine if conditions do the following:

 ✔ Reflect reasonable levels given past IV values

 ✔ Are relatively low making the option cheap

 ✔ Are relatively high making the option expensive

A cheap option in terms of relative implied volatility (IV) levels can remain cheap through the life of the option. Try to dig deeper into this measure to determine what's driving relative IV levels.

Before viewing the 12-month ATM IV for AKAM, look at the price chart to gain insight on what was happening to the stock during the most recent 12 months. Figure 15-2 displays the price chart for AKAM. Generally price charts are also available with volatility charts when accessing an options analysis package. This chart is courtesy of Optionetics Platinum.

Figure 15-2:
Twelve-month daily price chart for AKAM.

Option type refers to call or put.

Looking at the chart, you can see AKAM experienced two significant drops right before and after March 2007 — that's approximately 10% in a few days, which is pretty significant to me. After asking and answering, "Why did this happen?" don't forget to double-check news stories for that time period.

This first gap coincided with a market decline that occurred in late February on concerns a stock market bubble was bursting in China. Price recovered a bit, and then gapped down in late July, possibly in sympathy with a declining US market dealing with sub-prime mortgage problems.

When an at-the-money (ATM) implied volatility (IV) figure reflects a range of days, the value is a composite of call and put IV values expiring in that time period.

Was AKAM just a victim of a turbulent market or was something else going on? Checking headlines for AKAM the following was noted:

✔ In late February AKAM hosted a conference call and raised 2007 earnings expectations. No other significant news was found during the search, so it appears AKAM fell with the market.

✔ In mid-March news of significant insider selling during a six-month period made the headlines — this could potentially have amplified AKAM's losses as other technology stocks were also dropping.

✔ In late July AKAM had an earnings report that disappointed investors and analysts even though they were in line with expectations.

An option position that is delta neutral when created will become directionally biased as the price of the underlying changes and/or implied volatility levels change.

Figure 15-3 displays the 12-month ATM IV chart for AKAM. The chart includes composite IVs for both option types with expirations in 7 to 30 days, 30 to 60 days, and greater than 90 days, courtesy of Optionetics Platinum.

Figure 15-3:
Twelve-month ATM implied volatility chart for AKAM.

Spikes in the IV correspond pretty well with spikes in HV for AKAM, with HV spikes appearing slightly more extreme. If you compare the two y-axis volatility scales, you can see that the range for HV is greater.

Historical volatility is one component that impacts implied volatility values.

Suppose you were considering a long option expiring in 30 to 60 days with an IV of 57.9%, you note the following from the two volatility charts:

✔ The current composite IV value for options expiring in 30 to 60 days is 57.7%, so the option you're analyzing is very slightly above the average.

✔ Recent HV for the stock was approximately 54.0% (10-day) and 52.3% (20-day), so the IV in your option is above short-term movement.

✔ Longer term HV for the stock 53.8%, so the IV in your option is about 8% greater than longer term movement.

✔ The current IV levels for options expiring in 30 to 60 just recently spiked to 60%, up from 40% 2½ weeks ago.

✔ Although there have been times when IV remained at high levels, it seems IV returned towards longer term IV (>90 day) values more often.

A current relatively low implied volatility value can remain low.

After comparing current IV levels to past levels, as well as the current and past HV levels, does this appear to be an optimal time to purchase the option? Although you can't predict IV, its cyclic nature seems to favor selling the option rather than buying it. Because this may not be consistent with your directional outlook for the stock, you can consider the following:

- ✔ Monitoring the stock and option to see what happens to price and IV during the next few days
- ✔ Evaluating combination positions that are consistent with your outlook while allowing you to be a net seller of elevated IV
- ✔ Buying the option and hoping that when you wake up tomorrow IV has increased again or the stock has moved your way

Of course that last approach is not really one associated with disciplined trading. That said, it's something we've all experienced once or twice along the way in our careers. Anytime the word "hope" gets strongly associated with a position, alarm signals should go off in your head that it's a trade you need to avoid (or seriously consider exiting).

The margin requirement is the amount needed to establish a position while maintenance requirements are those needed to hold the position in the account.

Recognizing potential changes to volatility

When viewing IV charts you may notice seasonal tendencies. The most common reason for such periodic changes to volatility levels is the release of a quarterly earnings report.

Figure 15-4 displays a two-year IV chart for Cisco Systems, Inc. (CSCO). It provides a great example of seasonal tendencies for volatility.

Short options that are either naked or covered by another option generally have margin and maintenance requirements.

Figure 15-4:
Two-year
implied
volatility
chart for
CSCO.

A two-year chart was provided to show how consistent the increase in IV has been for CSCO, particularly for the shorter term options. The eight spikes on the chart coincide with earnings announcements for the company. This seasonality has persisted for years.

You may find you trade certain stocks and options, more frequently than others. By becoming familiar with IV charts and potential seasonality in this pricing component, you can better tailor strategies that meet current market conditions for the underlying and also anticipate future conditions. Although there are no guarantees IV will continue to exhibit a specific seasonal pattern, such an approach is consistent with putting the odds in your favor. If nothing else, you want to be aware that these conditions exist.

An implied volatility (IV) smile is the term used to describe the typical IV pattern for equity and index options, with IV levels lowest for the at-the-money (ATM) strike price options and increasing moderately as you move away from this central area.

When options are skewed

The Black-Scholes Option Pricing Model is the Nobel Prize-winning model created to price European Style options and serves as the basis for many other pricing models that followed. A significant model assumption is that implied volatility (IV) is constant across strike prices and expiration months. The reality is IV can vary across both, sometimes significantly. It's important to understand this so you can select the strategies and options that are the best given current conditions.

Skew is the term used to describe option IV levels that vary from normal conditions. The two types of skews include the following:

- ✔ **Price Skew:** Condition where certain options have atypically high IV compared to others expiring in the same month. The skew will often follow a pattern.

- ✔ **Time Skew:** Condition where options expiring in later months have atypically high IV compared to those expiring earlier.

Skews can exist when demand for specific contracts increase price. Calendar and diagonal spreads are optimal when the right time skew exists (see Chapter 12). Here strategies that have the most success when a price skew exists are discussed. There are two types of price skews:

- ✔ **Forward Price Skew:** Condition where higher strike price options of the same type have higher IV compared to those expiring in the same month.

- ✔ **Reverse Price Skew:** Condition where lower strike price options of the same type have higher IV compared to those expiring in the same month.

When trading option spreads, skews help increase the odds of profitability when you sell the relatively high IV options and buy the normal or relatively low IV options.

A forward price volatility skew exists when higher strike options have greater implied volatility than lower strike options.

Identifying volatility skews

A *skew chart* is a visual display of option IV versus strike price for each type of option by month. Figure 15-5 displays typical IV conditions with at-the-money (ATM) options having the lowest IV, increasing moderately as you move away from this strike price. Note the smile that results when a curved line is drawn through the data points.

Figure 15-5:
Typical
implied
volatility
skew for
CSCO.

A reverse price volatility skew exists when lower strike options have greater implied volatility than higher strike options.

Figure 15-6 displays a forward price skew and a reverse price skew. These skews can remain in place for extended periods of time and do not necessarily revert to the typical skew pattern. However, changing conditions can improve profits when using strategies that sell relatively high IV options and buy relatively low options.

Options analysis applications can save you a great deal of time searching for optimal market conditions for a specific strategy.

In addition to viewing a skew chart, you can locate volatility skews by using an options analysis application that scans the market for them. Figure 15-7 displays an output table for a basic IV scan seeking price skews. Positive values in the skew results reflects a price skew for the option pair listed.

Cisco Systems Inc.

Figure 15-6:
Forward
price skew
(left) and
reverse
price skew
(right) for
CSCO.

Click the option prices to get the Risk Graph.
Open Risk Graph in: ○ this window ● new window   New window size: [718x924 ▼]

Rank Close	Stock News	Strategy	Strike	Expire	Price (bid/ask)	Volume	Open Interest	Diff (Days)	Days to Expiration	IV (%)	Skew (%)	Ext Ratio
1 156.33	SPY news	Call Spread	Sell 155.00 Buy 163.00	Nov 2007 Nov 2007	4.35 0.65	998 66	39214 12823	0	35 35	18 14	30.74	4.65
2 156.33	SPY news	Call Spread	Sell 155.00 Buy 162.00	Nov 2007 Nov 2007	4.35 0.90	998 853	39214 15176	0	35 35	18 14	26.93	3.36
3 156.33	SPY news	Call Spread	Sell 155.00 Buy 161.00	Nov 2007 Nov 2007	4.35 1.22	998 2531	39214 9896	0	35 35	18 15	22.54	2.48
4 156.33	SPY news	Call Spread	Sell 155.00 Buy 160.00	Nov 2007 Nov 2007	4.35 1.59	998 1604	39214 42720	0	35 35	18 15	18.79	1.90
5 141.12	DIA news	Call Spread	Sell 140.00 Buy 146.00	Nov 2007 Nov 2007	3.35 0.65	1008 641	3506 3875	0	35 35	15 12	17.74	3.43
6 141.12	DIA news	Call Spread	Sell 140.00 Buy 142.00	Oct 2007 Oct 2007	1.77 0.58	4109 1470	14362 7435	0	7 7	14 12	16.20	1.12
7 165.90	MDY news	Call Spread	Sell 165.00 Buy 175.00	Nov 2007 Nov 2007	4.60 0.75	1 0	1107 148	0	35 35	19 17	14.43	4.93
8 156.33	SPY news	Call Spread	Sell 155.00 Buy 159.00	Nov 2007 Nov 2007	4.35 2.04	998 3475	39214 14101	0	35 35	18 16	14.38	1.48
9 141.12	DIA news	Call Spread	Sell 140.00 Buy 145.00	Nov 2007 Nov 2007	3.35 0.94	1008 610	3506 5665	0	35 35	15 13	13.83	2.37
10 165.90	MDY news	Call Spread	Sell 165.00 Buy 174.00	Nov 2007 Nov 2007	4.60 0.95	1 0	1107 117	0	35 35	19 17	13.01	3.89
11 97.22	HIG news	Call Spread	Sell 95.00 Buy 105.00	Nov 2007 Nov 2007	4.50 0.60	20 152	261 226	0	35 35	27 24	12.23	3.80
12 156.33	SPY news	Call Spread	Sell 155.00 Buy 158.00	Oct 2007 Oct 2007	2.17 0.59	11902 10020	58968 78933	0	7 7	16 14	11.79	1.42
13 101.09	PRU news	Call Spread	Sell 100.00 Buy 110.00	Nov 2007 Nov 2007	4.50 0.80	42 151	6041 1449	0	35 35	30 27	11.16	4.26
14 165.90	MDY news	Call Spread	Sell 165.00 Buy 173.00	Nov 2007 Nov 2007	4.60 1.20	1 0	1107 324	0	35 35	19 17	11.02	3.08

Figure 15-7:
Skew scan
output table
courtesy of
Optionetics
Platinum.

Taking advantage of skews

Trading opportunities emerge when a large IV skew exists, allowing you to
create combination positions for a smaller debit or a larger credit than when
normal conditions are in place. Skews can persist for the life of the option
in any expiration month, so there are no guarantees IV levels will return
to normal.

The ideal IV skew scenario is when the atypical IV results from temporary
contract demand — the demand may simply reflect institutional hedging for a
large stock position. In this instance the skew is likely temporary, allowing
you to capitalize as conditions return to normal.

Make sure you match your strategies to existing market conditions.

Understanding Ratio Spreads

Ratio spreads are similar to vertical spreads, but with an uneven number of long and short contracts. They are generally created for a net credit by selling more contracts than you buy. Unlike limited risk vertical spreads, the extra short contract(s) in a ratio spread creates risk that is either unlimited (call ratio spread) or limited, but high (put ratio spread). Given the high to unlimited risk for a ratio spread, you must know and execute your exit point for a loss prior to establishing a ratio spread. Trade management is key to risk management.

As part of the risk-reward trade-off, the maximum gain possible when creating a call ratio spread can actually exceed the initial credit you receive when establishing the position. Ratio backspreads, which are covered in the next section, arelimited risk alternative to ratio spreads.

Ratio spreads have an uneven amount of short and long options of the same type, with the number of short options exceeding the number of long options. As a result, the position incorporates naked options and has either unlimited risk (call ratio spreads) or limited but high risk (put ratio spread).

Reviewing ratio spread risk profiles

As you might expect by now, there are two types of ratio spreads you can create — one for each option type. So ratio spreads include

- ✔ Call ratio spreads
- ✔ Put ratio spreads

A review of these spreads follows, along with risk profiles and basic guidelines to consider when employing them. Always remember a ratio spread has limited reward with risk that is either high or unlimited.

Risk graphs provide a great, quick view of your potential risk and rewards with a strategy.

A call ratio spread has the following characteristics:

- ✔ Includes a long option plus a greater number of short options expiring the same month, with the short options having a higher strike price.
- ✔ Is used when your market outlook is bearish or moderately bullish for the underlying.
- ✔ Should be implemented for an initial credit.
- ✔ Generally uses a 1:2 or 2:3 ratio for long to short call options.

✔ Is best when a forward price skew exists for implied volatility (IV) because the higher strike price options are being sold.

✔ Is an unlimited risk position with high margins required due to one or more uncovered short calls.

The net credit for the position is the credit received from selling the short, higher strike calls minus the debit required to purchase the long, lower strike call. Although IV may be high for the short options when the position is initiated, maximum profits are achieved when the stock moves to the short option strike price at expiration.

Suppose XYZ is trading at $115.70 and you were evaluating this call ratio spread which expires in approximately 43 days:

✔ Buy 1 XYZ 110.00 Call @ $7.70 and simultaneously

✔ Sell 2 XYZ 115.00 Calls @ $4.20 each

Delta values may be measured on a scale from -100 to +100 or -10 or +1.0, both of which are acceptable.

Because a call ratio spread includes an unprotected short call, it's critical for you to identify and execute an exit criteria before you establish the position to minimize your risk if the stock moves upward.

The combined position brings in a credit of $70 and has a bearish directional bias (delta of ——38). It has unlimited risk, but limited reward. Calculating the potential reward is accomplished by breaking the position into a vertical debit spread (110-115) plus one short call (115) as follows:

Spread: $[(115 - 100) - (7.70 - 4.20)] \times 100 = \$150$

Short Call: $(4.20 - 100) = \$420$

Call Ratio Spread: $\$150 + 420 = \$570$

See Chapter 11 for details on calculating vertical spread risks, rewards and breakeven levels. Losses accumulate after XYZ moves above the upside breakeven which you calculate as follows:

Breakeven: Higher call strike + [(Difference in strikes × # of short calls) ÷ (# of short calls – # of long calls)] – net option prices*

Breakeven: $115.00 + (5 \times 2) \div (2 - 1) + 0.70 = 115.00 + 5.00 + 0.70 = 120.70$

* This is a negative value if there is a credit.

The worst-case scenario for the position is when XYZ moves upward above $120.70. Although your losses are capped for one of the short calls, they will accumulate as prices rise due to the remaining naked short call in the position.

The best-case scenario for the position is when XYZ closes at $115 on expiration, allowing you to keep the credit for the short calls while maximizing the value of the long call.

An option's intrinsic value is the value associated with the option's moneyness while the extrinsic value is the portion associated with time.

Figure 15-8 displays the risk graph for the XYZ call ratio spread.

Figure 15-8:
Risk graph
for 110–115
call ratio
spread.

Implementing this call ratio spread strategy provides you with a reasonably sized price range for profits given the time until expiration. The fact that profits can increase beyond the initial credit is also nice. Regardless, the thing that should really catch your attention is that downward sloping arrow displaying unlimited losses as prices rise.

Always contact your broker to obtain their specific margin and maintenance requirements for option combination positions.

A *put ratio spread* has the following characteristics:

- Includes a long option plus a greater number of short options expiring the same month, with the short options having a lower strike price.
- Is used when your market outlook is bullish or moderately bearish for the underlying.
- Should be implemented for an initial credit.
- Generally uses a 1:2 or 2:3 ratio for long to short put options.
- Is best when a reverse price skew exists for implied volatility (IV) because the lower strike price options are being sold.
- Is a limited, high-risk position with high margins required due to one or more uncovered short puts.

The net credit for the position is the credit received from selling the short, lower strike puts minus the debit required to purchase the long, lower strike put. Although IV may be high for the short options when the position is initiated, maximum profits are achieved when the stock moves to the short option strike price at expiration.

Because a put ratio spread includes an unprotected put option, it's critical for you to identify and execute an exit criteria before you establish the position to minimize your risk if the stock moves downward.

Always ask yourself, "What if I'm wrong on my outlook"? Know your risk.

Calculations for risk, reward, and breakevens for this position are similar to the call ratio spread, with some minor adjustments. A put ratio spread is a limited, but high risk as displayed by the risk graph in Figure 15-9.

Figure 15-9
Risk graph
for 110–105
put ratio
spread.

Ratio spreads generally rely on moderate movement once established.

The reward for the put ratio spread reaches the maximum when the stock trades at the lower strike price heading into expiration. Even though the stock can trade anywhere above the lower strike price to realize profits, the fact remains that a significant risk is taken for limited reward potential.

Identifying best conditions for ratio spreads

Because you are selling implied volatility (IV) on a net basis when using a ratio spread, optimal market conditions for either strategy is when IV is relatively high for the options being sold. This means the following:

- ✔ Capitalizing on a forward price skew when creating a call ratio spread
- ✔ Capitalizing on a reverse price skew when creating a put ratio spread

Elevated IV often accompanies elevated price volatility. However, both types of ratio spreads realize maximum reward when the stock settles down and its movement is limited to the short option strike price. Additional conditions to seek for ratio spreads include the following:

- **Call ratio spread:** When implementing this strategy you should also have a neutral to moderately bearish outlook on the stock because these conditions yield profits or limited risk. A strong bullish move for the underlying is extremely detrimental to the position, with unlimited losses possible.

- **Put ratio spread:** When implementing this strategy you should also have a neutral to moderately bullish outlook on the stock because these conditions yield profits or limited risk. A strong bearish move for the underlying is extremely detrimental to the position, with limited, but high losses possible.

When short options have very little time value remaining (say, less than $0.20), your chance of assignment goes up significantly.

The range of profitability for a ratio spread is dictated by both the long and short option strike prices, but generally tends to be narrow when implemented for a credit. As a result, the best conditions to implement a ratio spread is when there has been recent volatility in price of the underlying and that volatility is expected to subside.

Deciding your strategy

When deciding on which strategy to use, you need to consider both current market conditions and your future outlook for those conditions. Two areas to consider for option trading include

- Directional bias: bullish, bearish or sideways (neutral)
- Volatility bias: implied volatility and stock volatility

You can identify the current directional and volatility bias with price and volatility charts. Because volatility displays stronger seasonal tendencies and is often driven by scheduled reports, you can generally identify a more reliable IV outlook for the future than price.

The bottom line is that you want to use strategies that are consistent with current market conditions and can benefit if your outlook plays out. With this in mind, it's a good time to identify strategies that may be used in place of the unlimited risk call ratio spread or the limited but high risk put ratio spread.

When evaluating high or unlimited risk strategies, ask yourself if there are other strategies that can capitalize on the same market conditions.

Considering other bearish alternatives

A call ratio spread is best employed under forward volatility skew conditions (higher strike price options have higher IV) when you have a neutral to moderately bearish directional outlook for the stock.

Other strategies discussed that can also profit under such circumstances include

- ✔ Limited risk bearish call credit spread
- ✔ Limited risk bearish put debit spread
- ✔ Limited, but high risk covered call position
- ✔ Limited risk collar position

Although it generally takes more capital to initiate a combination position that includes stock (covered call or collar), keep in mind that a short option position has margin requirements that can increase the costs associated with a trade. Rather than an unlimited risk call ratio spread, it makes sense for you to consider alternate strategies that can reduce risk.

List the conditions that are optimal for each strategy you use in your trading.

Looking to gain with other bullish options

A put ratio spread is best employed under reverse volatility skew conditions (lower strike price options have higher IV) when you have a neutral to moderately bullish directional outlook for the stock.

Other strategies discussed that can also profit under such circumstances include:

- ✔ Limited risk bullish put credit spread
- ✔ Limited risk bullish call debit spread
- ✔ Limited, but high risk covered put position

Again while it takes more capital to initiate a combination position that includes stock (covered put), margin requirements for a put ratio spread must also be considered as part of the overall costs for the trade. Rather than a limited but high risk put ratio spread, it makes sense to consider other less risky strategies.

The next section identifies two strategies that take advantage of price skews when your directional outlook is stronger: ratio backspreads.

Exchange-traded funds (ETFs) can also be used in place of stocks for ratio spreads and ratio backspreads — just be sure to check implied volatility characteristics of the specific ETF.

Using Ratio Backspreads

Ratio backspreads are similar to ratio spreads because there are an uneven amount of long and short options of the same type. However this strategy has limited risk because you buy more option contracts than you sell. Although I generally avoid ratio spreads, I really like to trade ratio backspreads. Ratio backspreads are among my favorite strategies because the risk is limited while reward is potentially unlimited. Add to this the fact that you can create these positions for a credit, and then you get a sense of why I like them so much.

This section covers two types of ratio backspreads (call and put), along with risk profiles and optimal conditions for their use.

Ratio backspreads have an uneven number of short and long options, with the number of long options exceeding the number of short options. As a result, the position is like a vertical spread plus additional long option(s).

Defining ratio backspreads

You can create ratio backspreads using calls or puts, for either a debit or a credit. I prefer the latter because gains can actually go up from there. Here's some detail on the two types of backspreads:

A *call ratio backspread* has the following characteristics:

- ✔ Includes a short option plus a greater number of long options expiring the same month, with the long options having a higher strike price.
- ✔ Should be established when a reverse price skew exists for implied volatility (IV) because the lower strike price options are being sold.
- ✔ Is used when your market outlook is strongly bullish.
- ✔ Realizes the largest losses when the underlying closes at the long call strike price at expiration.
- ✔ Is most profitable when an explosive upward move occurs (increasing intrinsic and extrinsic long call value).
- ✔ Is best when implemented for an initial credit which allows the position to yield profits when the underlying declines modestly.
- ✔ Is a limited risk position with unlimited reward potential.

Ratio backspreads have risk that is limited while reward is potentially unlimited (call ratio backspread) or limited, but high (put ratio backspread).

A _put ratio backspread_ has the following characteristics:

- ✔ Includes a short option plus a greater number of long options expiring the same month, with the long options having a lower strike price.
- ✔ Should be established when a forward price skew exists for implied volatility (IV) because the higher strike price options are being sold.
- ✔ Is used when your market outlook is strongly bearish.
- ✔ Realizes the largest losses when the underlying closes at the long put strike price at expiration.
- ✔ Is most profitable when a strong bearish move occurs (increasing intrinsic and extrinsic long call value).
- ✔ Is best when implemented for an initial credit which allows the position to yield profits when the underlying rises modestly.
- ✔ Realizes the largest losses when the underlying closes at the long put strike price at expiration.
- ✔ Is a limited risk position with limited, but high reward potential.

Both positions can be established for a credit or debit. When paying a debit to enter the position, try to get as close to $0 as possible. In either case, it's best to maintain a short to long ratio multiple of 1:2 or 2:3 for these positions.

The most important thing to keep straight when entering a ratio backspread is that there are more long option contracts than short option contracts. This results in a position with short options that are covered.

Profiling call ratio backspread risk

When properly implementing a call ratio backspread you're taking advantage of a reverse price skew in volatility to improve trade odds and off-set long call costs. This is accomplished when you sell a lesser number of high implied volatility (IV) calls.

Your losses are greatest with a call ratio backspread when a moderately bullish move occurs and the underlying stock closes at the long call strike price at expiration. At this level the long calls expire worthless, while the short calls realize their maximum loss.

You may have more success finding ratio backspreads for a credit when you focus on stocks trading between $25 and $75 per share.

The trade does best when an explosive move upward occurs, increasing the long call moneyness and IV. Because long calls have unlimited profit potential, a call ratio backspread also has unlimited profit potential.

The initial credit for a call ratio backspread is

[(# of Short Calls × Short Call Price) – (# of Long Calls × Long Call Price)] × 100

The combination may result in a net debit rather than credit.

Your maximum risk occurs when the underlying expires at the long call strike price and is calculated as follows:

[(Number of Short Calls × Difference in Strike Prices) × 100] – Initial Credit (or + Initial Debit)

Your maximum reward is unlimited above the position breakeven level.

There are two breakevens for this position when it is established for a credit. The upside breakeven is calculated as follows:

Higher Strike Price + [(Difference in Strikes × # of Short Calls) ÷ (# of Long Calls – # of Short Calls)] + net option prices*

There is no downside breakeven if the trade is established for a debit. In the event the position is created for a credit downside breakeven is calculated as follows:

Lower Strike Price + (Net Option Prices* ÷ # of Short Calls)

* This is a negative value if there is a credit.

Margin requirements are dictated by your brokerage company.

Call ratio backspread example

While completing a volatility scan, you find a reverse skew for options on a consumer discretionary company that are expiring in 67 days. The longer term chart looks bullish, but because you're approaching a traditionally bearish period for the market you decide to evaluate a slightly out-of-the-money (OTM) call ratio backspread. Assume ABC is trading at $69.90 when you note the reverse price skew. You analyze the following trade:

- ✔ Buy 3 ABC 75.00 Calls @ $0.60 and simultaneously
- ✔ Sell 2 ABC 70.00 Calls @ $2.45

The net credit for the position is $310, [(2 × 2.45) – (3 × 0.60)] × 100. The best move for the stock is one that is strongly bullish, but if the stock follows the market downward, the position will still be profitable.

Using a delta neutral approach to ratio backspread positions may increase your strategy success.

Figure 15-10 displays the skew chart for the ABC options expiring in 67 days.

Figure 15-10:
Reverse
skew chart
for potential
call
backspread
trade.

Altria Group Inc.
Jun07 Implied Volatility Skew Chart

Identify your risk, reward, and breakevens when you evaluate a potential trade.

Calculating other important trade values you obtain the following:

✔ **Maximum Risk:** Your maximum risk occurs when the underlying expires at the long call strike price, or 75:

[(Number of Short Calls × Difference in Strike Prices) × 100] – Initial Credit (or + Initial Debit)

[(2 × 5) × 100] – $310 = $690

✔ **Maximum Reward:** Unlimited above the position breakeven level.

✔ **Upside Breakeven:** There are two breakevens for this position since it is established for a credit.

Higher Strike Price + [(Difference in Strikes × # of Short Calls) ÷ (# of Long Calls – # of Short Calls)] + Net Option Prices*

75 + [(5 × 2) ÷ (3 – 2)] – 3.10 = 81.90

* This is a negative value if there is a credit.

✔ Downside breakeven:

Lower Strike Price + (Net Credit / # of Short Calls)

70 + 1.55 = 71.55

The initial credit and debit amounts usually refer to the total amount received as a credit or paid as a debit. When calculating breakeven values, it refers to the option prices themselves, without the option contract multiplier.

Figure 15-11 displays the risk graph for the ABC call ratio backspread.

Risk management is an important aspect of all trades — including those with limited risk. Have an exit plan that includes purchasing the short leg of a ratio backspread when you want to avoid assignment.

From the time the position was established until the last trading day before expiration, this stock barely moved — it closed at $70.65. The short options were $0.65 in-the-money (ITM) and were bought back at $0.65 ($130) to avoid weekend assignment. These conditions are far from optimal for the strategy, but you ended up making $180 [$310 − $130]. That really is not too bad.

Sometimes it's exciting to see a textbook example of a trade, but in this case I think it's even better to see a trade where conditions aren't optimal or things don't really go as expected and you still have gains. That's pretty powerful. See the end of this chapter for hints on creating call ratio backspreads with the best chances of success.

Figure 15-11: Risk graph for the 70–75 call ratio backspread.

Profiling put ratio backspread risk

When evaluating a put ratio backspread, you want to look for a forward price skew on the implied volatility (IV) so that the higher strike price put — those being sold — have the higher IV. You then buy a larger number of lower strike prices, lower IV puts, ideally for a credit.

Your losses are greatest with a put ratio backspread when a moderately bearish move occurs and the underlying stock closes at the long put strike price at expiration. At this level the long puts expire worthless, while the short puts realize their maximum loss.

If placing a ratio backspread order with a broker, keep the order as simple as possible by specifying both the long and short options along with the number of contracts for each. Avoid a lot of terminology shortcuts that could result in placing the wrong type of ratio spread.

The trade does best when an explosive move downward occurs, increasing the long put moneyness and IV. Because long puts have limited but high profit potential, a put ratio backspread also has limited, but high profit potential.

The initial credit for a put ratio backspread is:

[(# of Short Puts × Short Put Price) – (# of Long Puts × Long Put Price)] × 100

The combination may result in a net debit rather than credit.

Your maximum risk occurs when the underlying expires at the long put strike price and is calculated as follows:

[(Number of Short Puts × Difference in Strike Prices) × 100] – Initial Credit (or + Initial Debit)

Your maximum reward is limited, but high to the downside since the underlying stock can only fall to zero.

Ratio backspreads have an upper and lower breakeven value.

There is no upside breakeven if the trade is established for a debit and two breakevens when created for a credit. The upside breakeven is calculated as follows:

Higher Strike Price + (Net Option Prices* ÷ # of Short Puts)

* This is a negative value if there is a credit.

In the event the position is created for a credit downside breakeven is calculated as follows:

Lower Strike Price – [(Difference in Strikes × # of Short Puts) ÷ (# of Long Puts – # of Short Puts)] – Net Option Prices*

* This is a negative value if there is a credit.

Margin requirements are dictated by your brokerage company — be sure to contact them for specifics!

This time when scanning IV you find a minor forward price skew for a stock with a pending news that could be bearish. The stock is in the brokerage business and is trading at $73.85. There's a moderate skew between the 75 and 65 strike price puts. Because the stock is volatile, you look at a shorter term ratio put backspread in case stock takes off higher instead. You consider the following trade:

Buy 2 XYZ 65.00 Put @ $2.75 and Sell 1 XYZ 75.00 Puts @ $7.20 each

The combined position brings in a credit of $170, $[(1 \times 7.20) - (2 \times 2.75)] \times 100$.

A typical ATM IV chart is said to display an IV smile which refers to the image produced when the IV points are connected. When you find volatility skews, identify the strategies you can implement to take advantage of the skew.

To evaluate other important trade data you obtain the following:

Your maximum risk occurs when the stock expires at 65. This maximum risk is:

[(Number of Short Puts × Difference in Strike Prices) × 100] – Initial Credit (or + Initial Debit)

$[(1 \times 10) \times 100] - \$170 = \$830$

Your maximum reward occurs if the stock goes to zero. You can calculate this maximum reward by breaking the position into a put credit spread and a long put, and assuming the stock goes to zero:

Spread: $[(7.20 - 2.75) - [(75 - 65)] \times 100 = (\$555)$

Put: $[(65 - 0) - 2.75] \times 100 = \$6,225$

Put Gain – Spread Loss = $6,225 – 555 = $5,670

There are two breakevens when created for a credit. The upside breakeven is calculated as follows:

Higher Strike Price + (Net Option Prices* ÷ # of Short Puts)

$75 - (1.70/1) = 73.30$

* This is a negative value if there is a credit.

The downside breakeven is calculated as follows:

Lower Strike Price – [(Difference in Strikes × # of Short Puts) ÷ (# of Long Puts – # of Short Puts)] – Net Option Prices*

$65 - [(10 \times 1) \div (2 - 1)] + 1.70 = 56.70$

* This is a negative value if there is a credit.

Always consider the margin requirements necessary to implement a trade.

Because the stock is already trading above the upside breakeven and the reward to risk is reasonable, you establish the position. You'll allow the trade to expire if the stock continues upward and exit one month prior expiration if a move down has occurred.

Figure 15-12 displays the risk graph for the XYZ put ratio backspread.

Figure 15-12: Risk graph for the 75–65 put ratio backspread.

Recognize that all trades don't play out in textbook fashion — manage your risk so you can build experience that allows you to most effectively manage different trades.

The stock was near a peak when the trade was put in place. About three weeks before your exit date the stock reaches a low and bounces back. On your planned exit date, the stock has reached the low again and is moving upward. It's possible a double-bottom has formed. Regardless, this is your planned exit date.

The stock is trading at $55.08 when exit the put ratio backspread. Both options were in-the-money (ITM) and the short options were bought back at $20.20 ($2,020) and the long options sold for $10.70 ($2,140) for an additional profit of $120. The position gain was $290 because it was initially established for a credit.

It can be difficult to find ratio backspreads for a credit, but by understanding the IV conditions that are optimal for these types of trades, you have a much better chance of locating credits. If you do establish the position for a debit, try to keep that debit as low as possible.

The trickiest option to manage at expiration is a barely out-of-the-money (OTM) short option leg that is covered by another expiring option. If the short option is at-the-money (ATM) or even slightly OTM while your long option is OTM, you could have the short option assigned after the long option has expired. Always manage your risk by actively managing the assignment possible as much as possible.

Spotting best conditions for ratio backspreads

Both ratio spreads and ratio backspreads rely on volatility price skews for best results. Although backspreads are clearly the preferred strategy — you have unlimited to high rewards for the ratio backspread versus unlimited to high risk for the ratio spread — your outlook for the stock ultimately determines which strategy is reasonable.

Price skews provide ratio backspread opportunities while time skews provide calendar spread opportunities.

Putting a call ratio backspread to work

A call ratio backspread combines a lower strike, short call with a greater number of higher strike, long calls that expire in the same month. The risk for the position is limited, while the potential gain is unlimited.

When seeking a call ratio backspread position, look for the following market conditions:

- ✔ A reverse price skew in implied volatility (IV) so the lower strike short calls have a greater IV than the higher strike long calls.
- ✔ Bullish conditions for the underlying stock, with the potential for an explosive move upward (i.e. very favorable report).
- ✔ A potential increase in IV for both options.

When noting the above conditions are in place, here are some additional tips to help you successfully implement a call ratio backspread:

- ✔ Even though the trade can be created for a credit, losses occur when there is limited movement in the stock. Identify a maximum loss amount for the combined position and exit the position if it is reached.
- ✔ Keep the ratios you use to multiples of 1:2 or 2:3 at most. Calculate net delta to determine which ratio best minimizes directional bias for the position.
- ✔ Seek an initial credit. If you create the trade for a debit, keep that debit as low as possible.

✔ Use options with 90 days to expiration when possible to allow time to for the stock to continue an upward move.

✔ Focus on stocks valued between $25 and 75 per share.

✔ Consider exiting an equal number of long and short calls when the position has 50% profit above the upper breakeven. This allows for profit-taking while leaving one or more long calls in place for additional profits.

✔ Exit the position with 30 days to expiration when time decay negatively impacts the long calls — be particularly diligent when the stock is trading between the two call strike prices which represents the area of maximum risk.

✔ Never hold an in-the-money (ITM), at-the-money (ATM) or slightly out-of-the-money (OTM) short option into expiration weekend. Manage your assignment risk by buying the short option back to cover the position.

Successfully implementing a call ratio backspread strategy takes a little time to find the proper market conditions and identify options that work best. This means it's perfectly suited to paper trading for honing your skills. You'll find the time you invest can be well worth it.

Paper trading is a great way to gain experience with different strategy dynamics.

Making the most of put ratio backspreads

A put ratio backspread combines a higher strike, short put with a greater number of lower strike, long puts that expire in the same month. The risk for the position is limited, while the potential gain is limited, but high.

When seeking a put ratio backspread position, look for the following market conditions:

✔ A forward price skew in implied volatility (IV) so the higher strike short puts have a greater IV than the lower strike long puts — generally low implied volatility conditions will help.

✔ Bearish conditions for the underlying stock, with the potential for an explosive move downward (i.e. unfavorable report).

✔ A potential increase in IV for both options.

Never assume a short out-of-the-money (OTM) option will expire worthless. Always monitor conditions through expiration weekend to confirm you have not been assigned on a short option.

When noting the above conditions are in place, here are some additional tips to help you successfully implement a put ratio backspread:

✔ Even though the trade can be created for a credit, losses occur when there is limited movement in the stock. Identify a maximum loss amount for the combined position and exit the position if it is reached.

✔ Keep the ratios you use to multiples of 1:2 or 2:3 at most. Calculate net delta to determine which ratio best minimizes directional bias for the position.

✔ Seek an initial credit. If you create the trade for a debit, keep that debit as low as possible.

✔ Use options with 90 days to expiration when possible to allow time for the stock to continue an upward move.

✔ Paper trade the strategy to hone your trade selection skills and understand how changes in the underlying impact the position value throughout its life.

✔ Consider exiting an equal number of long and short puts when the position has 50% profit below the lower breakeven. This allows for profit-taking while leaving one or more long puts in place for additional profits.

✔ Exit the position with 30 days to expiration when time decay negatively impacts the long puts — be particularly diligent when the stock is trading between the two put strike prices which represents the area of maximum risk.

✔ Never hold an in-the-money (ITM), at-the-money (ATM), or slightly out-of-the-money (OTM) short option into expiration weekend. Manage your assignment risk by buying the short option back to cover the position.

Again, successfully implementing a put ratio backspread strategy takes time and practice. If it didn't require an effort, everyone would be doing it.

Chapter 16

Capitalizing When Markets Move Sideways

. . . .

In This Chapter

▶ Boosting current returns

▶ Trading sideways markets

▶ Understanding spread impact

. . . .

*A*lthough people generally think about the markets moving in one of two possible directions, it also spends significant time moving in a third direction: sideways. Major averages, sectors, and individual securities all display varying degrees of trending (up or down) and trendless (sideways) conditions.

Option strategies are unique because they allow you to realize profits when sideways movement is in place. By using options, you can reap additional rewards on existing positions or trade the markets with limited risk. Long butterflies and condors are two such strategies introduced here.

Winning Positions in Sideways Markets

You have two dilemmas when the markets move sideways:

✔ Dealing with stagnant returns on existing positions

✔ Finding gains with new positions

You may find yourself getting restless when sideways movement persists, wondering whether you should close out current positions and when things will get moving again (and in which direction). Although I don't know the exact statistics on how much time the market spends in such a "trendless" mode, I do know that because I trade options it doesn't really matter all that much. Let's look first at position management when the market settles into a sideways trading range.

Managing existing positions

Long calls allow you to realize gains from bullish moves while long puts allow you to realize gains from bearish moves. When the markets are spending time moving sideways, you can realize gains by combining positions. Hopefully by now you're comfortable with combination positions because there are so many different ones available to you. As a starting point, options can be added to existing stock or exchange-traded funds (ETFs) to boost returns when the markets seem to be directionless.

As a general rule of thumb for initiating new positions, you want to sell premium when implied volatility is relatively high and buy it when it is relatively low.

Sideways gains: DELL case study

Suppose it's late 2001 and you purchased Dell Computer Corporation (DELL) for $24.00 because technology names were finally strengthening. This came after a long decline in this sector and you felt DELL was a leader in its field. You identify $22.00 as your stop-loss exit point, which represents a decline of 8.3%.

After a move upward in price, DELL has stalled a bit. You re-evaluate some of the technical indicators you prefer under such conditions and decide the longer term outlook for DELL remains bullish. Rather than having the asset just sit there, you evaluate a covered call strategy to increase your returns.

In March 2002, DELL is trading at $26.50, about 10% higher than where you purchased it. You note that historical volatility (HV) and implied volatility (IV) are relatively low for the stock compared to the last 12 months, so you monitor conditions to see if IV strengthens at all. You also note that the next quarterly earnings report for DELL is due in mid-May.

Leg is the term used to describe each individual security in a combined position.

Selling a call against a long stock position doesn't protect it — it moderately reduces risk by reducing your net costs.

Because you'd prefer to keep the shares of DELL, you rule out the two in-the-money (ITM) calls with a strike price of 25.00. You also note that the May earnings report is due one day prior to May expiration and decide to wait until you are closer to that time to capture an IV boost for options expiring in May. Instead of May options, you focus on the Apr 27.50 and 30.00 strike price calls expiring April 19.

After capturing the sideways price movement by drawing a linear regression channel from the share purchase date to the current date, you extend the channel lines to the right to monitor price changes. See Chapter 6 for more information on price movements and projections using this technical tool.

Selling the Apr 30.00 will barely break-even after commission, so you sell the Apr 27.50 call for $0.70. You note there is a 39% chance the shares will be called using pricing model assumptions (delta = 39.1). You also note the upward directional bias for the position has been reduced from +100 to +60.9.

Volume levels may provide hints about the direction of a breakout from a consolidation pattern, as well as its chance of success. Volume should increase with the breakout. Adding a moving average line to volume data helps with this approach.

DELL traded in a range from $27.13 to 27.70 on the Friday before expiration, closing at $27.34. You retained the shares. After April expiration, you note the following:

- ✔ Your indicators remain long-term bullish for DELL, while the short-term view remains flat.

- ✔ IV levels are relatively low and they will likely increase as you get closer to the quarterly earnings report.

- ✔ Because the earnings report is so close to expiration, you'll sell a May call when IV increases and roll that option to June after earnings are released. This assumes DELL remains within its sideways channel and you remain long-term bullish on the stock.

Bollinger bands are bands constructed above and below a simple moving average, using a standard deviation calculation. As a result, the expansion and contraction of the bands coincide with expanding and contracting volatility.

DELL moves down to its lower Bollinger band near the end of April, but remains well within its sideways channel. It then moves back to its 20-day simple moving average (SMA) with an increase in IV a couple of days later. Once again it is trading near $26.50 and you evaluate May 27.50 and 30.00 strike calls. Figure 16-1 displays the current 12-month at-the-money (ATM) IV chart for DELL.

Even if you can realize additional gains by selling calls against an existing stock position, it doesn't mean you should necessarily hold onto that position. Consider both your shorter term and longer term outlook for the security before you decide whether to offset position cost by selling calls against it.

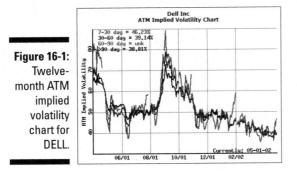

The cost basis for DELL is now $23.30, because the covered calls that were sold for $0.70 expired worthless. Although IV increased for the Apr 27.50 call, time decay had a greater impact on the option premiums. You decide to sell the May 27.50 strike call for $0.55.

Do not sell calls against a position you are not willing to part with. Although a stock can seem to spend lengthy periods of time moving sideways, it can explode upward at any time.

Four days after the call was sold, DELL declined rapidly through the lower regression channel line, but remained above your stop-loss exit price. The stock once again rebounds, but you do note there are wider Bollinger bands and longer daily price bars, indicating conditions are getting more volatile.

Expectations are bullish on the day earnings are set to be released (after the close) and DELL moves up to $27.85. The report is good and the stock opens up an additional $0.42 with movement remaining within the channel lines. You roll out the May call to June and also roll it up from 27.50 to 30.00 to minimize the risk of being called out of a longer term bullish position.

The IV for the May 27.50 call sky-rocketed with one day remaining to expiration, resulting in a $0.30 loss for the Apr 27.50 call. The position cost basis rises to $23.60. The June options did not realize the same magnitude spike in IV. You tell yourself to remember that for next time. As a result of selling the June call, your cost basis declines to $22.90.

Conditions deteriorate and DELL closes at 23.98 on the Friday of expiration weekend in June. You allow the Jun 30.00 strike price call option to expire worthless and decide to re-evaluate the stock position over the weekend. The short-term trend is downward and on a longer term basis it appears a more bearish picture has emerged. You elect to sell the stock at the open on Monday, rather than protecting the position with a collar (long put-short call).

Figure 16-2 displays the daily bar chart for DELL with a regression channel based on nearly five months of trading. The vertical lines denote stock entry and exit days, as well as short call transaction days. Volume data with a 20-day moving average and the directional movement indicator (DMI) are also included.

The stock was sold for $23.68 for a net gain of $0.78 per share, when the short call positions are included. These results do not include commissions, which would have added approximately $0.60 for an active trader (option and stock commissions). Although this is certainly significant, compare this to a net loss inclusive of stock commissions (approximately $0.52 per share) if the stock was held by itself until this time. These values translate to a 0.8% gain for the covered call approach versus a 2.2% buy and hold loss.

When a stock is consolidating and its volatility decreases, implied volatility (IV) for the stock's options will likely also decrease. This creates an environment that's not ideal for covered call strategies because premiums are decreasing. Regardless, the strategy can still be profitably implemented.

Figure 16-2: Daily price chart for DELL with regression channel.

Strategy comments

As it turns out, DELL had one more daily close below the lower regression channel line in late July 2002 and a few closes above the upper regression channel in early November 2002, before finally breaking out above the sideways consolidation pattern in May 2003. The price remained within the channel range all but a handful of days for 18 months.

The covered call strategy could have been continued for profits throughout this period. Had the stock been called away during the May 2003 breakout, it could have been purchased again later that month when DELL returned to test the upper channel line, which now serves as support.

Do not place a standing stop-loss order for the underlying stock used in a covered call strategy. In the event the stop is triggered, you'll be left holding a short, naked call which is an unlimited risk position.

While reviewing the DELL case study, hopefully you noted the following important points:

- The short call does not protect the stock position; it will typically just reduce the cost basis which moderately decreases risk

- You still need to manage your risk by identifying a stop-loss exit level, even if that means buying back a short call option to exit the stock

- Historical volatility and implied volatility both generally decrease when a stock is in a trading range

- Earnings reports and other company and economic-related news can significantly impact implied volatility even when price is basically moving sideways

- You should consider your longer term view for the long stock position because there is potential for limited, but high losses with such a strategy

- As an alternate approach, a long-term put can be purchased while the calls are sold each month to protect the downside

- Short calls that close in-the-money (ITM) may be rolled out a month and up a strike price for a modest gain when the stock moves upward

- Commissions can significantly impact trade results

- Other trading costs such as tax consequences need to be considered when implementing this or any trading strategy

- Trading rules based on stop-loss exits and regression channel breaks help implement a strategy successfully while managing risk

- Paper trading provides you with issues that can arise when implementing a new strategy, such as the price impact of IV versus time

- When a breakout away from a longer term consolidation occurs, it's common for the stock to return to test the pattern

If you exit or get called out of a position while implementing a covered call strategy during a consolidation, a move back to the pattern may provide you with an opportunity to establish a new directional position in the stock.

A LEAPS contract is a long-term option available for certain underlying indexes, exchange-traded funds, and stocks. These contracts generally have more than 9 months to 2½ years to expiration and become regular options after that time decreases.

When selling calls on a long stock or ETF position, you increase the number of ways the stock can move while still allowing for gains. You also limit your potential gains if an explosive upside move occurs. That's simply a strategy trade-off you need to weigh when considering different trade approaches.

Option strategies for sideways moves

The covered call strategy is just one that can yield gains during sideways trading periods. As mentioned in the Strategy Comments, you may elect to protect the stock position with a longer term put option, and then selling calls each month until a breakout occurs or the long put expiration month nears.

In addition to stock and option combination positions, you can extend the same concept to just option combination positions using a Long-term Equity AnticiPation Securities (LEAPS) contract in place of the stock leg. This approach will typically reduce risk by reducing the overall cost of the position.

Managing risk comes before bringing in income. If you feel prolonged sideways movement for a security you hold may set up a more bearish outlook for the stock, either exit the position or protect it with puts.

Things to consider with option combinations

One advantage options generally have over the individual stocks and exchange-traded funds (ETFs) that serve as the underlying for the options is that they generally require less of an investment. The end result is that you have less money at risk. The trade-off is that the entire asset can expire worthless. And so it goes for you on the trading side — there are a series of things to consider for every asset type you decide to use. That is why managing your risk is a common thread throughout. The only security considered to be risk-free is a U.S. Treasury Bill.

 When a stock moves sideways for a period of time it is said to be in a consolidation phase. The longer the consolidation, the greater the chance for a strong directional move away from this consolidation.

Rather than a portfolio of individual stocks or ETFs, you may hold LEAPS contracts for different sectors or stocks. A covered call strategy can also be implemented using the LEAPS option as the sideways moving asset from which you're boosting your income. There are a few things to consider if you go this route:

✔ Use a LEAPS contract as an underlying will subject you to margin requirements because the position technically represents a spread, not a pure covered call position.

✔ Spread strategies require a different option approval level from your broker — you may or may not be able to access these strategies depending on the account type (i.e. IRAs).

✔ Because LEAPS are also subject to the same pricing factors as a regular option contract, implied volatility (IV) conditions that are good for selling calls are not necessarily optimal for buying LEAPS. The strategy may work best on an existing position.

✔ The double-edge sword of IV may result in conditions where you're better off selling your LEAPS contract which may have declined less than the underlying asset itself.

In addition to a LEAPS strategy, additional income may be generated from a calendar strategy using simply an existing long call. In this case, shorter term calls are sold against a long call for the same underlying. Risk is moderately reduced by reducing your net investment in the position and the same considerations apply as those listed for a LEAPS short call approach.

The option term *roll out* refers to the process where an existing option position is closed with an off-setting transaction and a new similar position is created for a later expiration month.

Strategy short-list

A few strategies covered in this book that can either provide gains during sideways markets, moderately reduce risk, or both include the following:

✔ Long stock — covered call (limited but high risk position)

✔ Call credit spread (slightly out-of-the-money)

✔ Put credit spread (slightly out-of-the-money)

✔ Call calendar

✔ Put calendar

✔ Call ratio spread (unlimited risk position)

✔ Put ratio spread (limited but high risk position)

Next up, two limited risk strategies specifically designed to benefit from sideways market action — the butterfly and the condor.

Understanding Butterfly Positions

A butterfly is a strategy specifically designed to gain when a stock or ETF is trading sideways. Some characteristics of the strategy include the following:

- ✔ Limited risk and limited reward
- ✔ Can be created using calls or puts
- ✔ Combines two vertical spreads
- ✔ Is shorter term in nature
- ✔ Is generally created for a debit
- ✔ Maximizes gains when the underlying security remains within a trading range dictated by the option strike prices

A variation on the basic butterfly is the iron butterfly which combines calls and puts. This position is generally created for a credit with time decay working in its favor.

A sideways moving market can also be referred to as trendless or directionless.

Defining the long butterfly

As with most of the strategies in this book, the butterfly comes in two varieties:

- ✔ Long call butterfly
- ✔ Long put butterfly

Both of these strategies combine a vertical credit spread and a vertical debit spread to capitalize on sideways moves in the markets. The strategy name comes from the three options used to create the position, as follows:

- ✔ Body: two short options of the same type
- ✔ Wing 1: one long lower strike price option
- ✔ Wing 2: one long higher strike price option

Generally the short option strike prices are at-the-money (ATM) or near the money, with profits maximized when the underlying closes at expiration at the short option strike price.

Always consider different strategies suitable to current market conditions. You may decide that an alternate strategy does a better job of reducing your risk.

Call butterfly

A long call butterfly combines a bull call spread and bear call spread, using the same strike price for the short leg of each. It is a limited risk, limited reward position that is profitable during range-bound trading for the underlying stock or ETF.

The butterfly is constructed by creating two spreads:

- A bull call spread with a short option strike price that is near or at-the-money (ATM)
- A bear call spread with the same short option strike price as the bull call spread

The maximum risk for the position is the initial debit, which is determined by subtracting the bear call spread credit from the bull call spread debit. See Chapter 11 for more information on vertical spreads.

The best way to think about risks and rewards for a butterfly is to remember it combines two vertical spreads.

The long call butterfly strike prices compare to the spread strikes as follows:

- The lower strike price long call in the bull call spread is the lowest strike price call in the butterfly position and serves as the first wing.
- The two short options represent the next higher strike price and represent the body.
- The last call is the highest strike price in the group and comes from the long call in the bear call spread position.

Because the short options are approximately ATM, profits are maximized with the strategy when the stock moves very little and closes at the short option strike price on the last trading day before expiration. At this level three of the four options expire worthless. The lower priced long call will be ITM by an amount equal to the butterfly spread.

As price moves away from the short option strike price, profits diminish to the position breakeven levels where they are equal to zero. Beyond these price levels, the initial debit is the maximum risk.

Because a butterfly combines three different options, you must consider trading costs when evaluating a specific position.

Suppose it's late July and you feel the market has finally settled into vacation doldrums after some initial summer volatility. You note the ADX is declining below 20 and the 20-day and 30-day simple moving averages (SMAs) are relatively flat.

The Diamonds ETF (DIA), which is based on the Dow Jones Industrials, is trading at $106.48 and you evaluate a few long call butterfly alternatives with August 106 calls serving as the strike price for the short options (body).

Figure 16-3 displays the daily price chart for DIA with the ADX and SMAs.

Because butterflies combine vertical spreads there are margin requirements for the position.

Different DIA butterfly spreads are discussed in the next section, so for now, assume the Aug 103-106-109 call butterfly spread was established. This trade shorthand translates to the following:

- Long 1 Aug 103 Call @ $4.00
- Short 2 Aug 106 Calls @ $1.45
- Long 1 Aug 109 Call @ $0.30

Figure 16-3:
Daily price chart for DIA.

Calculating the net debit for these options you obtain the following:

[(Wing 1 Option Price + Wing 2 Option Price) – (2 × Body Option Price)] × 100

[(4.00 + 0.30) – (2 × 1.45)] × 100 = $140

To remember which options are long and short in the butterfly strategy, imagine a butterfly with a short body and long wings.

Figure 16-4 displays the risk chart for this butterfly position.

Figure 16-4: Risk chart for DIA Aug 103-106-109 call butterfly.

When maximum risk is identified for a position with short options, it's assumed that assignment risk will be managed properly by 1) meeting any assignment obligations with existing shares or exercising a long call, or 2) closing out any short options that could be potentially assigned over expiration weekend.

As always, you need to know the risk, reward, and breakevens for the position:

- ✔ **Maximum Risk:** The initial debit of $140 is the maximum risk for the DIA Aug 103-106-109 call butterfly position.

- ✔ **Maximum Reward:** There are a couple of ways to calculate the maximum reward for the position. You can either calculate each spread separately (as shown) or use a single butterfly formula (put butterfly example).

- ✔ **Bull call spread:**

    [(Difference Between Strikes) – (Long Option Price – Short Option Price)] × 100

    [(106 – 103) – (4.00 – 1.45)] × 100] = (3 – 2.55)] × 100 = $45.00

- ✔ **Bear call spread:** Initial credit

     ($1.45 − 0.30) × 100 = $115

- ✔ **Call butterfly:**

     Bull call spread maximum reward + Bear call spread maximum reward

     $45 + $115 = $160

- ✔ **Upper breakeven:**

     Highest strike price − initial debit

     109.00 − 1.40 = $107.60

- ✔ **Lower breakeven:**

     Lowest strike price + initial debit

     103.00 + 1.40 = $104.40

Options that are slightly out-of-the-money (OTM) on the last trading day before expiration will almost always have some offer price available, allowing you to buy it back at $0.05 or less plus commissions, to eliminate assignment risk.

As expiration approaches, the following four distinct areas are where the stock could be trading. If you elect to sell any long option legs to either realize gains or minimize losses, be sure to also buy back the corresponding short option. The four areas are

- ✔ **Underlying below lowest strike:** All options will expire worthless realizing the maximum loss.

- ✔ **Underlying from the lower breakeven to the short strike price:** Close out the bull call spread for profits and allow the bear call spread to expire worthless.

- ✔ **Underlying between the short strike price and upper breakeven:** Close out the bull call spread plus the additional short call for profits.

- ✔ **Underlying above highest strike price:** Close out both spreads and realize maximum loss.

If assigned early on a short option, use the corresponding long option or evaluate costs to buy shares in the market to meet the short obligation (see To Exercise or Not in Chapter 9).

Don't allow long options to expire worthless while you still have short option assignment risk. Properly manage a butterfly position into expiration weekend by focusing on potential risk.

In the DIA example provided, the ETF was trading at 105.73 into the close on the Friday before expiration. The bull call spread was closed out for $255 by completing the following transactions:

- ✔ Buy to Close 1 Aug 106 call @ $0.05 and simultaneously
- ✔ Sell to Close 1 Aug 103 call @ $2.60

Both options making up the bear call spread expired worthless. Because the initial debit was $140, the position gain was $115 ($255 – 140).

If you have a slightly bullish to neutral outlook you can purchase a call butterfly using an out-of-the-money (OTM) instead of at-the-money (ATM) body.

Put butterfly

A long put butterfly combines a bull put spread and bear put spread, using the same strike price for the short leg of each spread. It is a limited risk, limited reward position that is profitable during range-bound trading for the underlying stock or ETF.

The butterfly is constructed by creating two spreads:

- ✔ A bull put spread with a short option strike price that is near or at-the-money (ATM)
- ✔ A bear put spread with the same short option strike price as the bull put spread

The maximum risk for the position is the initial debit, which is determined by subtracting the bull put spread credit from the bear put spread debit. See Chapter 11 for more information on vertical spreads.

Calculate the net delta for the butterfly to identify the directional bias for the position.

Because both positions focus on range-bound markets, what would have happened if a put butterfly was used in place of a call butterfly for the DIA example? Before checking out an Aug 103-106-109 put butterfly for DIA, consider a few questions first — keep in mind DIA was trading at $106.48 when the position was initiated and closed at $105.73 going into expiration:

- ✔ Would you expect the put butterfly spread to be higher or lower than call butterfly spread, assuming the same strike prices were used?
- ✔ Using your first answer, would the range of profitability for the put butterfly be more or less than the call butterfly?
- ✔ Would you expect the gains for the put butterfly to be higher or lower?

Long put butterfly

Okay, it's late July . . . vacation doldrums . . . market's flat.

DIA is trading at $106.48 and you're evaluating a long put butterfly spread with August 106 puts serving as the short option strike price (body). Assuming you purchase the Aug 103-106-109 put butterfly spread, the following position was created:

- ✔ Long 1 Aug 109 Put @ $2.85
- ✔ Short 2 Aug 106 Puts @ $0.85
- ✔ Long 1 Aug 103 Put @ $0.30

WARNING!

Look for liquid options to avoid additional trading costs in the form of slippage, which is the difference between the bid-ask spread. These costs can be significant given the number of legs used to create butterflies.

Calculating the net debit for these options you obtain the following:

[(Wing 1 Option Price + Wing 2 Option Price) – (2 × Body Option Price)] × 100

[(2.85 + 0.30) – (2 × 0.85)] × 100 = $145

Figure 16-5 displays the risk chart for this butterfly position.

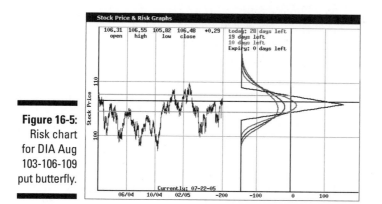

Figure 16-5: Risk chart for DIA Aug 103-106-109 put butterfly.

If you flip back quickly to Figure 16-4, you can hardly tell the difference between the two butterflies. Calculating the risk, reward and breakevens for the position you have:

- **Maximum risk:** The initial debit of $145 is the maximum risk for the DIA Aug 103-106-109 put butterfly position.

- **Maximum reward:** The maximum reward for a long butterfly position is a single spread value minus the initial debit.

   [(Difference Between Bull Put Spread Strikes × 100)] – (Initial Debit)

   [(106 – 103) × 100] – $145 = $155

- **Upper breakeven:** Highest strike price – initial debit

   109.00 – 1.45 = $107.55

- **Lower breakeven:** Lowest strike price + initial debit

   103.00 + 1.45 = $104.45

   The breakeven range is the same, but has shifted upward $0.05 reflecting the additional debit required to create the spread.

Many ETFs have dollar strike price increments giving you a great deal of flexibility when selecting butterfly options. By varying the long and short option strike prices, you vary your risk profile.

Approaching expiration, you have four distinct areas where the stock could be trading. If you elect to sell any long option legs to either realize gains or minimize losses, be sure to also buy back the corresponding short option. Here are your positions and options:

- **Underlying below lowest strike:** Close out both spreads and realize maximum loss.

- **Underlying between lower breakeven and short strike price:** Close out the bull put spread plus the additional short put for profits.

- **Underlying at short strike price to upper breakevens:** Close out the bull put spread for profits and allow the bear put spread to expire worthless.

- **Underlying above highest strike price:** All options will expire worthless realizing the maximum loss.

Because vertical spreads create a naturally hedged position for the floor trader they are desired orders. Try to execute the order below the market price by shaving a little bit off the debit limit amount for your order.

With DIA trading at 105.73 into the close on the Friday before expiration, the bear put spread was closed out for $295 by completing the following transactions:

- Buy to Close Aug 2 106 puts @ $0.35 and simultaneously

- Sell to Close Aug 109 put @ $3.30

The long option for the bull put spread expired worthless. Because the initial debit was $145, the position gain was $150 ($295 – 145). This higher return should be expected given the moderately bearish move for the ETF.

Combination orders may take additional time to execute, so keep this in mind if you want to cancel and replace the limit amount for the trade — the market may have moved by the time the order is updated.

In this example the short options were approximately ATM, so profits are maximized when the stock closes at the short option strike price on the last trading day before expiration. At this level three of the four options expire worthless. The higher priced long put will be ITM by an amount equal to the butterfly spread.

As price moves away from the short option strike price, profits diminish to the position breakeven levels where they are equal to zero. Beyond these price levels, the initial debit is the maximum risk.

Digging deeper into butterfly risk

When selecting a butterfly spread, you need to make some trade-offs in terms of risk and reward, along with the range of profitability for the position and its directional bias. This applies to both call and put long butterflies. In general, the following hold true:

- ✔ Using an OTM option for the body will increase directional bias
- ✔ Increasing the spread distance increases the range of profitability
- ✔ Increasing the spread distance decreases the reward-risk ratio

If you have a slightly bearish to neutral outlook you can purchase a put butterfly using an out-of-the-money (OTM) instead of at-the-money (ATM) body.

Paper trading helps you see how these trade-offs impact your trade success without having money on the line during your learning curve.

Narrow wings — smaller risk

When you decrease the spread distance for long butterflies, you also decrease the risk. This is true for vertical spreads as well. By using the DIA long call butterfly spread example and narrowing the spread, Table 16-1 provides the position impact.

Table 16-1	Narrowing the Spread for Aug DIA Butterflies				
Butterfly Strikes	Butterfly Risk	Max Reward	Reward-Risk	Breakeven Range	Butterfly Delta
105-106-107	30	70	2.33	1.3%	−3.7
104-106-108	75	125	1.67	2.4%	−10.1
103-106-109	140	160	1.14	3.0%	−16.6

In this table, the initial debit is the Butterfly Risk and the Breakeven Range is the difference in breakevens divided by the short option strike price of 106.

Calculate the range of profitability for a butterfly by obtaining the difference in breakevens and dividing it by the security's price to get a quick feel of whether the range is reasonable given past movement in the underlying security.

A few observations you should make as you decrease the butterfly spread distance:

- ✔ The risk decreases and the reward-risk increases
- ✔ The breakeven range decreases
- ✔ The directional bias generally becomes more neutral

You need to properly manage your risk, but also be realistic about the range in which the underlying will travel.

Wider wings — bigger risk

When you increase the spread distance for long butterflies, you also increase the position risk. Once again using the DIA call example as a starting point, Table 16-2 provides similar data to Table 16-1 creating wider spreads for the butterfly.

Table 16-2	Widening the Spread for Aug DIA Butterflies				
Butterfly Strikes	Butterfly Risk	Max Reward	Reward-Risk	Breakeven Range	Butterfly Delta
103-106-109	140	160	1.14	3.0%	-16.6
102-106-110	215	185	0.86	3.5%	-20.7
101-106-111	305	195	0.64	3.7%	-25.3

A few observations you should make as you increase the spread distance:

- ✔ The risk increases and the reward-risk decreases
- ✔ The breakeven range increases
- ✔ The directional bias generally becomes more bearish for a call butterfly and bullish for a put butterfly

In the case of the long call butterfly, as the bearish directional bias increases

- ✔ The position realizes increased losses for bullish moves in the underlying, to a point (the upper breakeven).
- ✔ The position realizes increased gains for bearish moves in the underlying, to a point (the lower breakeven).

If you're trading different underlying securities, explore different-sized spreads to get a feel for what's suitable for the security and your risk preferences. Fortunately, the limited risk nature of the strategy provides you with the time needed to build your butterfly skills.

Always check the news when you see big drops or advances in a company stock. You need to beware of adjusted option's resulting from a potential corporate action. It's also just as important to know significant news impacting the underlying for options you trade.

Creating an iron butterfly

The long iron butterfly is a twist on call and put butterflies that allows you to create the position for a credit. You do this by using a bear call spread and a bull put spread, both for a credit. The position remains one that has limited risk and limited reward. It also relies on sideways movement to maximize gains. In the category of "you don't get something for nothing," these spreads require additional margin because both vertical spreads are credit positions.

The put and call butterfly

The iron butterfly combines two vertical credit spreads to capitalize on sideways movement in a stock as follows:

- ✔ A bear call spread with a short option strike price that is near or at-the-money (ATM)
- ✔ A bull put spread with a short option strike price that is near or ATM and the same strike price as the short call

Brokers may base iron butterfly margin requirements on a short straddle — long strangle combination instead of two vertical credit spreads. Check with your broker on their specific requirements before creating a position.

The vertical spread differences are the same for the two credit spreads; the maximum risk for the position is the difference in strike prices for one vertical spread minus the initial credit. The long iron butterfly has strike prices that line up like this:

✔ The lowest strike price is a long put.

✔ The next lowest strike price is a short put.

✔ The same strike price is used for a short call.

✔ The highest strike price is a long call.

When creating the iron butterfly, you use the same strike price for the short option. The initial credit you receive when establishing the position is your maximum reward.

Iron butterfly risk

Using an iron butterfly with a wider spread reduces the reward-risk ratio for this position. This next example uses a stock that typically moves more quietly (100-day historical volatility 12%), with slightly low implied volatility (IV) levels relative to the last 12 months.

Corporate actions can lead to adjustments to existing option contracts. Be sure to check the specs for the options you use, especially when the prices seem off.

Long iron butterfly example

It's mid-June and after a big drop in the stock three months ago, MO has returned to a more typical trading range. It turns out it had a spinoff that changed the company's valuation (see Chapter 10 for information about adjustments to existing options due to corporate actions). MO is trading around $70 and after deciding the spinoff shouldn't impact the stock going forward, you evaluate the following iron butterfly:

✔ Long 1 Jul 60 Put @ $0.05

✔ Short 1 Jul 70 Put @ $1.20

✔ Short 1 Jul 70 Call @ $1.30

✔ Long 1 Jul 80 Call @ $0.05

So now instead of a $3 spread on index-based stock trading around $106, you've increased the spread to $10 on a $70 stock.

An iron butterfly combines four different options — remember to consider your trading costs before entering a position.

Calculating the net credit for these options you obtain the following credit, which is your maximum reward:

Bear Call Spread Credit + Bull Put Spread Credit

$$[(1.30 - 0.05) + (1.20 - 0.05)] \times 100 = \$240$$

Because both spreads are the same distance, the maximum risk is the difference between the two strike prices minus the initial credit.

[(Difference in Strike Prices × 100)] – Initial Credit

$$[(80 - 70) - \$240] = \$760$$

Butterflies and condors have two breakeven levels — one to the upside and one to the downside.

Figure 16-6 displays the risk chart for the MO iron butterfly position.

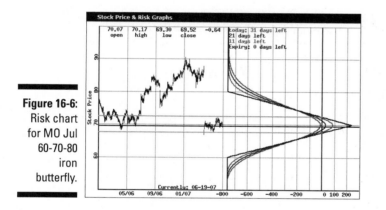

Figure 16-6:
Risk chart
for MO Jul
60-70-80
iron
butterfly.

The breakeven calculation is centered on the short option strike price:

✔ **Upper breakeven:**

Short call strike price + initial credit

$$70.00 + 2.40 = \$72.40$$

✔ **Lower breakeven:**

Short put strike price – initial credit

$$70.00 - 2.40 = \$67.60$$

Always manage your assignment risk into expiration weekend. Don't assume a short option will expire worthless when the underlying is trading near the short option strike price.

As expiration approaches, there are four distinct areas where the stock could be trading. If you elect to sell any long option legs to either realize gains or minimize losses, be sure to also buy back the corresponding short option. Here are your options:

- ✔ **Underlying below the long put strike:** Both put options are in the money and the maximum risk for the bull put spread is realized. The maximum reward is realized for the bear call spread.

- ✔ **Underlying from the lower breakeven to the short strike price:** Partial profits are realized for the bull put spread. The maximum reward is realized for the bear call spread.

- ✔ **Underlying from the short strike price to the upper breakeven:** Partial profits are realized for the bear call spread. The maximum reward is realized for the bull put spread.

- ✔ **Underlying above the call strike price:** Both call options are in the money and the maximum risk for the bear call spread is realized. The maximum reward is realized for the bull put spread.

If assigned early on a short option, use the corresponding long option or evaluate costs to buy shares in the market to meet the short obligation (see Chapter 9).

In the MO example provided, the stock was trading at 69.80 into the close on the Friday before expiration. The short put position was bought back for $20 and the remaining options expired worthless. Because the initial credit was $240, the net gain was $220 (240 – 20).

The impact of dividends already declared are priced into the value of existing call and put options if they expire after the dividend is issued. It is new dividend declarations that can affect the value of options you hold.

Understanding Condor Positions

The condor relates to a butterfly in the same way a strangle relates to a straddle — it splits the center strike price (see Chapter 14). The condor then combines two vertical spreads for the same type of option (call or put) using four different strike prices. Condors do the following:

- ✔ Increase the range of profitability versus a similar butterfly
- ✔ Decrease the maximum reward versus a similar butterfly

Condors are limited risk, limited reward positions that rely on sideways trading action in the underlying to maximize profits.

Evaluate limited risk positions before high- to unlimited risk positions so a strategy comparison can be made prior to establishing a new position.

Defining a condor spread

There are actually three types of long condors available to you for trading:

- ✔ Long call condor
- ✔ Long put condor
- ✔ Long iron condor

The iron condor combines a bear call credit spread and a bull put credit spread, with the short option legs at least one strike price apart.

Single type condors

Long call condors and long put condors allow for more movement in the underlying stock during the life of the trade than a similar call or butterfly position. This means you have a better chance of making a profit, but that profit will be smaller.

Historical volatility (HV) does not predict future prices and implied volatility (IV) may incorporate factors beyond HV. Regardless, using past HV and IV data provides you with valuable information when evaluating strategies.

Suppose a stock is trading at $134.45. You can create the following positions expiring in 31 days that include 10 point vertical spreads:

- ✔ A call or put butterfly using a short strike price of $135 (125-135-145)
- ✔ A call or put condor using $130 and $140 strike prices for the short options (120-130-140-150)

When evaluating strategies, you need to decide whether the higher probability gain using a condor is worth the additional risk. In this particular example, your risk is almost three times your potential reward. Your risk using a butterfly is less than your potential reward, but the stock can only travel in a range of 8% versus 11% for the condors.

Similar strategies will provide different advantages and disadvantages in terms of risk, reward and breakeven depending on a variety of factors. Be sure to evaluate a few alternatives.

The actual comparison between different strategy statistics are impacted by the specific underlying stock, option strike prices, and spreads used. The better risk-reward versus profitability range alternatives will not always be so clear. If the stock was trading at a midpoint between two strike prices, all the statistics for both strategies would be closer. The main point to keep in mind is that when you're selecting a trade that seeks to capitalize on sideways movement, explore different strategies and spread alternatives.

Iron butterflies and iron condors combine call and put vertical spreads rather than combining vertical spreads for just calls or just puts.

Iron condors

Throwing an iron condor into the mix for the butterfly-condor comparison, a similar table can be created using an iron butterfly versus an iron condor. Using a stock trading at $134.45, the following positions expire in 31 days:

- ✔ An iron butterfly using a short strike price of $135 (125-135-145)
- ✔ An iron condor using $130 and $140 strike prices for the short options (120-130-140-150)

Again, the iron condor increases the profitability range, but sacrifices potential gains while taking on additional risk. Both positions combine two vertical credit spreads (call plus put) so the margin requirement can be significant.

Always contact your broker prior to implementing new strategies to determine the margin requirement calculations and approval levels for the strategy.

Recognizing condor risks

Butterflies and condors are not all or nothing positions — you can close out either or both spreads for the position to reduce the maximum risk level if you choose to do so. Just remember that after creating a limited risk position, you want to keep it that way. Don't remove legs that will expose you to unlimited risk.

Condor risk profiles

As expiration approaches, there are four distinct areas where the stock could be trading relative to the condor strike prices. If you elect to sell any long option legs to either realize gains or minimize losses, be sure to also buy back the corresponding short option.

If assigned early on a short option, use the corresponding long option or evaluate costs to buy shares in the market to meet the short obligation (see Chapter 9).

Even if you don't have access to an options analysis software package, understand the risk graph for strategies you're evaluating.

Iron condor risk profile

The original example used in this chapter was for an ETF trading at 106.48 with $1 strike price increments. Using the same trade set-up, an iron condor can be created with slightly out-of-the-money short options to explore the iron condor risk profile.

Creating a $3 spread iron condor for DIA trading at $106.48, you have:

- ✔ Long 1 Aug 103 Put @ $0.30
- ✔ Short 1 Aug 106 Put @ $0.85
- ✔ Short 1 Aug 107 Call @ $0.85
- ✔ Long 1 Aug 110 Put @ $0.15

The maximum reward is the initial credit and the maximum risk is one spread difference minus this credit. Calculating these values you have:

- ✔ **Maximum reward:**

    $[(0.85 - 0.15) + (0.85 - 0.30)] \times 100 = \$125$

- ✔ **Maximum risk:**

    $(3 \times 100) - \$125 = \$175$

After calculating breakeven levels, ask yourself if the stock will realistically trade in the area(s) of profitability during the life of the trade.

Calculating the breakevens using short option strike prices and initial credit:

- ✔ **Lower breakeven:**

    Short Put Strike Price − Initial Credit = 106 − 1.25 = 104.75

- ✔ **Upper breakeven:**

    Short Call Strike Price + Initial Credit = 107 + 1.25 = 108.25

Figure 16-7 displays the risk chart for the DIA iron condor position.

By increasing the bear call spread by one point and combining puts and calls to create the position, the maximum risk was increased $35 (25%), the maximum reward reduced by $35 (22%), and the breakeven ranged increased 0.30 (9%). This reflects a pretty good improvement when you can better split the price of the underlying between the two short options.

Paper trading allows you to understand strategy mechanics without risking capital.

Because the underlying closed at 105.73 going into expiration weekend, the short 106 put would have been bought back at $0.35 for a net position profit of $90 versus $115 for the long call butterfly and $150 for the long put butterfly. The condor's sweet spot was a closing value between $106 and 107.

Figure 16-7:
Risk chart for DIA Jul 103-106-107-110 iron condor.

Part V:
The Part of Tens

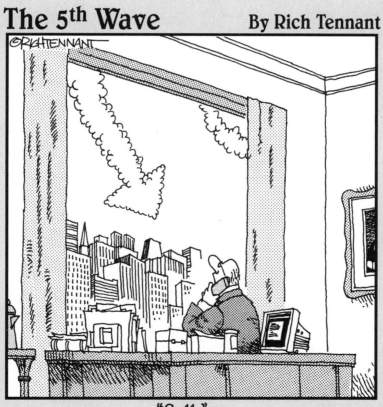

The 5th Wave   By Rich Tennant

"Sell."

In this part . . .

The chapters in this part include summaries for great option strategies aimed at reducing your risk. After you reduce your risk, you can look towards increasing reward . . . also covered here. I also discuss key elements all traders must address to be successful with a bent towards option traders.

Chapter 17

Ten Top Option Strategies

In This Chapter

▶ Developing an option strategy list

▶ Trading with a focus on risk

*T*rading is part art, part science. Developing specific rules and steps to follow is part of a process that gets you up and running on a path toward skillful trading. Implementing them with a focus on managing risk gives you the time needed to develop your craft. A great first step on the science side is creating a strategy list. This allows you to methodically approach a new type of trade so you gain the most knowledge and experience possible.

To get you started, I wanted to provide you with a list of ten great option strategies. The common thread with these strategies is that they have limited risk and are alternatives for you to consider. The unlimited risk or limited but high risk strategies they could potentially replaces are provided with the strategy summary.

Each top ten strategy includes:

- Strategy name and components
- Risks and rewards
- Optimal market conditions (trends, volatility)
- Advantages and disadvantages
- Basic risk profiles
- Additional information by strategy

By all means consider adding notes to these to make them your own.

Married Put

A married put combines long stock with a long put for protection. The position is created by purchasing the stock and put at the same time, but the key is creating put protection. Buying a put for existing stock or rolling out an option to a later expiration month remains true to that strategy goal. Long out-of-the-money (OTM) options should be sold 30 to 45 days before expiration. Table 17-1 gives you some ideas on strategy and Figure 17-1 shows you a a married put risk profile.

Table 17-1	Married Put Summary
Strategy	*Outcome*
Components	Long Stock + Long Put
Risk/Reward	Limited risk, unlimited reward
Replaces	Long stock with limited but high risk
Max Risk	[(Stock Price + Put Price) − Put Strike Price] × 100
Max Reward	Unlimited
Breakeven	Stock Price + Put Price
Conditions	Bullish, low IV
Margin	Not typically required — check with broker
Advantages	Changes limited but high risk to limited risk
Disadvantages	Increases cost of position by option premium

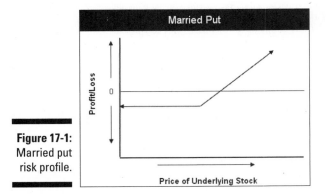

Figure 17-1:
Married put
risk profile.

Collar

A collar combines long stock with long put protection and a short call that reduces the cost of protection. An optimal scenario occurs when you can buy the stock and long put during low volatility conditions allowing you to buy longer term protection. Calls are sold as volatility increases and there is 30 to 45 days to expiration so that time decay accelerates short call gains. Check out the summary in Table 17-2 and the profile in Figure 17-2.

Table 17-2	Collar Summary
Strategy	*Outcome*
Components	Long Stock + Long Put + Short Call
Risk/Reward	Limited risk, limited reward
Replaces	Long stock with limited but high risk
Max Risk	[Stock Price + (Option Debit) − Put Strike Price] × 100
Max Reward	[(Call Strike Price − Stock Price) + (Option Debit)] × 100
Breakeven	Stock Price + (Option Debit)
Conditions	Bullish, low IV that increases
Margin	Not typically required — check with broker
Advantages	Changes limited, but high risk to limited risk
Disadvantages	Replaces unlimited reward with limited reward

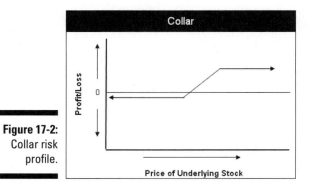

Figure 17-2:
Collar risk
profile.

Long Put Trader

A long put is a limited risk bearish position that gains when the underlying declines. This replaces an unlimited risk short stock position that requires more capital to establish. The bearish move must occur by option expiration and out-of-the-money (OTM) puts should be exited 30 to 45 days prior to expiration. See Table 17-3 for a summary of strategies and Figure 17-3 for an example of the profile.

Table 17-3	Long Put Summary
Strategy	*Outcome*
Components	Long put
Risk/Reward	Limited risk, limited but high reward
Replaces	Short stock with unlimited risk
Max Risk	Put Premium: (Put Price × 100)
Max Reward	(Put Strike Price − Put Price) × 100
Breakeven	Put Strike Price − Put Price
Conditions	Bearish, low IV that increases
Margin	Not required
Advantages	Changes unlimited risk to limited risk
Disadvantages	Time constraints for move to occur due to expiration

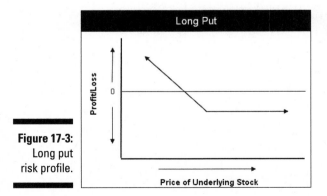

Figure 17-3: Long put risk profile.

LEAPS Call Investor

A Long-term Equity AnticiPation Security (LEAPS) call option reduces the cost and risk associated with a long stock position. The position is best established when implied volatility is relatively low. The LEAPS owner will not participate in dividend distributions which reduce the stock value. See Table 17-4 for a summary of investment strategies and Figure 17-4 for an example of the profile.

Table 17-4	LEAPS Call Investor Summary
Strategy	*Outcome*
Components	Long call with expiration greater than nine months
Risk/Reward	Limited risk, unlimited reward
Replaces	Long stock with limited but high risk
Max Risk	Call Premium: (Call Price × 100)
Max Reward	Unlimited
Breakeven	Strike Price – LEAPS Price
Conditions	Bullish, low IV that increases
Margin	Not required
Advantages	Changes limited but high risk to limited risk
Disadvantages	Pay for time value that erodes and misses dividends

Figure 17-4: LEAPS call risk profile.

Diagonal Spread

A diagonal spread combines a short near month option with a long later month option of the same type. When the strike prices are the same, it is referred to as a calendar spread. A near term neutral view allows you to sell the short option to offset the long option costs. A call diagonal is described here, but a put diagonal works equally well when you're bearish longer term. See Table 17-5 for a summary of investment strategies and Figure 17-5 for an example of the profile.

Table 17-5	Call Diagonal Spread Summary
Strategy	*Outcome*
Components	Long Lower Strike Call + Short, near month call
Risk/Reward	Limited risk, potential unlimited reward*
Replaces	Long call
Max Risk	(Long Call Price − Short Call Price) × 100
Max Reward	*Unlimited when short call expires worthless
Breakeven	Detailed
Conditions	Neutral with IV time skew, then trending
Margin	Required
Advantages	Reduces cost of long option
Disadvantages	A fast bullish move results in limited reward

Figure 17-5:
Call
diagonal
spread risk
profile.

Bear Call Credit Spread

A bear call spread combines a short, lower strike price call and a long, higher strike price call expiring the same month. It creates a credit and replaces a short call with unlimited risk. It's best applied when implied volatility is high and there are 30 or 45 days or less time to expiration. See Table 17-6 for a summary of investment strategies and Figure 17-6 for an example of the profile.

Table 17-6	Bear Call Credit Spread Summary
Strategy	**Outcome**
Components	Short Lower Strike Price Call + Long Higher Strike Price Call (same month)
Risk/Reward	Limited risk, limited reward
Replaces	Short option
Max Risk	(Difference between Strike Prices − Initial Credit) × 100
Max Reward	Initial Credit
Breakeven	Short Strike Price + Net Credit
Conditions	Bearish, high IV
Margin	Required
Advantages	Reduces risk from unlimited to limited
Disadvantages	Reduces reward from limited but high to limited

Figure 17-6:
Bear call credit spread risk profile.

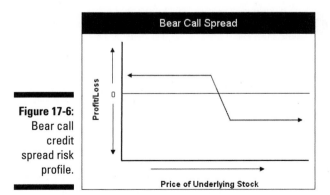

Bear Call Spread

Profit/Loss

Price of Underlying Stock

Straddle

A straddle combines a long call with a long put using the same strike price and expiration. It's created when volatility is low and expected to increase and gains when prices moves strongly up or down. Because there are two long options, exit the position with 30 to 45 days to expiration to avoid time decay. See Table 17-7 for a summary of investment strategies and Figure 17-7 for an example of the profile.

Table 17-7	Straddle Summary
Strategy	**Outcome**
Components	Long Call + Long Put (same strike price, month)
Risk/Reward	Limited risk, high to unlimited reward
Replaces	Single option with directional bias (call or put)
Max Risk	Net Debit: (Call Price + Put Price) × 100
Max Reward	Up: Unlimited, Down: (Strike Price − Net Debit) × 100
Breakeven1	Strike Price + Net Option Prices
Breakeven2	Strike Price − Net Options Prices
Conditions	Neutral, low IV with strong moves expected in both
Margin	Not required
Advantages	Reduces directional risk of single option position
Disadvantages	Increases cost of single option position

Figure 17-7:
Straddle risk
profile.

Call Ratio Backspread

A call ratio backspread combines long higher strike price calls with a lesser number of short lower strike calls expiring the same month. It's best implemented for a credit and is a limited risk, potentially unlimited reward position that is most profitable when a strong bullish move occurs. See Table 17-8 for a summary of investment strategies and Figure 17-8 for an example of the profile.

Table 17-8	Call Ratio Backspread Summary
Strategy	*Outcome*
Components	Long Calls + Less Lower Strike Short Calls (same month)
Risk/Reward	Limited risk, potential unlimited reward
Replaces	Bear call credit spread
Max Risk	Limited: Detailed, see in Chapter 15
Max Reward	Up: Unlimited, Down: Initial Credit
Breakevens	Detailed, see strategy discussion in Chapter 15
Conditions	Bullish, IV skew with strong increase in price and IV
Margin	Required
Advantages	Changes limited reward to unlimited reward
Disadvantages	Initial credit less, complex calculations

Figure 17-8:
Call ratio backspread risk profile.

Put Ratio Backspread

A put ratio backspread combines long lower strike price puts with a lesser number of short higher strike puts expiring the same month. It's best implemented for a credit and is a limited risk — limited, but a potentially high reward position. It is most profitable when a strong bearish move occurs. See Table 17-9 for a summary of investment strategies and Figure 17-9 for an example of the profile.

Table 17-9	Put Ratio Backspread Summary
Strategy	*Outcome*
Components	Long Puts + Less Higher Strike Short Puts (same month)
Risk/Reward	Limited risk, limited but potentially high reward
Replaces	Bull put credit spread
Max Risk	Limited: Detailed, see Chapter 15
Max Reward	Up: Initial Credit, Down: (Long Strike Price + Initial Credit) × 100
Breakevens	Detailed, see strategy discussion in Chapter 15
Conditions	Bearish, IV skew with strong decline and increased IV
Margin	Required
Advantages	Changes limited reward to limited but high reward
Disadvantages	Initial credit less, complex calculations

Figure 17-9:
Put ratio backspread risk profile.

Long Put Butterfly

A long put butterfly combines a bull put spread and a bear put spread expiring the same month for a debit. The two short puts have the same strike price and make up the body. The two long puts have different strike prices (above and below the body) and make up the wings. Time decay helps the trade. See Table 17-10 for a summary of investment strategies and Figure 17-10 for an example of the profile.

Table 17-10	Long Put Butterfly Summary
Strategy	*Outcome*
Components	Bear Put Spread + Bull Put Spread (same month)
Risk/Reward	Limited risk, limited reward
Replaces	Short straddle
Max Risk	Net Debit: [(Lowest Strike Put Price + Highest Strike Put Price) − (2 × Middle Strike Put Price)] × 100
Max Reward	[(Highest Strike Price − Middle Strike Price) × 100] − Net Debit
Breakeven 1	Highest Strike Price − Net Debit Price
Breakeven 2	Lowest Strike Price + Net Debit Price
Conditions	Sideways to moderately bearish, IV skew
Margin	Required
Advantages	Changes unlimited risk to limited risk
Disadvantages	Trading costs associated with three positions

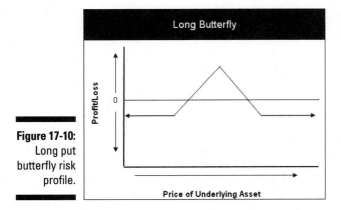

Figure 17-10:
Long put butterfly risk profile.

Chapter 18

Ten Do's and Don'ts in Options Trading

*T*rading is part art, part science. Developing as a trader begins with using a formula-type approach to the markets and different strategies. Skillfully applying it as a seasoned pro requires practice, patience, and experience. It's a journey and one you ideally welcome.

Hopefully there are plenty of rules, steps, and concrete methods you can take away with you from this book. I genuinely hope I've also provided you with some important nuances of trading . . . things that can't quite be mechanically applied. It seems the perfect point to focus on those here.

Do Focus on Managing Risk

Managing risk is the name of the game. In fact, when people ask you about your trading and what you do, tell them you're a risk manager. Become one with it. Now if that isn't nuance, I don't know what is.

By just exploring option strategies you are actively addressing other financial risks in your life. These include inflation risk, income risk, and even market risk associated with buy and hold investing.

When your trading is built on risk management you

- ✔ Understand the risks and rewards associated with the markets you trade

- ✔ Learn and test strategies before putting money on the line

- ✔ Create a plan that identifies trade sizes entry and exit approaches and maximum loss allowed

✔ Identify how the plan will be implemented to honor your risk parameters

✔ Understand how to establish positions and manage a trade

✔ Have a plan for taking profits

✔ Ask yourself, 'What if I'm wrong?'

Other more general risk considerations include diversifying sectors and strategies traded. You may properly allocate trade sizes, but if you enter five trending trades using the same strategy on stocks in the same sector, well then, you've kind of gone against that trade sizing rule. That's the nuance. By extending these guidelines on a portfolio basis you're acting more as an effective risk manager.

Don't Avoid Losses

One way or another you will have losses in your trading. It's not a beginner's trait; it's simply a cost of doing business. As a matter of fact taking small losses is a skill that's developed by experienced traders. Try to get to that level sooner than later.

Avoiding losses is a sure way to make them bigger. You can follow your rules and see positive results with a series of small gains and losses, only to have the slate wiped clean (and then some) with one big loss. It's a discouraging setback.

By shifting your view of what constitutes a successful trade from one that is profitable to one that follows your rules, you're on your way to true success. Initially you can tell yourself to do this, but often you become a true believer with experience. As this happens you become more committed to a rules-based approach and that's when the shift occurs.

Do Trade with Discipline

Trading with discipline means following your rules on each and every trade. Not some of the time, or most of the time, but every time. Will you have a perfect record on the discipline front? Probably not . . . somewhere along the way your human emotions will get the better of you. If you lack discipline early on and you're fortunate enough to remain in the trading game, your discipline better continually improve. Otherwise it's just a matter of time before your luck will run out.

Unfortunately those experiencing initial success may delay an appreciation and commitment to disciplined trading. Early success can give you a false feeling of being right, which is not what trading is about.

Characteristics of trading with discipline on each trade include the following:

- Allocating a reasonable amount of money to a trade
- Identifying a maximum risk for the trade
- Identifying entry and exit signals
- Executing an order when your plan requires it

Those are the checklist items, but trading with discipline goes beyond this. Doing your homework, reviewing your trades, assessing your plan . . . I don't think I could create a comprehensive list. It's about learning what you have to do to trade successfully, mapping out how you'll do it, and then putting it into practice.

Don't Expect to Remove Your Emotions

Some traders assume that trading successfully means completely conquering your greed and fear emotions. I'm here to tell you, when that day comes it means you won't have any emotions at all . . . definitely not a good thing. Eliminating emotions when trading is not a reasonable goal; however, managing them is.

Things that can elevate emotions include:

- Trading using a discretionary approach
- Making trading decisions when the markets are open
- Using an underlying stock or sector that 'owes' you on a trade due to previous losses

Ways to address these specific items include:

- Focusing on more systematic approaches
- Identifying an after-hours time for trade review and management
- Stepping away from a specific stock or sector, even if you typically trade with it successfully

There are even times when stepping away from trading for a period of time is the best way to adjust your attitude and approaches.

Monitoring your emotions is the first step to managing them. Consider adding a note to your trade management sheets to track them. Also note your emotions during off-market hours . . . if you wake up cranky or even worse, can't get to sleep at night, your emotions are managing you.

Do Have a Plan

Many Wall Street sayings have been around for awhile because they simply remain true to form year after year. Other adages do as well including one that fits perfectly here, 'when you fail to plan, plan to fail'.

Creating a base plan should definitely be considered a process rather than a one-time event. Think "draft" and start by writing an outline. Completing it with an easily edited word processing document or spreadsheet may be great, but if you feel you're at the computer too much, a plain old piece of paper and pen is fine. The old-fashioned approach allows you to jot notes along the way without procrastinating because your computer is off. The bottom line is, create something.

When working on your first trading plan, set a timeframe for completion and re-visit it about three months later. This gives you a chance to kick the wheels, identifying what seems to be working and not working. It also highlights what elements may be missing. Anticipate a second review about six months later, and then get on a regular schedule that makes sense.

In addition to primary risk management elements, start incorporating items such as general rules (i.e. buying low implied volatility options and selling high implied volatility options when feasible) and the steps you'll be taking to accomplish this (i.e. reviewing historical and implied volatility charts and checking implied volatility levels with an options calculator).

Identifying other aspects of your trading job helps too (i.e. analyzing market conditions for long-term investments separately from short-term trading) and again, how you'll be accomplishing this (i.e. monthly Saturday analysis for investments, weekly Sunday analysis for trades).

Because both the markets and your personal situation change over time, expect your trading plan to change as well. Better yet, plan on it.

Do Be Patient

Because so much emphasis is placed on managing risk and creating a plan, you may feel a lot of pressure to create the "right" plan. Try to understand that there's almost always more at stake when there is no plan as opposed to a plan that needs some work.

Part of the trading plan process includes making adjustments to your rules. That's definitely something you do outside of market hours and is the result of assessing strategy performance and works toward improving your overall trading plan. It may mean increasing trade allocations or your stop loss percentages or trading fewer strategies at one time.

Your plan may be too aggressive or too conservative, but at least it serves as a base for making adjustments. Will draft two be better? Probably, but changing market conditions could impact the effectiveness of your adjustments. It's okay; at some point you will have traded under a variety of conditions and will have learned techniques to capitalize on them. It's called experience and it takes time.

Patience is not just for trading plans. Sometimes the best thing a trader can do is nothing . . . waiting for the trade or waiting to take profits are useful skills that can have a big impact on trading profitability.

Don't Suffer Analysis to Paralysis

If you like playing around with numbers, the economy and financial markets provide you with an endless supply of them. You could probably go years seeking out relationships between different measures trying to obtain market timing signals. Then you can backtest and forward test every existing indicator to see which ones give you the optimal trading signals.

Paper trading it the whole time won't necessarily get you any closer to successfully trading. At some point you need to experience the markets where you, the human trader, will respond differently when in a live trade.

As mentioned, part of trading successfully means managing your emotions not removing them. There's another side to that, because there are also great emotions and traits you bring to the trading table. Confidence becomes so important when the market picture begins to get hazy — it's what keeps you following your reasonably tested rules.

So the market with all its data can provide some interesting diversions, but it does keep you from the task at hand. After all your learning, reviewing, testing, practicing, and analyzing are done for a strategy, taking it live provides experience that solidifies your understanding of it all. If it's your first time trading options, use limited risk strategies and proper trade sizes to gain that experience. And if all goes well, you'll also make some money along the way.

Do Take Responsibility for Your Results

Never, ever, ever shift any responsibility for your trading results on anyone or anything but you. Why put your success in someone else's hands? It makes it too elusive.

Along your trading career different situations or problems will certainly arise that impact trade profitability. If there's a problem with executions consider how you're placing the orders and discuss it with your broker. If problems persist, remedy it by shifting a portion of your assets to another broker and measure those results.

When you don't have sufficient time for your standard analysis due to work constraints, personal commitments . . . whatever, shift to strategies that you do have time to do the right way. If there is still insufficient time, stepping away from trading is your only responsible choice. Don't worry, the markets will still be there chugging away when you're able to get to them. And when you do, you will have preserved some assets for trading.

By always acknowledging the fact that you are responsible for your own results, you seek out solutions faster and take control. You don't have to wait for someone else to take action or some event to occur. Doing this early in the game helps you assert much greater command over your learning curve and accelerates successful trading.

Don't Stop Learning

The changing nature of the markets make it almost impossible to avoid this one. Because economic conditions, bullish and bearish phases for the market and international markets never repeat themselves exactly, there's always the opportunity to learn.

There are a variety of analytical approaches to trading, and within each of them a bigger variety of techniques and tools for you to explore. Add to the mix new products periodically introduced, and you have your work cut out for you.

There may seem to be a conflicting message here; I've suggested focusing on a couple of strategies rather than taking on a variety of different approaches. The goal there was strategy mastery and remains important. However, when you're on that path, a manageable number of new strategies should be explored. Market conditions will simply dictate it.

It's helpful to have a game plan regarding continued education . . . especially if you want to stay on good terms with your friends, family, work colleagues, etc. (a.k.a. balance in your life). Here are some quick thoughts to help you when creating yours:

- ✔ When mastering strategies you'll find topics you want to understand better. Address those in a focused manner through self-study (books, CDs, periodicals).

- ✔ Move on to additional analysis forms and strategies, through more formal education if needed (live courses or via DVD, books manuals) or self-study.

> ✔ Start the year with general topic goals (i.e. learn two strategies and more on technical analysis), along with more specifics (i.e. find strategies benefiting in sideways trending markets; better understand intermarket analysis).

Most traders naturally continue learning because they gravitate toward books, articles, news programs, conversations . . . dealing with the markets. This is a perfect lead-in to my closing comment on what I believe is critical for your success in trading . . .

Do Love the Game

As with many other traders, I enjoy reading about the markets, trading and other traders. When checking out discussions on traits of successful traders, I see "loving the game" time and time again. Believe it.

Primary drivers for successful traders include really enjoying the challenge of understanding the markets, applying the right approach and being disciplined. It's not about getting even or making money for them. That's partially because you have to love something that requires such intense work — not necessarily long hours, but certainly focused ones. And in terms of making money, that singular driver will eventually lead to large losses for most traders. The long, practiced road for everyone else should be enjoyed.

There's a chance you think you know what I mean, but I have a feeling you know exactly what I mean. Be passionate about your trading and embrace its challenge. There's a healthy excitement about this lifelong pursuit you've chosen.

Glossary

adjusted option: An option contract that underwent changes to its underlying package, number of contracts, multiplier, and/or strike price due to a corporate action causing significant changes to the value of the underlying stock. The adjustment is made so the option contract retains its value.

American Stock Exchange (AMEX): A stock, ETF, and option exchange in the U.S., it includes a trading floor and electronic trading. Find out more at www. amex.com.

American style: An option style that allows rights to be exercised at any point up to the exercise cutoff time, which varies by broker.

ask: Best price available from sellers and is part of a market quote. It is also referred to as the offer.

assignment: When an option seller must meet the obligations of an option contract. A call seller must sell the underlying option package, and a put seller must buy the underlying option package when assigned.

assignment value: The amount received by a call seller or put holder when the rights of the option contract are evoked. It is equal to the strike price multiplied by the multiplier and is the same as the exercise value for a call holder and put seller.

at-the-money (ATM): A call or put option with a strike price equal to the current price of the underlying security. An option strike price may also be near the current price of the underlying (near the money).

backtest: Using historic data to generate trading signals so system performance can be measured in the past.

bear call spread: A vertical call spread created for a credit. It is a limited risk, limited reward position that benefits from a bearish move in the underlying stock. The long call has a higher strike price than the short call, minimizing short-call risk.

bear put spread: A vertical put spread created for a debit. It is a limited risk, limited reward position that benefits from a bearish move in the underlying stock. The short put has a lower strike price than the long put, reducing the long put cost.

bid: Best price available from buyers and is part of a market quote.

booked order: An order that improves the current quote for a security and is entered into the market by the market maker or specialist as the new best bid or offer.

Boston Options Exchange (BOX): An option exchange in the U.S. that uses electronic trading: www.bostonoptions.com.

breakeven: The stock price level where an option position yields profits. Combined option positions may have upper and lower breakeven price levels.

bull call spread: A vertical call spread created for a debit. It is a limited risk, limited reward position that benefits from a bullish move in the underlying stock. The short call has a higher strike price than the long call, reducing the long-call price.

bull put spread: A vertical put spread created for a credit. It is a limited risk, limited reward position that benefits from a bullish move in the underlying stock. The long put has a lower strike price than the short put, minimizing short-put risk.

butterfly (long): A limited risk, limited reward strategy that combines the same type option for a vertical debit spread and a vertical credit spread. It benefits from sideways moves in the markets. The two short options in the spreads are approximately at-the-money (ATM) with the same strike price (body) and the long option strike prices are above (wing 1) and below (wing 2) the short strike price.

calendar spread: A limited risk, potentially high- to unlimited-reward strategy combining a short option with a long option of the same type that has the same strike price and a later month expiration. The strategy benefits when a volatility skew exists. Option analysis software is the best way to view a position risk graph because the different expiration dates impact the risk-reward profile.

call calendar spread: A calendar spread using call options. It benefits from short-term neutral moves for the underlying that become longer term bullish.

call diagonal spread: A diagonal spread using call options. It benefits from short-term neutral moves for the underlying that become longer term bullish.

call option (stock): A security that gives the owner (seller) the right (obligation) to buy (sell) a specified number of shares for the underlying stock at a specified price, by a predetermined date.

call ratio backspread: A limited risk, limited reward strategy that includes a short call plus a greater number of long calls expiring the same month. The long options have a higher strike price and brings in a credit when a reverse price skew exists for implied volatility (IV). It benefits most from a strong bullish move in the underlying and realizes the largest losses when the underlying closes at the long call strike price at expiration.

call ratio spread: An unlimited risk, limited reward strategy that includes a long option plus a greater number of short options with a higher strike price, expiring the same month. The position has high margin requirements due to the uncovered short call(s) and is not recommended because other limited risk strategies are available for the same market outlook.

cancel order: An order that requests cancellation of an existing, standing order in the market. The cancellation may or may not be possible because the order may have already been executed.

cash settlement: An option settlement process that uses cash to satisfy obligations rather than a physical asset.

CBOE equity only put/call ratio: Total volume for all equity options trading on the Chicago Board Options Exchange.

change order: An order that requests cancellation of an existing, standing order in the market and the replacement of that order with a new one. In the event it is too late to cancel the original order, the replacement order is cancelled. This prevents trade executions from being duplicated.

Characteristics and Risks of Standardized Options: A publication written by the Options Clearing Corporation that must be distributed by a broker to his client prior to allowing option trading. It describes option contract specifications, mechanics, and the risks associated with the security.

Chicago Board Options Exchange (CBOE): The first stock option exchange in the U.S., it includes a trading floor and electronic trading. For more information, see www.cboe.com.

collar: A hedged position that has limited risk and limited reward. It combines a long put and a short call with a long stock position. The put provides protection for the stock while the call reduces the cost of that protection. It significantly reduces long stock risk and potential gains.

combined position: A position created using stock and options for the stock or multiple options for the same stock.

commission: The amount charged by a broker when a stock or option transaction is executed.

conditional order: An order that uses on movement in one security to trigger an order in another. A variety of criteria can be used including stock price level, movement, or quote prices. It is also known as a contingent order.

condor (long): A limited risk, limited reward strategy that combines the same type option for a vertical debit spread and a vertical credit spread. It is similar to a butterfly with reduced risk and reward. The condor also benefits from sideways moves. The two short options in the spreads are approximately at-the-money (ATM) with different strike prices and the long option strike prices are above and below the short strike prices.

correlation: Measure of movement for one data set relative to another that identifies magnitude and direction. Values ranging from –1 (perfect negative) to +1 (perfect positive). Correlation is not causal.

covered call: A position that combines a short call option with long stock to provide assignment protection for the call. It incrementally reduces long stock risk and significantly limits potential stock gains. High risk remains for the stock position.

covered option: A short option position with an obligation that can be satisfied using a stock position or a long option, with the same or later expiration date, which is also held in the account.

covered put: A position that combines a short put option with short stock to provide assignment protection for the put. It reduces short stock risk incrementally and significantly limits potential stock gains. Risk that is near unlimited remains for the stock position.

credit trade: A trade that results in funds added to the account. The sale of a long stock position is a credit trade, as is the short sale of stock.

current market: Best bid and best ask for a security.

day order: An order that is eligible for execution for the current trading session (or next session if the market is closed).

debit trade: A trade that results in funds being removed from the account. The purchase of stock is a debit trade.

delta: An option Greek measure that represents the *expected* change in the option value for each $1 change in the price of the underlying stock. Delta is positive for calls and negative for puts. Stock has a +1 delta per share.

delta neutral position: A combined position with a net delta value as close to zero as possible. It uses further out expirations to give the position time to yield profits.

derivative: A security that is valued primarily by the market value of the security in which it is based. A stock option is an example of a derivative that derives its value from a specific underlying stock.

diagonal spread: A limited risk, potentially high- to unlimited-reward strategy combining a short option with a long option of the same type that has a different strike price and later month expiration. The strategy benefits when a volatility skew exists. Option analysis software is the best way to view a position risk graph because the different expiration dates impact the risk-reward profile.

diversification: Allocation of investment dollars across and within different asset types (i.e. stocks, bonds, and commodities).

drawdown: Cumulative account losses from consecutive losing trades. High drawdowns can be unsustainable even if a system backtest is ultimately profitable.

duration: The period of time an order is in place, including day and good 'til canceled (GTC).

European style: An option style that only allows rights to be exercised on a designated date.

exchange-traded fund (ETF): A security that is based on the value of a basket of stocks, bonds, or commodities, similar to a mutual fund. ETFs do not necessarily hold the underlying assets they track. They can be traded throughout the day just as a stock and have options available for trading.

execution quality: A broker's ability to complete trades at, or better than, the current market for the security in a timely manner.

exercise: To evoke the rights of an option contract. A call buyer purchases the underlying option package, and a put buyer sells the underlying option package when the option is exercised.

exercise by exception (auto-exercise): A stock option that is in-the-money by 5¢ or more at expiration is exercised on the holder's behalf by the Options Clearing Corporation (OCC) over expiration weekend without specific exercise instructions submitted. The OCC assumes the holder did not want an option with value to expire worthless. Auto-exercise can create a short stock position for put contracts.

exercise date: The date in which a long, European style contract holder can exercise his or her rights under the contract.

exercise instructions: Formal request submitted to broker to evoke the rights of an option contract. Exercise cutoff times vary by broker.

exercise value: The amount received by a call holder and put seller when the rights of the option contract are evoked. It is equal to the strike price multiplied by the multiplier and is the same value as the assignment value for a call seller or put holder.

expiration date: The date an option contract no longer exists. Monthly stock option expiration dates are the Saturday following the third Friday of the month.

extrinsic value: The portion of the option price attributed to time. It's the price remaining after intrinsic value is removed.

fast markets: A security is in a fast market when a very large volume of orders is flowing to the market and it's difficult for the market maker or specialist to maintain an orderly market for the security. Volume is high and quotes and execution reports are delayed. Standard rules for execution are waived at this time.

Fibonacci ratios: Ratios derived from the Fibonacci series when dividing an integer in the series by previous or subsequent integers in the series. The primary Fibonacci ratios used in technical analysis include: 0.382, 0.500, 0.618, 1.00, 1.618 and 2.618.

Fibonacci series: An integer series used in technical analysis originally defined by Leonardo Fibonacci that is generated when starting the series with 0 and 1, and adding the two previous integers to obtain the next integer. 0, 1, 1 (0 + 1), 2 (1 + 1), 3 (1 + 2), 5 (2 + 3), 8 (3 + 5), 13 (5 + 8), ...

fill: A term for order execution.

filter: A trading rule or system parameter that is added to minimize entry and exit from false signals. A filter is used to improve system profitability.

float: The amount of authorized shares available to the public for trading.

forward price skew: Condition where higher strike price options of the same type have higher implied volatility (IV) compared to others expiring in the same month.

forward test: Using past data to generate trading signals so a backtest can be evaluated with more recent data.

gamma: An option Greek measure that represents the *expected* change in delta for each $1 change in the price of the underlying stock. Gamma is positive for both calls and puts.

good 'til canceled order (GTC): An order that is eligible for execution until it is canceled by the customer. The broker may cancel a GTC order.

hedge: A position that protects a stock or portfolio against an adverse move.

historical volatility (HV): A measure of past movement in a stock that uses an annualized standard deviation for daily price changes during a given period of time. Higher HV stocks are expected to make bigger daily moves that are less predictable than those with a smaller HV. Lower HV stocks have daily changes that stay close to the average daily change. HV is also referred to as statistical volatility (SV).

implied volatility (IV): Part of an option price that represents the markets' expectations for future volatility in the underlying. IV is based on past volatility for the stock (HV) along with other factors. It is the volatility that is implied by an option's price after all these other factors have been accounted for.

index: A measure calculated using the value of its component securities including individual stocks, bonds, or commodities. A single value allows easier tracking of a particular market or sector.

International Stock Exchange (ISE): The first electronic stock option exchange in the U.S. For more information check out www.ise.com.

in-the-money (ITM): A call option with a strike price that is below the stock price or a put option with a strike price that is above the stock price. ITM options have intrinsic value.

intrinsic value: The option price attributed to its rights. It's the amount gained when the option is exercised then the underlying position is immediately closed by selling or buying shares in the market.

iron butterfly (long): A limited risk, limited reward strategy that combines two vertical credit spreads using different option types to capitalize on sideways moves in the markets. The two short options are approximately at-the-money (ATM) with the same strike price (body), and the long option strike prices are above (call, wing 1) and below (put, wing 2) the short strike price.

iron condor (long): A limited risk, limited reward strategy that combines two vertical credit spreads using different option types to capitalize on sideways moves in the markets. The two short options are approximately at-the-money (ATM) with different strike prices, and the long option strike prices are above and below the short strike prices.

last day to exercise: The last day to trade (usually a Friday) is usually the last day for retail traders to exercise stock option rights. Typical cutoff times to submit instructions to the broker is one hour after the markets close, but that time varies by firm. Contact your broker to obtain specific cutoff times and instruction requirements.

last trading date (index): The last date an index option can be traded in the market — it is identified in the contract specification, varies by options, and may be two days prior to expiration.

last trading day: For stock options, usually the third Friday of the month. Occasionally holidays push this last trading day further up the week to Thursday.

leg: Each option and/or stock in a combined position.

limit order: An order that guarantees price, but not execution. It identifies the lowest price the security can be sold or the highest price it can be purchased, and it may be placed for the current trading session or longer.

liquidity: The ease you can enter and exit a trade without impacting its price — the depth of a market.

long call: Right to buy shares of a specified number of shares for the underlying stock at a specified price by a predetermined date.

long put: Right to sell shares of a specified number of shares for the underlying stock at a specified price, by a predetermined date.

Long-term Equity AnticiPation Security (LEAPS): An option contract with an extended period to expiration — anywhere from more than six months to as much as 2½ years. Not all stocks with options have LEAPS available, but for those that do the expiration month is almost always January.

maintenance call: Additional funds that must be brought into an account to hold a margin position when account equity falls below the maintenance requirement. A call is generated when adverse moves occur in one or more securities in the account and must be satisfied immediately.

maintenance requirement: The amount of equity required in an account to hold a margin position after it is purchased. Federal regulations allow for some adverse movement against a margin position so the maintenance requirement is less than the initial margin requirement. Thirty-five percent is a typical requirement for stocks, but individual broker rates may be more stringent.

margin requirement: The initial amount of available funds required when a margin position is established. Federal regulations typically require a 50% requirement for stocks, but individual broker rates may be more stringent.

market capitalization: A measure used to define a company's size. It is calculated by multiplying the current stock price by the total number of shares outstanding. Typical market cap sizes include small-, mid-, and large.

market maker: Professional exchange trader responsible for providing current quotes and executions for a select list of securities. They also keep the markets orderly, handling trades by price and time priority.

market order: An order that guarantees execution at the current market for the security given its priority in the trading queue (a.k.a. trading book) and the depth of the market.

market quote: The current price bid by buyers to purchase a security and offered (asked) by sellers to give up the security.

marketable order: An order that can be filled given the current market quote. These include standard market orders as well as limit orders with a limit to buy above or sell below the current market.

maximum adverse excursion/move: The largest loss per position based on a percentage of the initial trade size. This value is an unrealized value — it does not reflect the actual trade exit.

maximum favorable excursion/move: The largest gain per position based on a percentage of the initial trade size. This value is an unrealized value — it does not reflect the actual trade exit.

mean: Measure of central tendency, also known as average.

median: Measure of central tendency, it is the middle value(s) in a sequential data series.

minimum account balance: An account value required to trade different strategies. These are broker requirements that vary by firm and are different than margin or maintenance requirements.

moneyness: The option strike price relative to the current price of the under-lying, determined by option type. An option can be in-, at-, out-of-the-money, or near the money.

multiplier: The value used to determine option premium and deliverable amounts. It's usually 100 for stock and index options.

naked option: A short option position with an obligation that cannot be satisfied using a stock position or a long option with a later expiration date also held in the account.

National Best Bid and Offer (NBBO): The best market quote. It represents composite information from the various option or stock exchanges trading a particular security.

near month option: An option that has the closest month for its expiration date.

neutral approach: A combination of stock and options or options only that limits directional bias. Trading a neutral approach allows you to realize gains whether the market goes up or down.

New York Stock Exchange (NYSE/ARCA): A stock, ETF, and option exchange in the U.S., it includes a trading floor and electronic trading. For more information, go to www.nyse.com.

next month option: An option that expires in the month that follows the next month.

one cancels other (OCO): An order designation that allows two different orders for one security. If and when one of those orders is executed, the system automatically cancels the other order. It prevents strong swings from resulting in execution of both orders.

open interest: The number of contracts in existence for a specific option. On a given day, it reflects the total number of options that are not closed out or delivered the previous day.

option: A derivative security that represents a contractual right to the buying party and an obligation to the selling party.

option calculator: A tool used to input option and stock market data to obtain theoretical option pricing or volatility values. It is based on an option pricing model.

option chain: All options available for a specific underlying stock or index.

option cycle: The method of creating quarterly expiration months for an option beyond those that are near or next month. Three option cycles exist.

option package: The security in which an option contract bases holder's rights and seller's obligations. It identifies the name and number of shares for the security, as applicable. A package is usually 100 shares for stock options.

option pricing model: A series of calculations using stock data and assumptions to obtain a theoretical price for an option. The first model was developed by Fischer Black and Myron Scholes and received a Nobel prize.

option root: A unique identifier (one to three letters long) for stock options. The root may match the stock ticker symbols (i.e. General Electric's stock symbol and option root is GE). Option roots are expected to disappear with the Options Symbology Initiative.

Options Clearing Corporation (OCC): The clearing firm that performs option contract administration and guarantees option contracts for buyers and sellers.

Options Industry Council (OIC): An entity formed by the Options Clearing Corporation and six option exchanges that provide investor education.

Options Symbology Initiative: A formal effort within the marketplace to update the system used to identify stock options. A new system is expected to be approved in mid-2008 for implementation in 2009.

out-of-the-money (OTM): A call option with a strike price that is above the stock price or a put option with a strike price that is below the stock price. OTM options have no intrinsic value.

paper trading: A method of simulating trades to practice strategies.

parameter: A rule for a trading system.

partial hedge: A security that gains value when the hedged security loses value. The movement between the two is less than one-to-one, which occurs when the cumulative delta for the position is something other than zero.

Philadelphia Stock Exchange (PHLX): A stock, ETF, and option exchange in the U.S., it includes a trading floor and electronic trading. You can find out more information by visiting www.phlx.com.

physical settlement: An option settlement process that uses a physical asset to satisfy obligations.

premium: The total value of an option in the market based on its quote and multiplier.

price skew: A condition where options expiring in the same month have implied volatilities that deviate from normal.

probability: A measure of an expected outcome.

proxy security: A security that behaves similarly and is well correlated to another security or measure.

put calendar spread: Hey, who said options weren't sexy? I bet you didn't realize you'd come up against a calendar spread (tastefully done, of course) using put options. It benefits from short-term neutral, longer term bearish moves in the underlying.

put diagonal spread: A diagonal spread using put options. It benefits from short-term neutral, longer term bearish moves in the underlying.

put option (stock): A security that gives the owner (seller) the right (obligation) to sell (buy) a specified number of shares for the underlying stock at a specified price, by a predetermined date.

put ratio backspread: A limited risk, limited reward strategy that includes a short put plus a greater number of long puts expiring the same month. The long options have a lower strike price and bring in a credit when a forward price skew exists for implied volatility (IV). It benefits most from a strong bearish move in the underlying and realizes the largest losses when the underlying closes at the long put strike price at expiration.

put ratio spread: An unlimited risk, limited reward strategy that includes a long option plus a greater number of short options with a lower strike price, expiring the same month. The position has high margin requirements due to the uncovered short put(s) and is not recommended because other limited risk strategies are available for the same market outlook.

relative ratio: A value calculated by dividing one security into another. It allows you to compare the performance of one security versus another. A rising relative ratio indicates outperformance of the top security (numerator) while a declining line indicates underperformance. A relative ratio is also referred to as relative strength comparison.

relative strength: Comparison of upward movement in two stocks, sectors, or markets. It can also be a comparison of upward movement for one stock using two different time periods.

reverse price skew: Condition where lower strike price options of the same type have higher implied volatility relative to those expiring the same month.

rho: An option Greek measure that represents the expected change in the option value due to a 1% change in the risk-free interest rate (usually T-bills).

risk: The potential for losses or the inability of your savings to outpace inflation.

risk graph (also risk profile): A graphical view of potential risk and reward in option trading. It is created by plotting position gains or losses for varying prices in the underlying stock.

roll: An option transaction that involves closing one position and opening a similar one for the same stock. This process is used to push expiration further out in time or to change the strike price.

selling short: Reversing the typical sequence for a stock transaction. Rather than buying first and selling later, you sell first and buy the stock at a later time. To short sell a stock, the shares must be borrowed from a broker and may or may not be available.

settlement date: The date (and time) specifications used to determine the index closing value at expiration.

settlement value (SET): Index closing value used to determine intrinsic value for index options.

short call (stock): Obligation to sell a specified number of shares for the underlying stock at a specified price by a predetermined date.

short put (stock): Obligation to buy a specified number of shares for the underlying stock at a specified price by a predetermined date.

skew chart: A visual display of option implied volatility versus strike price for each type of option by month.

slippage: A transaction cost associated with the security's quoted spread. The loss realized if you were to buy a security on its ask then immediately turn around and sell it on the bid.

specialist: Professional exchange trader responsible for providing current quotes and trade executions for a select list of securities. They also keep the markets orderly, handling trades by price and time priority.

stability: In a trading system, refers to the consistency of results and can be measured using a standard deviation calculation on individual returns.

standard deviation (SD): A measure calculating the distance data in a set is from the set's average value. Higher SD is associated with data that is more dispersed.

statistical volatility (SV): Another term for historical volatility.

stop order: An order that serves as a risk management tool by identifying a trigger price for a market order. The trigger price is inferior to the current market and is typically used to minimize losses for an existing position. It is also referred to as a stop-loss order.

straddle (long): A limited risk, high to unlimited reward combination position using a long call and long put for the same underlying, with the same expiration month and strike price. The strategy benefits when a big move occurs in the underlying stock, either up or down, and is best established when implied volatility is low.

strangle (long): A limited risk, high to unlimited reward combination position using a long out-of-the-money (OTM) call and long OTM put for the same underlying with the same expiration month and different strike prices. The strategy benefits when a big move occurs in the underlying stock, either up or down, and is best established when implied volatility is low.

strike price: The predetermined price level used to exercise option rights.

system: A set of strictly followed rules for trade entry and exit. The trader must establish a position when each buy signal is generated and exit each position when the exit signal is generated.

theta: An option Greek measure that represents the expected daily decline in option premium due to time. Theta is negative for both calls and puts.

time skew: A condition where options expiring in different months have implied volatilities deviating from normal.

time value: The portion of an option's price the remains after intrinsic value is removed. It is associated with the number of days until expiration. It is also known as extrinsic value.

trade size: The number of shares or contracts used for a position based on predetermined dollar amounts or trade allocations.

trading halt: An official stop in trading for a specific security put in place by an exchange when the market is open.

type: The kind of option by right — a call or put.

underlying security: The stock or index used to derive an option's value.

vega: An option Greek measure that represents the expected change in the option value due to a 1% change in implied volatility for the option. Vega is positive for both calls and puts.

vertical spread: A limited risk, limited reward position combining two options of the same type, one long and one short. The same expiration month and different strike prices are used to create a debit or credit trade.

volatility skew: A condition where options for the same underlying stock have significantly different implied volatilities. This can occur for options expiring in the same month (price skew) or different months (time skew).

volume: The total number of stock shares or option contracts traded during a given period.

Index

• Z •

BUSINESS, CAREERS & PERSONAL FINANCE

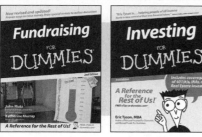

0-7645-9847-3

0-7645-2431-3

Also available:
- Business Plans Kit For Dummies
  0-7645-9794-9
- Economics For Dummies
  0-7645-5726-2
- Grant Writing For Dummies
  0-7645-8416-2
- Home Buying For Dummies
  0-7645-5331-3
- Managing For Dummies
  0-7645-1771-6
- Marketing For Dummies
  0-7645-5600-2

- Personal Finance For Dummies
  0-7645-2590-5*
- Resumes For Dummies
  0-7645-5471-9
- Selling For Dummies
  0-7645-5363-1
- Six Sigma For Dummies
  0-7645-6798-5
- Small Business Kit For Dummies
  0-7645-5984-2
- Starting an eBay Business For Dummies
  0-7645-6924-4
- Your Dream Career For Dummies
  0-7645-9795-7

HOME & BUSINESS COMPUTER BASICS

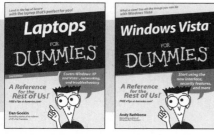

0-470-05432-8

0-471-75421-8

Also available:
- Cleaning Windows Vista For Dummies
  0-471-78293-9
- Excel 2007 For Dummies
  0-470-03737-7
- Mac OS X Tiger For Dummies
  0-7645-7675-5
- MacBook For Dummies
  0-470-04859-X
- Macs For Dummies
  0-470-04849-2
- Office 2007 For Dummies
  0-470-00923-3

- Outlook 2007 For Dummies
  0-470-03830-6
- PCs For Dummies
  0-7645-8958-X
- Salesforce.com For Dummies
  0-470-04893-X
- Upgrading & Fixing Laptops For Dummies
  0-7645-8959-8
- Word 2007 For Dummies
  0-470-03658-3
- Quicken 2007 For Dummies
  0-470-04600-7

FOOD, HOME, GARDEN, HOBBIES, MUSIC & PETS

0-7645-8404-9

0-7645-9904-6

Also available:
- Candy Making For Dummies
  0-7645-9734-5
- Card Games For Dummies
  0-7645-9910-0
- Crocheting For Dummies
  0-7645-4151-X
- Dog Training For Dummies
  0-7645-8418-9
- Healthy Carb Cookbook For Dummies
  0-7645-8476-6
- Home Maintenance For Dummies
  0-7645-5215-5

- Horses For Dummies
  0-7645-9797-3
- Jewelry Making & Beading For Dummies
  0-7645-2571-9
- Orchids For Dummies
  0-7645-6759-4
- Puppies For Dummies
  0-7645-5255-4
- Rock Guitar For Dummies
  0-7645-5356-9
- Sewing For Dummies
  0-7645-6847-7
- Singing For Dummies
  0-7645-2475-5

INTERNET & DIGITAL MEDIA

0-470-04529-9

0-470-04894-8

Also available:
- Blogging For Dummies
  0-471-77084-1
- Digital Photography For Dummies
  0-7645-9802-3
- Digital Photography All-in-One Desk Reference For Dummies
  0-470-03743-1
- Digital SLR Cameras and Photography For Dummies
  0-7645-9803-1
- eBay Business All-in-One Desk Reference For Dummies
  0-7645-8438-3
- HDTV For Dummies
  0-470-09673-X

- Home Entertainment PCs For Dummies
  0-470-05523-5
- MySpace For Dummies
  0-470-09529-6
- Search Engine Optimization For Dummies
  0-471-97998-8
- Skype For Dummies
  0-470-04891-3
- The Internet For Dummies
  0-7645-8996-2
- Wiring Your Digital Home For Dummies
  0-471-91830-X

* Separate Canadian edition also available
† Separate U.K. edition also available

Available wherever books are sold. For more information or to order direct: U.S. customers visit www.dummies.com or call 1-877-762-2974.
U.K. customers visit www.wileyeurope.com or call 0800 243407. Canadian customers visit www.wiley.ca or call 1-800-567-4797.

SPORTS, FITNESS, PARENTING, RELIGION & SPIRITUALITY

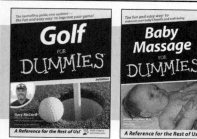

0-471-76871-5   0-7645-7841-3

Also available:
- Catholicism For Dummies
  0-7645-5391-7
- Exercise Balls For Dummies
  0-7645-5623-1
- Fitness For Dummies
  0-7645-7851-0
- Football For Dummies
  0-7645-3936-1
- Judaism For Dummies
  0-7645-5299-6
- Potty Training For Dummies
  0-7645-5417-4
- Buddhism For Dummies
  0-7645-5359-3

- Pregnancy For Dummies
  0-7645-4483-7 †
- Ten Minute Tone-Ups For Dummies
  0-7645-7207-5
- NASCAR For Dummies
  0-7645-7681-X
- Religion For Dummies
  0-7645-5264-3
- Soccer For Dummies
  0-7645-5229-5
- Women in the Bible For Dummies
  0-7645-8475-8

TRAVEL

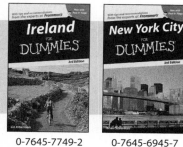

0-7645-7749-2   0-7645-6945-7

Also available:
- Alaska For Dummies
  0-7645-7746-8
- Cruise Vacations For Dummies
  0-7645-6941-4
- England For Dummies
  0-7645-4276-1
- Europe For Dummies
  0-7645-7529-5
- Germany For Dummies
  0-7645-7823-5
- Hawaii For Dummies
  0-7645-7402-7

- Italy For Dummies
  0-7645-7386-1
- Las Vegas For Dummies
  0-7645-7382-9
- London For Dummies
  0-7645-4277-X
- Paris For Dummies
  0-7645-7630-5
- RV Vacations For Dummies
  0-7645-4442-X
- Walt Disney World & Orlando
  For Dummies
  0-7645-9660-8

GRAPHICS, DESIGN & WEB DEVELOPMENT

0-7645-8815-X   0-7645-9571-7

Also available:
- 3D Game Animation For Dummies
  0-7645-8789-7
- AutoCAD 2006 For Dummies
  0-7645-8925-3
- Building a Web Site For Dummies
  0-7645-7144-3
- Creating Web Pages For Dummies
  0-470-08030-2
- Creating Web Pages All-in-One Desk
  Reference For Dummies
  0-7645-4345-8
- Dreamweaver 8 For Dummies
  0-7645-9649-7

- InDesign CS2 For Dummies
  0-7645-9572-5
- Macromedia Flash 8 For Dummies
  0-7645-9691-8
- Photoshop CS2 and Digital
  Photography For Dummies
  0-7645-9580-6
- Photoshop Elements 4 For Dummies
  0-471-77483-9
- Syndicating Web Sites with RSS Feeds
  For Dummies
  0-7645-8848-6
- Yahoo! SiteBuilder For Dummies
  0-7645-9800-7

NETWORKING, SECURITY, PROGRAMMING & DATABASES

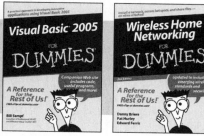

0-7645-7728-X   0-471-74940-0

Also available:
- Access 2007 For Dummies
  0-470-04612-0
- ASP.NET 2 For Dummies
  0-7645-7907-X
- C# 2005 For Dummies
  0-7645-9704-3
- Hacking For Dummies
  0-470-05235-X
- Hacking Wireless Networks
  For Dummies
  0-7645-9730-2
- Java For Dummies
  0-470-08716-1

- Microsoft SQL Server 2005 For Dummies
  0-7645-7755-7
- Networking All-in-One Desk Reference
  For Dummies
  0-7645-9939-9
- Preventing Identity Theft For Dummies
  0-7645-7336-5
- Telecom For Dummies
  0-471-77085-X
- Visual Studio 2005 All-in-One Desk
  Reference For Dummies
  0-7645-9775-2
- XML For Dummies
  0-7645-8845-1

HEALTH & SELF-HELP

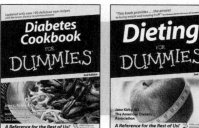

0-7645-8450-2

0-7645-4149-8

Also available:
- Bipolar Disorder For Dummies
  0-7645-8451-0
- Chemotherapy and Radiation
  For Dummies
  0-7645-7832-4
- Controlling Cholesterol For Dummies
  0-7645-5440-9
- Diabetes For Dummies
  0-7645-6820-5* †
- Divorce For Dummies
  0-7645-8417-0 †

- Fibromyalgia For Dummies
  0-7645-5441-7
- Low-Calorie Dieting For Dummies
  0-7645-9905-4
- Meditation For Dummies
  0-471-77774-9
- Osteoporosis For Dummies
  0-7645-7621-6
- Overcoming Anxiety For Dummies
  0-7645-5447-6
- Reiki For Dummies
  0-7645-9907-0
- Stress Management For Dummies
  0-7645-5144-2

EDUCATION, HISTORY, REFERENCE & TEST PREPARATION

0-7645-8381-6

0-7645-9554-7

Also available:
- The ACT For Dummies
  0-7645-9652-7
- Algebra For Dummies
  0-7645-5325-9
- Algebra Workbook For Dummies
  0-7645-8467-7
- Astronomy For Dummies
  0-7645-8465-0
- Calculus For Dummies
  0-7645-2498-4
- Chemistry For Dummies
  0-7645-5430-1
- Forensics For Dummies
  0-7645-5580-4

- Freemasons For Dummies
  0-7645-9796-5
- French For Dummies
  0-7645-5193-0
- Geometry For Dummies
  0-7645-5324-0
- Organic Chemistry I For Dummies
  0-7645-6902-3
- The SAT I For Dummies
  0-7645-7193-1
- Spanish For Dummies
  0-7645-5194-9
- Statistics For Dummies
  0-7645-5423-9

Get smart @ dummies.com®

- **Find a full list of Dummies titles**
- **Look into loads of FREE on-site articles**
- **Sign up for FREE eTips e-mailed to you weekly**
- **See what other products carry the Dummies name**
- **Shop directly from the Dummies bookstore**
- **Enter to win new prizes every month!**

* Separate Canadian edition also available
† Separate U.K. edition also available

Available wherever books are sold. For more information or to order direct: U.S. customers visit www.dummies.com or call 1-877-762-2974.
U.K. customers visit www.wileyeurope.com or call 0800 243407. Canadian customers visit www.wiley.ca or call 1-800-567-4797.